D␣
LONDON

MW01251354

—— 30 ——

**One Day Adventures
In and Around
London by
Underground,
Rail or Car**

4/92

To the Hatens —

Here's to an adventure.

Eileen

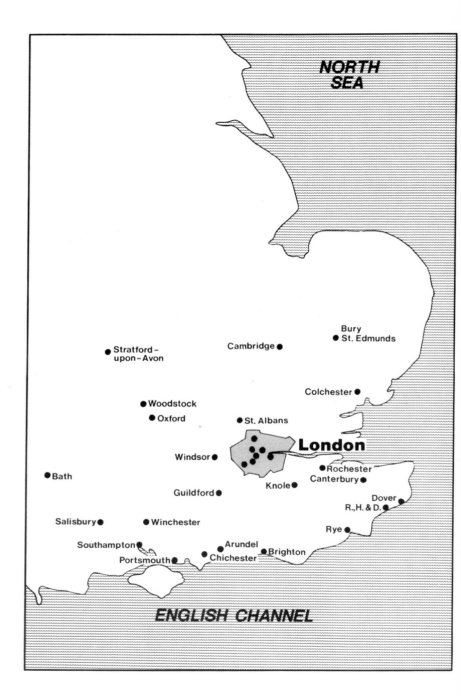

NORTH
SEA

Bury
St. Edmunds

Cambridge ●

● Stratford –
upon-Avon

Colchester ●

● Woodstock

● Oxford

● St. Albans

London

Windsor ●

● Rochester
Canterbury ●

Knole ●

● Bath

Guildford ●

Dover
R.,H. & D. ●

Salisbury ●

● Winchester

Rye ●

Southampton ●

Arundel
● ● Brighton
Chichester

Portsmouth ●

ENGLISH CHANNEL

DAYTRIPS
LONDON
—— 30 ——
One Day Adventures In and Around London by Underground, Rail or Car

by
Earl Steinbicker

HASTINGS HOUSE
MAMARONECK, NEW YORK

The author would like to thank the following people, whose
generous help and encouragement made this book possible:
John Lampl, of British Airways.
Patricia B. Titley, of BritRail Travel International.

All photos are by the author except as noted.

Distributed to the trade by Publishers Group West, Emeryville, CA

ISBN 0-8038-9329-9

Printed in the United States of America
10 9 8 7 6 5 4 3 2 1

Contents

Introduction

If ever a place was made for daytripping, it is southeastern England. By basing yourself in London you are within easy striking distance of many of Europe's most desirable attractions, where language is no problem and where getting around on your own is as simple as it is back home. This book takes a fresh look at 30 of the most intriguing destinations, including seven within Greater London itself, and describes in step-by-step detail a pleasurable way of exploring them on self-guided walking tours.

Walking is by far the best way to probe most places. Not only is it undeniably healthy, but it also allows you to see the sights from a natural, human perspective; and to spend just as much or as little time on each as you please. The carefully tested walking tours were designed to take you past all of the attractions worth seeing without wasting time, effort, or money. Which of these you actually stop at is up to you, but you won't have any trouble finding them with the large, clear maps provided. There is never a need to rush as you'll have plenty of time for each walk, taking pleasant rest stops along the way.

The destinations were chosen to appeal to a wide variety of interests. In addition to the usual cathedrals, castles, art galleries, and stately homes there are such attractions as country walks, colorful London neighborhoods, maritime museums, canals, Roman ruins, places where history was made, places of literary association, quaint fishing villages, great seaports, resorts, elegant spas, and even an exciting railfan excursion. Not only do these reflect a delightful sense of the past, but several of the daytrips also expose you to the excitement of a changing Britain that is finding its role in a newly unified Europe.

Dining (and drinking) well is a vital element in any travel experience. For this reason, a selection of particularly enjoyable restaurants and pubs along the walking routes has been included for each of the daytrips. These are price-keyed, with an emphasis on the medium-to-low range, and have concise location descriptions that make them easy to find.

All of the daytrips can be made by rail, and all of those outside London itself by car as well. Specific transportation information is given in the "Getting There" section of each trip, and general information in the "Getting Around London" and "Getting Around Southeastern England" chapters. A feature called "Links" shows you how to go directly from one out-of-town destination to another without returning to London in case you'd like to spend one or more nights at country inns instead of sticking strictly to daytrips.

Time and weather considerations are important, and they've been included in the "Practicalities" section of each trip. These let you know, among other things, on which days the sights are closed, when the colorful outdoor farmers' markets are held, and which places should be avoided in bad weather. The location and telephone number of the local Tourist Information Centre is also given in case you have questions.

Many of the attractions have a nominal entrance fee—those that are free will come as a pleasant surprise. Cathedrals and churches depend on small donations in the collection box to help pay their maintenance costs, so it is only fair to leave some change when making a visit.

Finally, a gentle disclaimer. Places have a way of changing without warning, and errors do creep into print. If your heart is absolutely set on a particular sight, you should check first to make sure that it isn't closed for renovations, or that the opening times are still valid. The local tourist offices are always the best source of such up-to-the-minute information.

One last thought—it isn't really necessary to see everything at any given destination. Be selective. Your one-day adventures in and around London should be fun, not an endurance test. If it starts becoming that, just stroll over to the nearest café, tea shop, or pub and enjoy yourself. There will always be another day.

Happy Daytripping!

Section I

This street scene in Canterbury is typical of the sights you'll find close to London

DAYTRIP
STRATEGIES

The word "Daytrip" may not have made it into dictionaries yet, but for many experienced travelers it represents the easiest, most natural, and often the most economical approach to exploring a European country. This strategy, in which you base yourself in a central city and probe the surrounding country on a series of one-day excursions, is especially effective in the case of London and southeastern England.

ADVANTAGES:

  While not the answer to every travel situation, daytrips offer significant advantages over point-to-point touring following a set plan. Here are a dozen good reasons for considering the daytrip approach:

1. Freedom from the constraints of a fixed itinerary. You can go wherever you feel like going whenever the mood strikes you.
2. Freedom from the burden of luggage. Your bags remain in your hotel while you run around with only a guidebook and camera.
3. Freedom from the anxiety of reservation foul-ups. You don't have to worry each day about whether that night's lodging will actually materialize.
4. The flexibility of making last-minute changes to allow for unexpected weather, serendipitous discoveries, changing interests, new-found passions, and so on.
5. The flexibility to take breaks from sightseeing whenever you feel tired or bored, without upsetting a planned itinerary. Why not sleep late in your base city for a change?
6. The opportunity to sample different travel experiences without committing more than one day to them.
7. The opportunity to become a "temporary resident" of your base city. By staying there for a while you can get to know it in depth, becoming familiar with the local restaurants, shops, theaters, night life, and so on—enjoying them as a native would.
8. The convenience of not having to hunt for a hotel each day, along with the security of knowing that a familiar room is waiting back in your base city.
9. The convenience of not having to pack and unpack your bags each day. Your clothes can hang in a closet where they belong, or even be sent out for cleaning.
10. The convenience (and security!) of having a fixed address in your base city, where friends, relatives, and business associates can reach you in an emergency. It is exceedingly difficult to contact anyone who changes hotels daily.
11. The economy of staying at one hotel on a discounted longer-term basis, especially in conjunction with airline package plans. You can make advance reservations for your base city without sacrificing any flexibility at all.
12. The economy of getting the most value out of a railpass. Day-tripping is ideally suited to rail travel as the best train service operates out of base-city hubs. This is especially true in the case of London.

Above all, daytrips ease the transition from tourist to accomplished traveler. Even if this is your first trip abroad, you should be able to handle an uncomplicated one-day excursion such as the one to Canterbury or Bath on your own. The confidence gained will help immensely when you tackle more complex destinations, freeing you from the limitations of guided tours and putting you in complete control of your own trip.

DISADVANTAGES:

For all of its attractions, the daytrip concept does have certain restrictions. There are always a few areas where geography and the available transportation have conspired to make one-day excursions impractical, or at least awkward. In Britain, these include the Cotswolds, the West Country, the Lake District, much of Wales, and the Highlands of Scotland. Fortunately, only the first of these is anywhere near London.

Another disadvantage is that you will have to forego the pleasures of staying at country inns, which can be delightful experiences. Should this deter you from making daytrips, you can still get the most from this guidebook by referring to the "Links" feature on page 102. You might use daytrips part of the time and touring the rest.

GETTING TO LONDON:

Plenty of airlines fly the North Atlantic route to London, with fares, schedules, and package deals constantly changing to meet the competition. As seasoned travelers know, there are certain advantages to flying the major airline of the country you're visiting. For one thing, they are more familiar with your destination and can supply reliable advice and information about it. For another, despite a certain sameness of all aircraft, native lines do provide a touch of in-flight ambiance that eases the passage from one culture to another. They also tend to get the most favorable landing slots and airport facilities at their home bases.

These pluses would be negated if the airline itself were not up to snuff; fortunately **British Airways** is a consistent favorite among frequent travelers, offering more flights to London from more North American gateways than any other carrier, with 17 departure cities in all. If speed is more important than price, they are also the only airline with supersonic Concorde flights to London, arriving there only $3\frac{1}{2}$ hours after leaving New York. British Airways' own **Terminal 4** at London's Heathrow Airport was designed for convenience and rivals the best in the world today. It has direct bus and Underground service (see pages 19 and 21) to central London, as well as frequent shuttle buses to terminals 1, 2, and 3. Some other transatlantic carriers land at London's Gatwick Airport instead, which has excellent rail service to Victoria Station in London.

GETTING SETTLED:

Since your London accommodations will be your "home" for a while, you'll want to be especially careful in choosing a place that is pleasant, priced right, and conveniently located for your daytrip plans, both within and beyond London. This doesn't mean that they must be near a train station if you're traveling by rail, but should be close to an Underground (subway) stop that connects easily to the various stations.

Advance reservations for regular **hotels** are best made through your travel agent, who has access to more hotel information than any guidebook could possibly include. Be sure to ask about the economical **package plans** offered by several transatlantic airlines in conjunction with their flights. British Airways is the leader in this field, with a wide choice of hotels and lengths-of-stay in different price categories. If you wish, you can add on discounted car rentals, guaranteed theater tickets to the most popular shows, or sightseeing arrangements— all at a considerably lower price than they would cost if purchased separately. To take maximum advantage of this, it is important that you consult your travel agent as far in advance as possible and study the brochures carefully. Note that these packages require you to fly both ways on the issuing airline, and that they can be used with any applicable fare, from the speedy Concorde to the least expensive excursion.

You can save even more money by staying at a "**Bed-and-Breakfast**" establishment. These places often call themselves hotels but in fact are more like rooming houses. Private baths are rare, and usually the only meal offered is breakfast, but the bedrooms are almost always clean and pleasant enough. If you're willing to use the bath and toilet "down the hall," you'll find that bed-and-breakfast places are not only a good value but, being mostly family-operated, they provide a far more personal touch than you'll ever get in a hotel. Indeed, many travelers prefer "B&Bs" over hotels and return to the same ones year after year.

If you arrive in London without reservations, you'll find several organizations ready and willing to secure immediate lodging for you. Among these are the offices of the **London Tourist Board** in the Underground Station Concourse of terminals 1, 2, and 3 at Heathrow Airport and in the forecourt of Victoria Station, as well as the **British Travel Centre** at 12 Regent Street, two blocks south of Piccadilly Circus. These are both official agencies who are especially adept at finding budget accommodations. Their fees are reasonable, but expect to wait in line for service. More information about London's tourist offices will be found on page 22. **Commercial hotel booking agencies** have convenient service counters at the airports, and at Victoria, King's

Cross, and Liverpool Street train stations. They tend to favor mid-to-upper-price hotels, and sometimes charge exorbitant booking fees. Be sure to ask about the terms first.

GETTING AROUND:

Transportation within London is discussed in the short chapter beginning on page 19. Details about rail and road travel throughout the rest of southeastern England, including railpass plans, will be found on pages 97 through 103.

FOOD AND DRINK:

Several choice restaurants and pubs are listed for each destination in this book. Many of these are long-time favorites of experienced travelers and serve typically English food unless otherwise noted. Their approximate price range, based on the least expensive complete meal offered, is shown as:

$	—	Inexpensive, but may have fancier dishes available.
$$	—	Reasonable. These establishments may also feature daily specials.
$$$	—	Luxurious and expensive.
$$$+	—	Very expensive.
X:	—	Days or periods closed.

The quality of restaurant food in England has been getting better, although there is still plenty of room for improvement, especially in the middle price range. If you're really serious about dining, you should consult an up-to-date guide such as the red-cover *Michelin Great Britain and Ireland* or any of the *Egon Ronay* guides. It is always wise to check the posted menus before entering, paying particular attention to any daily set-meal specials. Some restaurants add a service charge to the bill, in which case there is no need to tip unless the service was extraordinary. Where no service charge is added, the waiter expects a gratuity of 10–15%.

Besides restaurants specializing in traditional English fare, you will find a great many featuring foreign cuisines, most notably French, Italian, Indian, and Chinese. American favorites such as hamburgers, chili, pizza, and the like are extremely popular.

For many, the traditional **English Breakfast** is the great treat of the day. Usually consisting (more or less) of fruit juice, cereal, eggs, bacon or sausages, grilled tomatoes or baked beans (!), toast with butter and marmalade, and tea or coffee, it is served by numerous hotels, especially in the "Bed-and-Breakfast" category. Be sure to ask about this before booking so you don't get stuck with the anemic "Continental" breakfast.

Having lunch at a **pub** will save you time and money, and is often a very pleasant experience. Not all pubs serve meals, and of those that do, not all serve especially good food. A reliable way to judge quality before eating is to size up the other customers and note whether the pub makes a special point of preparing meals. A great many pubs, especially in cities, do not serve evening meals. Most pubs are self-service in that you buy drinks at the bar, usually order food at a separate counter, and take both to a table. Tipping in this case is neither expected nor encouraged. Some pubs have full-service restaurants attached to them as well. Pubs in London are usually open on Mondays through Saturdays from 11 a.m. to 11 p.m., and on Sundays from noon to 3 p.m. and 7–10:30 p.m.

Beer, happily, remains the national beverage of Britain. It comes in a bewildering variety of tastes and local specialties. The most common types, at least on tap, are *lager*, which is somewhat similar to American and Continental beers and should be served cool; and *bitter*, the richly flavored traditional British brew, always served at cellar temperature. The latter is an acquired taste, but once you get used to it you'll probably be back for more. The best of these come from small local breweries, and are virtually never exported. "Real Ale," a term sponsored by the CAMRA organization, denotes cask-conditioned beer made the old-fashioned way without chemical additives. It is worth seeking out. A "free house" is a pub not owned or otherwise associated with a particular brewery—it is free to sell various brands. Asking the bartender for his—or her—advice will not only get you some interesting brews, it will often open the way to spirited conversations as well.

WHEN TO GO:

The best time to visit southeastern England is between mid-spring and early fall. The extra hours of sunlight in these months will greatly enhance your daytrips, as will the mild weather. While periods of rain are fairly frequent, the showers are also brief and usually blow over quickly. Always carrying a folding umbrella is good insurance against getting wet. A light jacket or sweater will also be welcome, sometimes even in the middle of July. England's fast-changing weather is utterly unpredictable but rarely given to extremes.

HOLIDAYS:
Legal holidays in England are:

January 1 (New Year's Day)	August Bank Holiday
Good Friday	(last Monday in
Easter Monday	August)
May Day (first Monday in May)	Christmas
Spring Bank Holiday (last Monday in May)	Boxing Day
	(December 26)

SUGGESTED TOURS:
Most of the do-it-yourself walking tours in this book are relatively short and all are easy to follow. On the assumption that you will probably be using public transportation, they always begin at the local train station, Underground, or bus stop. Those going by car can make a simple adjustment. Suggested routes are shown by heavy broken lines on the maps, while the circled numbers refer to major attractions or points of reference along the way. Remember that the tour routes are only suggestions—you may prefer to wander off on your own using the maps as a guide.

As a way of estimating the amount of time that any segment of a walking tour will take, you can look at the scale on the map and figure that the average person covers about 100 yards in one minute.

Trying to see everything in any given town could easily become an exhausting marathon. You certainly will enjoy yourself more by being selective and passing up anything that doesn't catch your fancy in favor of a friendly pub. Not all museums will interest you, and forgiveness will be granted if you don't visit *every* church.

Practical information, such as the opening times of various attractions, is as accurate as was possible at the time of writing, but everything is subject to change. You should always check with the local tourist information office if seeing a particular sight is crucially important to you.

*OUTSTANDING ATTRACTIONS:
An * asterisk before any attraction, be it an entire daytrip or just one painting in a museum, denotes a special treat that in the author's opinion should not be missed.

TOURIST INFORMATION:
Local sources of tourist information within London are discussed on page 22. Each of the daytrip destinations outside London has its own **Tourist Information Centre**, the location and phone number of which are listed in the "Practicalities" section for that daytrip, and the

location marked on the appropriate map by the word "**info**." These
local offices are usually closed on Sundays, and sometimes on Saturdays as well. To **phone** them from another town in England you must
first dial the area code, which always begins with 0 and is shown in
parentheses, followed by the local number. Note that London now
has two area codes; (071) for Inner London and (081) for Outer London. Most pay phones use coins and have operating instructions on
them, but some of the newer ones accept only the "Phonecard," a
pre-paid card available in various denominations at post offices and
newstands. The cost of each call is subtracted from the value of the
card as it is used.

ADVANCE PLANNING INFORMATION:
    The **British Tourist Authority** has branches throughout the world
to help you plan your trip. In North America these are located at:

40 West 57th St.,
New York, NY 10019-4001
Phone (212) 581-4700—FAX (212) 265-0649

875 North Michigan Ave., Suite 3320
Chicago, IL 60611
Phone (312) 787-0490—FAX (312) 787-7746

2305 Cedar Springs Road, Suite 210
Dallas, TX 75201-1814
Phone (214) 720-4040—FAX (214) 871-2665

350 South Figueroa, Suite 450
Los Angeles, CA 90071
Phone (213) 628-3525—FAX (213) 687-6621

94 Cumberland St., Suite 600
Toronto, Ont. M5R 3N3, Canada
Phone (416) 925-6326—FAX (416) 961-2175

COMMENTS:
    We are always grateful for comments from readers, which are ex-
tremely useful in preparing future editions of this or other books in
the series. Please write directly to the author, Earl Steinbicker, c/o
Hastings House, 141 Halstead Avenue, Mamaroneck, NY 10543; or FAX
(914) 835-1037. Thank you.

Section II

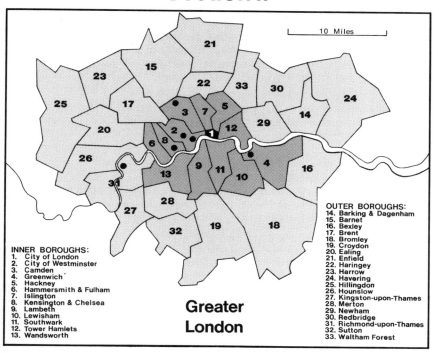

10 Miles

21
15
23
22 33 30
25 17 24
3 7 5
20 2 12 29 14
6 8 1
26 13 9 11 10 4 16
31
27 28
32 19 18

INNER BOROUGHS:
1. City of London
2. City of Westminster
3. Camden
4. Greenwich
5. Hackney
6. Hammersmith & Fulham
7. Islington
8. Kensington & Chelsea
9. Lambeth
10. Lewisham
11. Southwark
12. Tower Hamlets
13. Wandsworth

OUTER BOROUGHS:
14. Barking & Dagenham
15. Barnet
16. Bexley
17. Brent
18. Bromley
19. Croydon
20. Ealing
21. Enfield
22. Haringey
23. Harrow
24. Havering
25. Hillingdon
26. Hounslow
27. Kingston-upon-Thames
28. Merton
29. Newham
30. Redbridge
31. Richmond-upon-Thames
32. Sutton
33. Waltham Forest

Greater London

DAYTRIPS IN LONDON

Not only is London surrounded by dozens of tantalizing daytrip destinations, but it is also in itself the most varied and arguably the most interesting city on Earth. Once the heart of a far-flung Empire Upon Which the Sun Never Set, London is today the dynamic, vital, and rapidly changing metropolis of a newly unified Europe. Although many of its tourist attractions are rooted in timeless tradition, there is infinitely more to London than just the preserved past, as you will quickly discover.

The key to understanding Greater London (as the whole is called) is to realize that this is not just one homogenous city, but rather a mosaic of often unrelated villages and towns, each with its own distinct character, spread over some 620 square miles stretching about 35 miles from end to end. An incredibly large amount of it is given over to green parks and even forests. Within its boundaries can be found anything from high-rise office complexes to quaint rural hamlets; from elegant residential areas to colorful working-class neighborhoods. Greater London is divided into 12 Inner Boroughs and 20 Outer Boroughs, plus the tiny City of London, a self-governing ancient enclave of only one square mile in the very center of things. The population is about as cosmopolitan as you'll find, with people from all over the globe filling the air with the sounds of nearly every imaginable language.

Not content to be the world's best base for daytripping, London also offers within its borders some of the most enjoyable opportunities for one-day excursions to be found anywhere. The seven walking tours described in this section each cover a different aspect of London's seductive personality, and are designed to take you to nearly all of the most famous attractions as well as to a multitude of little-known discoveries. The actual walking distance of each tour can be comfortably covered in under two hours, leaving plenty of time for the sights, shopping, or just relaxing at a pub. Walking is by far the best way to explore the nooks and crannies of this most likable of cities and, besides, it will help undo the consequences of a full English breakfast.

The start and finish points of each of the walking tours can be easily reached by public transportation, and there are plenty of places along the way for cutting them short if you get tired. Additional attractions that could not be fit into the tour routes are described in the chapter beginning on page 89.

An Underground Train at Piccadilly Circus Station

Getting Around London

Although all of the tours are designed for walking, you will still need to use some form of transportation to get to their starting points, and later back to your hotel. Here are the options:

THE UNDERGROUND:

The **Underground**, also known as the **Tube**, is one of the best and most comprehensive subway systems in the world. Quite crowded during rush hours, it is otherwise a comfortable way to travel. Most of the lines are deeply underground and are reached by long escalators or elevators (lifts), except for the Circle, District, and Metropolitan lines, which operate nearer the surface. Each of the 11 separate **lines** has a name, is color coded, and connects with other lines at frequent interchange stations. Ask for a free **pocket-size map** with a station index, which makes everything perfectly clear. The system runs from around 5:30 a.m. until about midnight. For further information, phone (071) 222-1234.

Fares are calculated on a zone basis, and **tickets** can be purchased from booths in the stations or from vending machines. To use these, just push a button for your destination and insert the required amount in coins or bills. Most of them make change. On some machines you must first check the posted station list to determine the fare. The tickets operate turnstiles and are then returned to you. Hang onto yours as it is needed to go through the exit turnstile, after which it will be returned only if it is still valid for further travel. Economical **passes** are described below.

Be aware that at some stations the same platforms are used for several different final destinations. An illuminated sign indicates the routing for the next two or three trains, along with the number of minutes until their arrival.

The Piccadilly Line of the Underground extends all the way to **Heathrow Airport**, stopping first at the outlying Terminal 4 and then at the junction of terminals 1, 2, and 3. Trains run frequently, but make sure that the one you are boarding is going all the way. The journey from central London takes about 45 minutes. Those with heavy or bulky luggage will find the "Airbus" service to be more manageable.

BUSES:

London's famous **buses**, mostly red double-deckers, offer a view along with the ride. **Bus stops** are indicated by red-and-white signs; at those marked "Request" you must hail the bus by raising your hand. Be careful to note the route number and be sure that you're going in the right direction. Free **route maps** are available at Underground stations and tourist information offices, or you can get further information by phoning (071) 222-1234. Buses are particularly useful in those parts of London, such as Chelsea or Greenwich, that are not really served by the Underground. **Fares** are determined by distance, and tickets sold by the conductor or sometimes by the driver. Keep yours until the end of the journey. Economical **passes** are described below.

DOCKLANDS LIGHT RAILWAY:

Opened in 1987, this is London's newest form of public transportation. Offering spectacular vistas from its elevated tracks, the high-tech automated system at present operates from near the Tower of London eastwards through the revitalized Docklands area, with a useful line serving Island Gardens adjacent to the Greenwich Foot Tunnel under the Thames. In the near future the railway will be extended to the Bank station of the Underground, and then to the new London City Airport. Tickets are sold by vending machines and can also be valid for continuation on the Underground. Travel passes covering the appropriate zone are accepted.

BRITISH RAIL:

Regular commuter trains may seem like an odd way to get around London, but in some cases they are very practical, especially for those with a BritRail Pass. The starting and finishing points of the walking tours in Greenwich, Hampstead Heath, and Richmond are easily reached by frequent trains. A careful study of the British Rail Passenger Network Map (see page 98) or the Network SouthEast Map will reveal many interesting possibilities, including the new **ThamesLink** line between stations south of the river and King's Cross Station, the **North London Link**, and the decrepit but useful **Waterloo & City** line. A new high-speed line from Heathrow Airport to Paddington Station is due to open in 1993.

British Rail has an enormous number of stations within London itself, most of which are for local commuter trains only. Some of these double as Underground stations. Rail services for the daytrips outside of London (see Section III) depart from the mainline stations, which are shown on the map on page 99. These are all connected to the Underground system.

PASSES:

Passes for unlimited travel on London's Underground, buses, and in some cases the Docklands Railway and local British Rail trains, are a good way to save time and money if you intend to take more than 3 or 4 trips a day. They include the **Visitor Travelcard**, which can be purchased in North America and other overseas locations from travel agents or BritRail offices (see page 100). These come with a set of discount vouchers for selected tourist attractions (a nice little bonus), and are also valid for transfers to and from Heathrow Airport by Underground. This card is not sold in Britain.

A standard **Travelcard** for specific zones (or all zones) can be purchased at major Underground stations, London Transport information centers, British Rail ticket offices in London, or London Tourist Board offices. They are valid for either 1 or 7 days; the 7-day pass requiring a passport-size photo available from photomat machines in nearly all stations. The 1-day pass is not valid until after the morning rush hour on working days.

The **London Extra** is an interesting and economical arrangement for travelers who plan to both explore London and make daytrips throughout the southeast of England. It is described on page 100 and must be purchased from a travel agent or overseas BritRail office before leaving for Britain.

BOATS:

Floating on the Thames is a slow but highly enjoyable way to get to your destination while seeing the sights. Boats can be used on both the Greenwich and Richmond walking tours in this book, as well as to Hampton Court and other attractions. The most convenient departures are from Westminster Pier (near Parliament), with others from Charing Cross and Tower piers. For further information and schedules phone (071) 730-4812.

TAXIS:

Taxis are a favorite way of getting around town, and not too expensive if two or more travel together. You can hail cabs in the street when their "For Hire" sign is lit, go to a taxi rank, or phone for one. Fares are metered, higher between 8 p.m. and 6 a.m. and on weekends, and supplemented by charges for waiting, luggage, and additional passengers. A tip of 15% is expected.

AIRPORT BUS:

The express **Airbus** service provides an easy way to get to and from **Heathrow Airport**. It is particularly useful if you have too much luggage to handle easily on the Underground, and is vastly cheaper than taking a taxi. The A-1 route goes to Victoria Station and the A-2 to Russell Square, both with stops along the way. A brochure outlining this service is available at Underground stations and tourist information offices. The best way to and from **Gatwick Airport** is to use the Gatwick Express train, which connects the terminal building with London's Victoria Station in 30 minutes flat.

BY CAR:

In a word, don't. Only a native can possibly unscramble the maze of one-way streets or magically find a legitimate parking place. Illegally parked cars either get their wheels clamped by the police or are spirited away by an amazing truck that plucks it out of its space and dumps it onto a trailer. If you insist on facing this torture, remember that you have been warned. Save the car for out-of-town trips.

TOURIST INFORMATION:

London abounds in tourist offices. For general information concerning all of Britain you should visit the **British Travel Centre** at 12 Regent Street, two blocks south of Piccadilly Circus. Their phone number is (071) 730-3400. Open from 9 a.m. until 6:30 p.m. on Mondays through Fridays and from 10 a.m. until 4 p.m. on weekends, the center includes branch offices of the British Tourist Authority, British Rail, American Express, a hotel booking agency, a travel book store, and a gift shop.

More specific information about London is available from the **London Tourist Board**, with offices located in the forecourt of **Victoria Station** (also makes hotel bookings), in both **Harrods** and **Selfridges** department stores, at the West Gate of the **Tower of London** (Easter through October only), and in the Underground Station Concourse at terminals 1, 2, and 3 as well as the Terminal 2 Arrivals Concourse at **Heathrow Airport**. For phone inquiries dial (071) 730-3488.

Some districts of London have their own tourist information offices, as noted in the "Practicalities" section for each of the walking tours.

London
*The City

Visitors often (and quite understandably) confuse the City of London with London itself. Actually, the City (with a capital "C") refers to the semi-autonomous square mile extending from Temple Bar east to the Tower of London, and from the Thames north to the Barbican. This is the ancient core of London, the site of a prehistoric Celtic settlement and the walled Roman city of *Londinium*. It is today the commercial heart of Britain, and one of the most important financial centers on Earth.

With its own Lord Mayor and a separate police force, the City occupies a unique position in Britain's political structure. Its own local government, headquartered at the Guildhall, is elected by commercial interests, not by residents—of whom there are precious few. Even the sovereign of England cannot enter the City without symbolic permission from its Lord Mayor. You, however, can.

Over the centuries, the City has been continually destroyed and rebuilt, suffering especially from the Great Fire of 1666, the bombs of World War II and, more recently, from the hands of overzealous developers. Yet it remains an exceptionally interesting place, with many first-rate attractions such as St. Paul's Cathedral and the Tower of London scattered between the gleaming modern skyscrapers.

GETTING THERE:

The **Underground** station closest to the start of this walking tour is at Temple, on the Circle and District lines. Note that this station is closed on Sundays and holidays. During workday rush hours you could also take the Piccadilly Line extension to Aldwych. On Sundays and holidays the Embankment or Charing Cross stations should be used. A great many **bus** routes also serve this area. By **taxi**, ask the driver for The Temple. The nearest **British Rail** stations are Blackfriars and Charing Cross.

PRACTICALITIES:

The City is best seen on a working day, when the streets are alive with the sound of commerce. The Museum of London is closed on Mondays and holidays, while some other sights are closed on Sundays and/or holidays. Oddly, even some of the churches are locked on

Sundays, as are many pubs. The **City of London Information Centre**, phone (071) 606-3030, is located on St. Paul's Churchyard, opposite the south side of the cathedral. Information is also available at **London Tourist Board's** branch office by the West Gate of the Tower of London, open daily between Easter and the end of October.

FOOD AND DRINK:

Restaurants and pubs in the City cater primarily to businessmen and are usually closed on weekends, holidays, and in the evenings. Some choices are:

> **Le Poulbot** (45 Cheapside, 2 blocks northeast of St. Paul's Cathedral) This highly regarded basement restaurant features French cuisine. Proper dress expected, reservations needed, phone (071) 236-4379. X: Sat., Sun. $$$

> **Corney and Barrow** (109 Old Broad St., a block northeast of the Stock Exchange) Open for lunch only, this modern establishment is famed for its highly inventive dishes. Proper dress expected, reservations suggested, phone (071) 638-9308. X: Sat., Sun., holidays, $$$

> **Whittington's** (21 College Hill, a block west of Cannon Street Station) Inventive light lunches at a wine bar in a vaulted cellar. $$

> **Sweetings** (39 Queen Victoria St., 2 blocks southwest of the Bank of England) Long a lunchtime favorite among City businessmen, noted for its fish dishes. X: Sat., Sun., holidays. $$

> **El Vino** (47 Fleet St., 3 blocks east of Temple Bar) This famous old wine bar, a traditional lunchtime venue for businessmen, has caught up with the times and now serves women as well, provided they're dressed properly. Men must wear a jacket and tie to get in. $$

> **Ye Olde Cheshire Cheese** (145 Fleet St.) An historic pub and restaurant, last rebuilt in 1667. It seems that everyone born since then has been there at least once for a beer or the traditional English fare. X: Sun. $ and $$

> **Dickens Inn** (St. Katharine's Way, at St. Katharine's Docks) A pub and restaurant in an 18th-century warehouse, with indoor and outdoor tables overlooking the marina. Traditional English foods and real ale. $ and $$

> **Balls Brother** (2 Old Change Court, a block southeast of St. Paul's Cathedral) An old-fashioned wine bar with good lunches. X: Sat., Sun., holidays. $

> **Black Friar** (174 Queen Victoria St., opposite Blackfriars Station) Have lunch in an old pub with a stunning Art Nouveau interior and plenty of atmosphere. X: Sat., Sun., holidays. $

SUGGESTED TOUR:

Begin your walk at the **Church of St. Clement Danes** (1), close to both the Temple and Aldwych Underground stations and a bit over a half-mile northeast of Trafalgar Square. Strangely situated in the middle of the Strand, an ancient thoroughfare linking the City with Westminster, it was built by Sir Christopher Wren in 1682 on the site of earlier churches dating as far back as the 9th century. Practically destroyed during a 1941 air raid, the church was beautifully restored in 1958 and is now the central church of the Royal Air Force. It is perhaps best known for its carillon, heard on weekdays at 9 a.m., noon, and at 3 and 6 p.m., playing the tune of the nursery rhyme, "Oranges and lemons, say the bells of St. Clement's." Outside the rear of the church, facing Fleet Street, is a statue of Samuel Johnson, who was a member of the congregation.

Continue up the Strand to the site of the **Temple Bar** (2), the western boundary of the City of London ever since the Middle Ages. By tradition, this is the spot where the sovereign of England must halt and receive permission to enter the City. The gate itself—a traffic bottleneck—was removed in 1878 and replaced by the present monument in the center of the road, which at this point changes its name to Fleet Street.

Turn right and pass through a small gateway into Middle Temple Lane, leading to the quiet enclave of two of London's four Inns of Court, these two known collectively as **The Temple**. The name derives from the Order of Knights Templars, a religious and para-military organization that established its seat in England here in 1185. After the order was suppressed in the 14th century, the complex of monastic buildings fell into the hands of a group of lawyers who, as lawyers are wont to do, have occupied the premises ever since. Most of the present structures date from Elizabethan times and later, but a few are medieval. On the west side of the lane is the **Middle Temple** (3), whose Fountain Court is an oasis of calm in the midst of the bustling City. The adjoining Middle Temple Hall was built between the 14th and 16th centuries and restored after suffering terrible bomb damage in World War II. Tradition has it that Shakespeare performed in his own *Twelfth Night* here in 1602. The fine interior, seldom open, is well worth seeing if you get the chance.

Now pass through the Pump Court cloisters and into the grounds of the **Inner Temple** (4). The **Temple Church**, built in the 12th century by the Knights Templars, is among the most interesting medieval buildings in London. Its highly unusual round nave is based on the Church of the Holy Sepulchre in Jerusalem, and is perhaps the finest of the five surviving circular churches in England. An oblong chancel, in the Gothic style, was added in 1240. Severely damaged in 1941, the

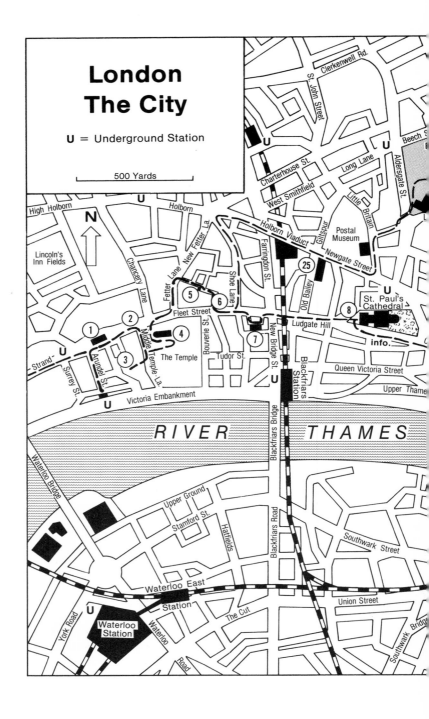

London
The City

U = Underground Station

|———— 500 Yards ————|

church has since been fully renovated and is usually open daily from 10 a.m. to 4 p.m., except during services.

Leave The Temple by way of Inner Temple Lane and turn right, going through an attractive 17th-century gateway and onto **Fleet Street**, named for the small river it once crossed, which now runs underground. Until a few years ago this was the center of England's newspaper business, but most of the publishers have since moved east into the Docklands and other areas. The fictional Sweeney Todd, the "Demon Barber of Fleet Street," was supposed to have had his shop next to **St. Dunstan's Church**. A left turn on Fetter Lane and a right at Trinity Church Passage brings you through some narrow alleyways to **Dr. Johnson's House** (5) on Gough Square. The first definitive dictionary of the English language was compiled here by Dr. Samuel Johnson, the literary giant of the 18th century, who lived in this typical late-17th-century town house from 1749 to 1759. His spirit is still to be felt throughout the neighborhood. You can step inside to see various memorabilia, as well as a first edition of the famed *Dictionary*. The house is open on Mondays through Saturdays, from 11 a.m. to 5:30 p.m., closing at 5 p.m. in winter.

Now follow the map to another place associated with Johnson, **Ye Olde Cheshire Cheese** pub (6), which was rebuilt in 1667. Dickens downed the occasional ale here, too, but the pub was most famous for its foul(fowl?)-mouthed parrot whose vocabulary of four-letter words astonished patrons for many years until 1926, when the bird finally expired. The attached restaurant is popular with tourists, but perhaps you'd like to step into the highly atmospheric bar for some real ale. Its entrance is on Wine Office Court, just off Fleet Street.

Continue down Fleet Street and turn right to **St. Bride's Church** (7), traditionally the house of worship for journalists. Although churches have stood on this site since Saxon times, the present structure was designed in 1675 by Wren, who rebuilt so many of the churches in the City after the disastrous Great Fire of 1666. St. Bride's is famous for its incredibly ornate steeple, at 226 feet the tallest of Wren's spires. The interior was badly damaged in World War II, and during reconstruction in the 1950s several interesting Roman and Saxon remains were discovered under the floor. These can be seen by visiting the **Crypt**, which also has an exhibition on the development of printing in Fleet Street. The church is open daily from 8:30 a.m. to 5:30 p.m.

Return to Fleet Street and turn right, continuing under the railway viaduct and up Ludgate Hill to one of London's stellar attractions. ***St. Paul's Cathedral** (8) has long been a monument to Britain's fortitude, a testimony to its stiff upper lip. Time and again the church was destroyed by fire, decay, and bombs; yet it has always come back to remind Britons of their heritage. The first house of worship on this site appeared in the 7th century but soon succumbed to flames, as did its successors. During the 12th century an immense cathedral was begun, one whose steeple eventually reached the amazing height of 489 feet before being demolished by lightning in 1561. In 1666 the Great Fire finished off the rest of the building, which was already in a state of sad neglect following the Civil War and the Great Plague.

The magnificent Renaissance structure you see today is the supreme masterpiece of **Sir Christopher Wren**, perhaps the greatest English architect of all time. His plan for rebuilding the entire burned-out City was never adopted, but St. Paul's and the many other Wren churches and secular buildings throughout London and elsewhere are evidence of a unique genius.

Begun in 1675, the new cathedral was completed by 1708. Although hit by several bombs during World War II, it survived the conflict thanks to the continual presence of a fire brigade determined to save this symbol of British perseverance. A postwar renovation has once again restored all of its former splendor.

The most outstanding feature of St. Paul's is its famous **Dome**, visible from all over London. Patterned after the great domes of St. Peter's in Rome and the Cathedral of Florence, it was the first of its type in Britain. Like those Renaissance domes of Italy, it is partly an illusion—a dome within a dome, supported by a hidden superstructure and crowned with a stone lantern. You can climb up through it for both a better understanding of its remarkable construction and for a marvelous view of the City.

Enter the cathedral through the elaborately decorated **West Front**, flanked by two Baroque towers. Wren originally designed the interior in the form of a Greek cross, but the Latin cross arrangement that was finally used was forced on him by the authorities, who may have been anticipating a possible return to Catholicism under James II. The accession to power in 1689 of William III, a staunch Protestant, insured that this would not happen.

If Wren had first conceived of the interior as being one of uncluttered elegance, it has since been filled with all kinds of monuments to national heroes, some of which are quite splendid. Don't miss Holman Hunt's piously Victorian painting, *The Light of the World,* in the south aisle of the nave. At the crossing you can look up into the interior dome, suspended beneath the hidden brick cone that supports the stone lantern and the lead-covered wooden outer dome. The early-18th-century monochromatic **frescoes** of the inner dome depict scenes from the life of St. Paul.

There is a small admission charge for entry into the **Chancel**, well worth it for the delightful **choir stalls** and organ case carved by Grinling Gibbons, the most famous English sculptor of the 17th century.

Under the Dome inside St. Paul's

The baldachin over the **High Altar** is a postwar addition, more or less following Wren's original drawings. Behind it, in the apse, is the **American Chapel** commemorating the names of 28,000 Americans based in Britain who fell in World War II. Along the south choir aisle is the only monument to have survived intact from the medieval cathedral, a macabre figure of the poet John Donne clad in a shroud. It still shows traces of the Great Fire.

The enormous ***Crypt**, believed to be the largest in Europe, is entered from the south transept upon payment of a modest charge. Fittingly, it contains the tomb of Sir Christopher Wren under the famous Latin inscription *Si monumentum requiris, circumspice*—"If you seek his monument, look around you." Wren died in 1723 at the ripe old age of 91. At the east end of the crypt is the Chapel of the Order of the British Empire, and nearby are the grandiose tombs of the **Duke of Wellington** and **Lord Nelson**. The **Treasury**, beneath the north transept, displays ecclesiastical vestments, illuminated manuscripts, and religious objects. Be sure to examine Wren's **Great Model**, a earlier design for the cathedral that was rejected. It is now on view beneath the nave, near the **Lecture Room** with its interesting audiovisual show. As you stroll around the crypt you will come across literally hundreds of memorials to famous English men and women.

Returning from the depths of the crypt, you may want to climb up into the ***Dome**, for which there is a separate entrance fee. The stairs for this are at the corner of the nave and the south transept. An easy climb brings you to the **South Triforium Gallery**, after which you continue upwards to the renowned **Whispering Gallery** with its peculiar acoustics. The slightest sound made near its wall travels completely around the dome without being heard elsewhere. A steeper climb now leads to the **Stone Gallery** for a fine view of London. Those endowed with excessive energy will, of course, want to continue all the way to the top, where the panorama from the **Golden Gallery** is unmatched.

St. Paul's Cathedral is open daily from 8 a.m. to 6 p.m., closing at 5 p.m. in winter. The Chancel, Crypt, and Dome may usually be visited between 10 a.m. (11 a.m. on Saturdays) and 4 p.m., on Mondays through Saturdays daily, but not on Sundays, Good Friday, or Christmas Day. Access is limited during services, and guided tours are offered on Mondays through Saturdays.

The route now leads past the City Information Centre on St. Paul's Churchyard and continues down Cannon Street, passing the train station. Turn right on King William Street and amble out onto **London Bridge** (9) for a good view of activities on the River Thames. The first bridge on this approximate site was a wooden structure erected after A.D. 43 by the Romans and rebuilt many times after frequently falling down, as recalled in the famous nursery rhyme. In the 12th century it was replaced by a stone bridge whose piers blocked the flow of water to such an extent that the Thames often froze over in winter. This span carried on it a number of houses and shops, a chapel, and two gatehouses decorated with the severed heads of traitors. Until 1729 it remained the only bridge across the river. Finally, it became inadequate for the traffic and a new bridge was built in the early 19th century, which in turn proved to be too small. Carefully dismantled in 1970, its numbered stones were sold for some one million pounds to the developers of Lake Havasu City, Arizona, where it was re-erected over a small lake. The present London Bridge was opened in 1973. Tourists often confuse the name with the more spectacular Tower Bridge, located a half-mile downstream.

Now retrace your steps and turn right to the **Monument** (10), a 202-foot-tall Doric column designed by Wren and erected to commemorate the Great Fire of 1666. According to tradition, the conflagration began exactly 202 feet from its base, in Pudding Lane. An inscription, removed in 1831, once unjustly attributed the tragedy to a Catholic plot. Yes, you can climb all 311 steps to the platform near its top, but the view is somewhat obstructed by modern office buildings. Ascents—on foot—may be made from April through September, on Mondays through Fridays from 9 a.m. to 6 p.m. and on Saturdays and Sundays from 2–5:30 p.m.; and also from October through March on Mondays through Saturdays from 9 a.m. to 4 p.m.

Fish Street leads to the busy Lower Thames Street, across which stands the **Church of St. Magnus the Martyr** (11). Rebuilt by Wren in 1676, it is noted for its formidable 185-foot steeple as well as for its splendid interior. The rector of the pre-fire church on the site, who published the first complete English Bible in 1535, is buried within. Take special note of the church's porch, through which passed the approach to the medieval Old London Bridge.

Recross Lower Thames Street and follow Pudding Lane, Monument Street, and Botolph Lane to the **Church of St. Mary at Hill** (12) on Lovat Lane. Yet another Wren church, it is well hidden but worth seeking out for its unusual box pews, fine woodwork interior, and genuine Dickensian atmosphere.

The route now takes you down Great Tower Street to the **Church of All Hallows-by-the-Tower** (13), which (surprise!) is not by Wren. In fact, its major attraction has little to do with religion, the **Undercroft** being an *in situ* **museum of Roman London**. Among the ruins of a Roman house are ashes from Boadicea's sack of *Londinium* in A.D. 61, bits of a Saxon church from the 7th century, an altar from the Crusades, and a model of Roman London. The aboveground part of the church, except for its 17th-century **Tower** from which Samuel Pepys witnessed the Great Fire, was almost totally destroyed during a 1940 air raid and rebuilt in the 1950s. It has historical connections with the United States, being the church where William Penn was baptized in 1644 and President John Quincy Adams was married in 1797. Although the church proper is new, it contains several treasures including a magnificent wooden font cover attributed to Grinling Gibbons, superb ship models, and a fine collection of brasses—some of which may be rubbed to make your own souvenirs.

And now on to one of England's most important tourist sights— the ***Tower of London** (14). Actually located just east of the City limits, this massive fortress was begun by William the Conqueror in 1067, shortly after the Battle of Hastings had established Norman rule in England. Its initial purpose was to protect the conquerors from the vanquished Anglo-Saxons, but throughout most of its bloody history it has been used more as a prison and place of execution. It also served as a sometimes royal residence until the reign of James I, although the palatial buildings have long since disappeared along with the royal menagerie. Among the other functions it once had were those of a mint, an observatory, a treasury, an arsenal, and a military garrison.

The Tower of London is an extremely popular place, attracting huge

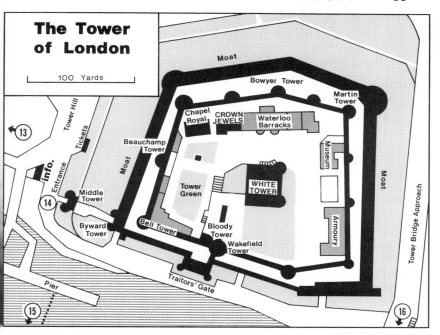

The Tower
of London

100 Yards

crowds during the height of the tourist season. Depending on the
length of the waiting lines and the number of sights you plan to see,
a visit here can easily take several hours. You may prefer to return on
another day, preferably early in the morning and hopefully not on a
Sunday. In any case, the opening times are: from March through October, Mondays through Saturdays from 9:30 a.m. to 5 p.m. and Sundays from 2–5 p.m.; and from November through February, Mondays
through Saturdays from 9:30 a.m. to 4 p.m., closed on Sundays. It is
also closed on a few major holidays. The Crown Jewels cannot be seen
during February. Those returning at another time can easily reach the
Tower by taking the Underground (Circle and District lines) to Tower
Hill.

Purchase your ticket and enter via the **Middle Tower**, across from
the tourist information office. Guided tours led by Yeoman Warders
(Beefeaters) in historic costume are usually available here and make
an excellent way to start your visit, after which you can poke about on
your own. A causeway leads across the former moat that was drained
in 1843 and is now a grassy ditch. The 13th-century **Byward Tower** still
retains its portcullis machinery. Pass through it and continue to the
Traitors' Gate, the medieval entrance from the Thames, where boats
bearing prisoners once docked.

A left turn brings you past the **Wakefield Tower**, where the saintly Henry VI was murdered in 1471. The **Bloody Tower**, under which you pass, was the scene of the murder of the Little Princes—the deposed child-king Edward V and his younger brother, the Duke of York, in 1485, supposedly on orders from Richard III. This was also the place where Sir Walter Raleigh wrote his *History of the World* while imprisoned from 1603 until 1615. Released to undertake an expedition to the New World, he was later executed in 1618 after returning empty handed.

You have now entered **Tower Green**, a large open space where the scaffold was located, its site marked by a brass plate. To the left stands the **Queen's House**, now the residence of the Governor, the **Yeoman Gaoler's House**, where the captured Nazi leader Rudolf Hess was incarcerated in 1941; the 13th-century **Beauchamp Tower**, long a prison; and the **Chapel Royal of St. Peter ad Vincula**, rebuilt in 1307 and used as the burial place for such beheaded victims as Anne Boleyn and Catherine Howard—both wives of Henry VIII—and many other illustrous names. Be on the lookout for some of the six **ravens** who officially inhabit the Tower's precincts; legend has it that if they leave the Tower will fall. To forestall this possibility, they are fed a generous allowance of meat.

The east side of Tower Green is totally dominated by the massive ***White Tower**, the oldest remaining part of the fortress complex. Begun in 1078 by William the Conqueror to replace his wooden structure of 1067, it was covered with whitewash in 1241, hence the name. Sir Christopher Wren enlarged the windows during the late 17th century, and a few other modifications were made, but basically the tower is the same today as it was in Norman times. The immensely strong walls are between 12 and 15 feet thick and rise to a height of 90 feet.

Enter by way of the staircase on the north side and climb to the first floor, where the **Sporting and Tournament Galleries** display weapons from the crossbow to pistols, along with armor for jousting. The second floor contains the **Chapel of St. John**, the oldest existing church in London, where medieval kings spent the night before their coronations. There is also another exhibition of arms and armor. The third floor is devoted to armor from Tudor and later times. Be sure to examine the various suits made for Henry VIII, which became larger and larger as the king grew fatter and fatter. Now descend to the ground floor for a look at weapons from the 16th through the 19th centuries.

Leave the White Tower and stroll over to the Jewel House, where you can join the inevitable queues for a hurried look at the ***Crown Jewels**, the most popular attraction at the Tower of London. Nearly all of the treasures date from after the Restoration of 1660, most of the earlier regalia having been plundered by Cromwell. The displays begin with a collection of banqueting plate, swords, maces, coronation robes, and other accoutrements of royalty. From here you move into a well-guarded vault protecting the Crown Jewels themselves. The **Royal Sceptre** contains the 530-carat Star of Africa, the largest diamond ever cut; while the Queen Mother's Crown of 1937 is fitted with the fabulous **Koh-i-Noor** diamond. All around these glitter other priceless objects, but you'll have little time to examine them as the line is kept moving at top speed.

There are several other attractions at the Tower of London that might interest you. The **Wall Walk** atop the curtain wall of the Inner Ward between the Wakefield and Martin towers provides exceptionally nice views of both the precincts and the Thames. Near its northern end stands the **Bowyer Tower** with its gruesome collection of torture instruments, while just south of this the Waterloo Barracks house the **Oriental Gallery** of arms and armor from Asia, North Africa, and eastern Europe. Adjacent to it is the **Heralds Museum** of British heraldry. Along the eastern wall you will find the **Royal Fusiliers Museum**, which traces the history of the famous City of London Regiment, and the **New Armoury** with its collection of small arms.

Every evening at 10 p.m. the Tower is officially locked up for the night with the colorful **Ceremony of the Keys**, an event that can be attended upon written application only. Ask at the information office for current details.

While still in a military mood, you might want to cross the Thames by ferry to visit **H.M.S. *Belfast*** (15), a World War II cruiser permanently moored in the river as an extension of the Imperial War Museum. Built in 1938, she saw action with the Arctic convoys, the D-Day landings, and in the Korean War. You can climb all over it following a marked route, but be aware that some of the passageways and ladders are a bit cramped. The ferry service to it operates from Tower Pier (next to the Tower of London) daily during the summer and on weekends in winter. You can also get there via Tower Bridge. This proud fighting ship is open every day except for a few major holidays, from 11 a.m. until 5:20 p.m., closing at 4 p.m. in winter.

The wharf along the south side of the Tower of London leads to ***Tower Bridge** (16), easily one of the most recognizable landmarks in town. This bascule-type drawbridge, with its tall Gothic Revival towers and elevated walkway, was built around the end of the 19th century as the most easterly span over the Thames. At one time it was raised quite frequently, but since large ships seldom sail this far up the river anymore, it is now operated only about five times a week.

The familiar overhead walkway, closed to the public since 1909 after it became too popular a spot for suicides and prostitutes, has now been enclosed in glass and reopened as part of an **exhibition of the bridge**. The panoramic views from it, especially of the Tower, are quite

The Tower Bridge

stunning and there are special open windows for picture taking. Well-marked steps from the wharf lead to the base of the north tower, from which you ascend by lift to the walkway after first purchasing a ticket. As a special treat, the original Victorian steam engines that operated the bascules until 1975—when they were replaced by electric motors—have been preserved and are now part of the fascinating **Engine Room Museum** at the south end of the bridge. Visits to the walkway and the museum can be made daily except on a few major holidays, from 10 a.m. to 5:45 p.m., closing at 4 p.m. from November through March.

Return across the bridge and follow the map to **St. Katharine's Dock** (17). Once a prosperous dock serving the City of London, it was severely damaged in World War II and finally closed in 1968. Now restored as a marina and pleasure area, St. Katharine's is a delightful place to visit. One of the original 19th-century warehouses has been tastefully converted into apartments, shops, and restaurants; and an older wooden brewery into a pub. The new structures, including a hotel and the World Trade Centre, are in a style that complements the Victorian atmosphere. An extra bit of color is added by the presence of several old Thames sailing barges, which are available for hire.

Cross the Tower Bridge approach road through an underground passage to the north side of the Tower of London, then take another underpass to the **Tower Hill Underground Station**, near which is a

In the Engine Room Museum

section of the ancient **Roman Wall**. You have now passed the halfway point of this walking tour. The attractions that lie ahead will take considerably less time than those already covered, but if you're tired, this is a good place to stop.

The route now leads into the heart of the financial district, passing the attractive old **Church of St. Olave** (18) to which the diarist Samuel Pepys belonged in the 17th century. Its churchyard was immortalized as "St. Ghastly Grim" in Dickens' novel *The Uncommercial Traveller*, and is appropriately decorated with skulls. Just north of this is the nicely-restored **Fenchurch Street Station** of 1840, the first rail terminal to be built in the City. Continue past it and turn right on Fenchurch Street, then left onto Leadenhall Street.

The stunning new **Lloyd's of London Building** (19), opened in 1986, has a 200-foot-high glass atrium, six tall towers of shiny steel, and external lifts. You can ride one of these to the 4th floor for a look at the **Visitors' Gallery** and the famed 18th-century Lutine Bell, which is struck once for a disaster at sea and twice for a safe arrival. This world-famous insurance organization traces its roots all the way back to the 17th century. Visits can be made on Mondays through Fridays, from 10 a.m. to 2:30 p.m..

Now head north on St. Mary Axe to the **Church of St. Helen Bishopgate** (20). Begun in the 13th century, it is one of the most appealing in the City, and is noted for its intact medieval interior, monuments (note especially the one to the 16th-century financier Sir Thomas Gresham who first postulated that "bad money drives out good"), brasses, wood carvings, and a remarkable poor box of 1620.

From across Bishopgate you get a good view of the 600-foot **National Westminster Tower**, opened in 1981 as the tallest office building in Britain. Turn left and continue down Threadneedle Street past the modern **Stock Exchange** and the 19th-century **Royal Exchange**, which now deals in international financial futures and whose Visitors' Gallery is open on Mondays through Fridays, from 11:30 a.m. to 1:45 p.m. Opposite this stands the stately **Bank of England** (21), the renowned "Old Lady of Threadneedle Street," founded in 1694 to finance England's wars against France. Nationalized in 1946, it is the central bank, manages the national debt, and issues notes for England and Wales. Its arcane workings are explained in the bank's new **museum**, whose entrance is around the corner on Bartholomew Lane. Visits may be made from Good Friday through September, on Mondays through Saturdays, from 10 a.m. to 6 p.m., and on Sundays from 2–6 p.m. During the rest of the year it is open on Mondays through Fridays, from 10 a.m. to 6 p.m. **Mansion House**, on the south side of the intersection, is the official residence of the Lord Mayor and may be visited only on prior written application. The **Bank Underground Station** is unusual in that it is also the terminus of British Rail's strange Waterloo and City Line, otherwise known as "The Drain." Railfans may want to ride it to Waterloo Station and back for a singular experience. The Bank Station is also due to become the City terminus of the Docklands Light Railway.

From here the route leads to the **Guildhall** (22), seat of government for the Corporation of the City of London ever since the Middle Ages. The present structure dates in part from 1411, but has been substantially altered over the years, especially after the Great Fire of 1666 and the bombs of World War II. You can usually enter its magnificent 15th-century **Great Hall**, used for meetings and state banquets, on Mondays through Saturdays, from 10 a.m. to 5 p.m., and also on Sundays in summer, but not during special functions. Be sure to inspect the two giant wooden statues of Gog and Magog mounted on the Musicians' Gallery at the west end. Depicting legendary characters from pre-Roman Britain, these are actually post-war replicas of a pair destroyed in the Blitz. The large **Crypt**, with its columns of Purbeck marble, has survived intact since the 15th century. It is not normally open to visitors, but the officer in charge may let you go down if you ask.

The **Guildhall Library**, in an adjacent building to the west, was first founded in 1425 and has a wonderful collection of old books, maps, drawings and the like. Next to it is the **Guildhall Clock Museum**, where hundreds of ancient timepieces from the 15th century to the present are on display.

Now carefully follow the map around the rear of the Guildhall, up steps and across two overpasses to the **Barbican** (23). Occupying a 60-acre site that was totally devastated by World War II bombs, this monumental construction project incorporates apartment buildings of up to 40 stories, an artificial lake, gardens, covered walkways on several levels, and the Museum of London. It is virtually the only residential area within the City. Depending on your view of 1960s modern architecture, it can seem to either represent a bold new utopia or appear to be a bleak and even brutal mass of windswept concrete. Fortunately, its coldness has been relieved by the opening in 1982 of the lively **Barbican Arts Centre** at the northern end. Home to the London Symphony Orchestra and the Royal Shakespeare Company, this complex contains a concert hall, several theaters, a library, an art gallery, exhibition halls, restaurants, and shops. The new **Royal Britain** exhibition is nearby on Aldersgate Street, just north of Beech Street. Using the latest in theatrical technology, it re-creates scenes from over a thousand years of royal history and is open daily from 9 a.m. to 5:30 p.m.

Thread your way through the maze of walkways to the **Museum of London** (24), housed in a stunning modern structure in the southwest corner. The fascinating displays trace the history of London from prehistoric times to the present, with an emphasis on the social context. Just a few of the highlights include sculptures from the Roman Temple of Mithras, the Cheapside Hoard of 16th-century jewelry, an audio-visual representation of the Great Fire, a cell from Newgate Prison, shop interiors, a Victorian pub, and a 1920s elevator from a department store. The 18th-century **Lord Mayor's Ceremonial Coach**, still used once a year, ends the exhibition on a note of grandeur. The museum is open on Tuesdays through Saturdays from 10 a.m. to 6 p.m., and on Sundays from 2–6 p.m.

Cross the busy intersection on the walkway, descend to street level, and follow the map to the **Old Bailey** (25). Built on the site of the infamous Newgate Prison, outside of which public hangings were held until 1868, this early-20th-century building houses the Central Criminal Court for Greater London. Fans of the fictional barrister Horace Rumpole may want to stop in to watch the proceedings, which are open to the public on Mondays through Fridays, from 10:30 a.m. to 1 p.m. and 2–4 p.m.

You have now reached the end of this walking tour. The nearest Underground station, St. Paul's, is at the intersection of Newgate Street and Cheapside, just a short stroll to the east. Alternatively, you might prefer to follow the map back to Fleet Street where one of the historic pubs can provide a well-earned reward.

London

*Westminster

This classic walk takes you through the heart of official London and the seat of the British government, passing such famous sights as Trafalgar Square, the Houses of Parliament, Westminster Abbey, Buckingham Palace, and St. James's Park as well as world-class museums including the Tate Gallery and the National Gallery. This is also where you can best witness the ceremonial pomp for which England is renowned, and delight in the colorful trappings of an empire that has long since faded.

Westminster is the royal and political district of the much larger City of Westminster, which evolved considerably later than its rival to the east, the City of London. Both cities are among the 33 boroughs that make up Greater London. Westminster first developed around an isolated 8th-century abbey then known as the West Minster for its location in relation to the City. A royal palace was built in the early 11th century on the site of what are now the Houses of Parliament. In 1529, Henry VIII confiscated the archbishop's palace on nearby Whitehall and made it into his own residence, of which only a small part remains. Throughout most of its history, the area of Westminster has been the administrative center of England, a role it continues to play today.

Expect to encounter a great many tourists along the route of this walking tour, and don't forget to have your picture taken on the bridge, with "Big Ben" in the background.

GETTING THERE:

The **Underground** station nearest to the beginning (and end) of this walk is Charing Cross, served by the Bakerloo, Northern, and Jubilee lines. Those using the Circle or District lines may prefer to get off at the nearby Embankment station. A great many **bus** routes converge on this area. By **taxi**, ask the driver for Trafalgar Square. The closest **British Rail** station is Charing Cross.

PRACTICALITIES:

Any time is a good time to explore Westminster, but note that some of the sights are closed on major holidays and/or Sunday mornings. Both the Banqueting House and the Queen's Gallery are closed on Mondays, and the Royal Mews are open only on Wednesday and

Thursday afternoons. Most of the attractions in Westminster Abbey are closed on Sundays. The **British Travel Centre** at 12 Regent Street, phone (071) 730–3400, is just a few blocks northwest of Trafalgar Square. Another good source of information is the **London Tourist Board** office in the forecourt of Victoria Station.

FOOD AND DRINK:

Restaurants and pubs in this area cater mainly to government workers, businessmen, and tourists. A few good choices are:

Suntory (72 St. James's St., just north of St. James's Palace) First-rate Japanese cuisine served with great style. X: Sun., holidays. $$$

Tate Gallery Restaurant (in the Tate Gallery) Excellent English cuisine in a beautiful setting, with a formidable wine list. Reservations advised, phone (071) 834–6754. X: Sun. $$$ and $$

Gran Paradiso (52 Wilton Rd., 2 blocks southwest of Victoria Station) Superb Italian cuisine in cheerfully eclectic surroundings. X: Sat. lunch., Sun., late Aug. $$

Sherlock Holmes (10 Northumberland St., 2 blocks southeast of Trafalgar Square) A famous old pub and restaurant filled with Holmes memorabilia, even an upstairs re-creation of 221B Baker St. Sir Arthur Conan Doyle was a regular when it was called the Northumberland Arms. $$ and $

Cask and Glass (39 Palace St., 2 blocks east of the Royal Mews) Light lunches in a cozy, bright little pub. X: Sun. $

Field's (in the Church of St. Martin-in-the-Fields, Trafalgar Sq.) Light lunches and hot meals in the crypt, under a vaulted brick ceiling. $

Tate Gallery Coffee Shop (in the Tate Gallery) Not to be confused with the famous restaurant adjacent, this self-service cafeteria offers delicious light lunches in a suitably artistic setting. X: Sun. $

SUGGESTED TOUR:

All distances to and from London are measured from **Trafalgar Square** (1), making this the true center of the capital as well as the starting point of this walking tour. It is also a favorite gathering place for Londoners and the rallying point for political demonstrations. The square, laid out in the mid-19th century, is dominated by **Nelson's Column**, an immense 172-foot-hight monument to the victor at the Battle of Trafalgar, in which British naval supremacy was firmly established in 1805.

On the north side of the square stands the **National Gallery**, the **National Portrait Gallery**, and the famous **Church of St. Martin-in-the-**

Fields. Visits to these are best saved until the end of the walk, as you'll be coming back this way. At the extreme south end, on a traffic island, is the 1633 equestrian **Statue of Charles I**, with the king looking down Whitehall to the scene of his martyrdom at the hands of Cromwell. In 1655 the statue was sold for scrap by Parliament, but secretly saved and re-erected after the Restoration. It stands on the site of the 13th-century Charing Cross, which was destroyed by the Puritans. An 1865 replica of this is now in front of the nearby Charing Cross Station.

The broad thoroughfare known as **Whitehall** leads south towards Westminster Abbey and the Houses of Parliament, thus linking the government with the commercial interests of the City. Its very name has become synonymous with British administration, and the street is today lined with ministries.

Until the end of the 17th century, the great **Palace of Whitehall** complex occupied nearly all of the space on either side of the present road. Begun in the 13th century as a mansion for the Archbishop of York, it was enlarged by Cardinal Wolsey and seized in 1529 by Henry VIII, who gave it the name. Whitehall was a residence for all of the subsequent monarchs of England until William and Mary moved into Kensington Palace, after which it accidentally burned down and was never rebuilt. The only part to have survived intact is the Banqueting House, described below.

Stroll down the street, passing the handsome Old Admiralty of 1726 on the right. Just beyond this is the 18th-century **Horse Guards Building** (2), where a mounted changing-of-the-guard ceremony is held by the Household Cavalry on Mondays through Saturdays at 11 a.m., and on Sundays at 10 a.m., except in very wet weather. The Horse Guards Parade, beyond the arch, is the setting for the annual Trooping of the Color ceremony held each June.

Across the street stands the elegant Palladian-style **Banqueting House** (3), the only structure remaining from the former Palace of Whitehall. Built in 1625 for James I by the noted architect Inigo Jones, it features a fabulous **painted ceiling** by Rubens celebrating in allegorical terms the merits of the Stuart dynasty. This was commissioned by Charles I who, ironically, was led to his beheading in 1649 through a window in this very hall. The king died with great dignity on a scaffold outside, after which royalty was abolished during the 11 years of the Commonwealth. The Banqueting House is open to visitors on Tuesdays through Saturdays, from 10 a.m. to 5 p.m.; and on Sundays from 2–5 p.m. It is closed on a few major holidays and for special functions.

Continue down Whitehall to the next right turn, which is often blocked off for security reasons. There, at **Number 10 Downing Street** (4), is the official residence of the Prime Minister. Its deceptively sim-

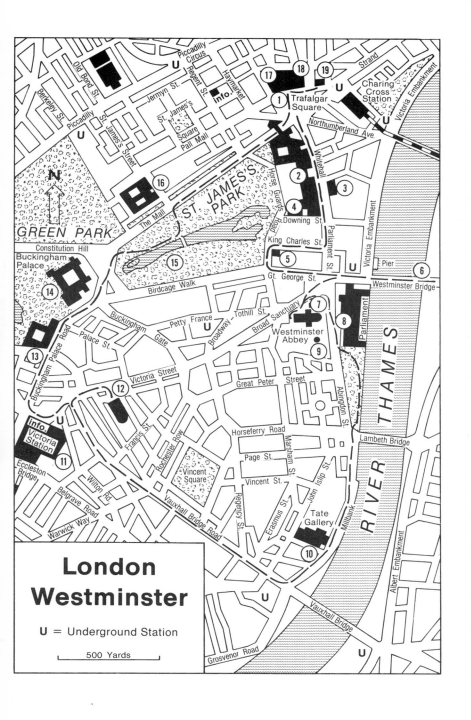

London
Westminster

U = Underground Station

500 Yards

ple façade belies a large and elegant interior, which also houses the Cabinet Room. With a great deal of luck, you might be able to catch a glimpse of some dignitary coming or going. The Chancellor of the Exchequer lives next door at number 11.

Whitehall becomes Parliament Street at the Cenotaph, an austere monument to Britain's war dead. Turn right on King Charles Street and descend the steps at its far end to visit the **Cabinet War Rooms** (5), an underground command center from which Sir Winston Churchill, his cabinet, and the chiefs of staff of Britain's armed forces directed the war effort from 1939 until 1945. Time has stood still since then, and in 1981 some 19 of the cramped rooms in this fortified bunker were opened to the public under the auspices of the Imperial War Museum. Among the highlights are the Cabinet Room, the Transatlantic Telephone Room from which Churchill could hold scrambled conversations with President Roosevelt, the Map Room, and the Prime Minister's Room, which provided office space and an emergency bedroom for Churchill. This fascinating place is open daily from 10 a.m. until 6 p.m., except on a few major holidays.

Now follow the map to **Westminster Bridge** (6) and walk out on it for a splendid view of the Houses of Parliament and the world-famous Clock Tower commonly (though incorrectly) known as ***Big Ben**. Actually, that name refers only to the largest bell in the clock, so-called after a rather corpulent man named Ben. There are several versions of the story, but no one really knows who Ben was. At the northwest foot of the bridge is **Westminster Pier**, from which boats depart frequently for various places along the Thames.

Retrace your steps to Parliament Square, a large open area with statues of famous statesmen including Churchill and Lincoln. South of this stands ***Westminster Abbey** (7), surely the most important house of worship in Britain. It is, in effect, the entire nation's church and a great repository of English history. This is where nearly all of the kings and queens since William the Conqueror have been crowned, and where a great many of them up to George II are buried along with leading statesmen and other notables. As a "Royal Peculiar" serving the Crown and the State, Westminster Abbey is independent of both the Bishop of London and the Archbishop of Canterbury.

The first abbey on this then-isolated site was probably built during the 8th century. This was replaced by a new church in the Norman style, started in 1050 by Edward the Confessor, who had erected his new royal palace nearby. Henry III, inspired by the magnificent French Gothic style, began in 1245 to rebuild the entire structure in the form you see today, a task that took some 250 years. The marvelous chapel of Henry VII was added in the early 16th century, and the west towers in the 18th century. Despite these and other changes, the abbey has

Inside the Cabinet War Rooms

a remarkable sense of unity about it.

Enter through the west front and step into the lofty **nave**. Just inside the door is a simple memorial to Winston Churchill, beyond which is the **Tomb of the Unknown Warrior** of World War I. On the first pier to the right hangs the famous medieval portrait of Richard II, the earliest known painting of an English sovereign. All around you are memorials to famous people, not all of whom are actually buried here.

An admission charge is made to go beyond the choir screen, or you might prefer to take one of the excellent guided **Super Tours** conducted by vergers. These last about 90 minutes and are booked from a desk in the south aisle. They include visits to areas that are not otherwise accessible and are operated fairly frequently on Mondays through Fridays, and less so on Saturdays. There are no tours on Sundays.

Continue up the north aisle to the north transept, burial place of several eminent statesmen. To the right is the Choir and the **Sanctuary**, where coronations take place. The north ambulatory has several interesting chapels, after which you step up into the utterly fantastic and profusely decorated early-16th-century ***Chapel of Henry VII**, with its high fan-vaulted ceiling and colorful banners. The exceptionally beautiful tomb of Henry VII is in front of the **Royal Air Force Chapel**, which commemorates the 1940 Battle of Britain. Don't miss the wonderfully carved misericords in the choir stalls. Along the north aisle is the somewhat modest tomb of **Elizabeth I**, which she shares with her sister, Mary I. In the south aisle is buried, among others, **Mary, Queen of Scots** for whom James I erected a grand tomb.

A bridge leads to the ***Chapel of Edward the Confessor**, raised between the two ambulatories. The shrine of this saint and king was once adorned with precious jewels, but these were looted during the Reformation. In front of it is the **Coronation Chair**, containing the fabled **Stone of Scone**. Stolen from Scotland by Edward I in 1297, this coronation stone was the mystical symbol of Scottish independence since ancient times. In 1950 it was again stolen, this time by Scottish nationalists who took it back to its native land, but was returned a few months later.

The ***Poets' Corner**, in the south transept, commemorates (and in some cases is the final resting place of) such renowned writers as Chaucer, Ben Jonson, Samuel Johnson, Milton, Shakespeare, Browning, Byron, Keats, Shelley, Dickens, Kipling, and just about all of the other famous names in English literature.

Exit into the medieval **Cloisters**, which date primarily from the 13th and 14th centuries. There is a good brass-rubbing center here in case you would like to make your own distinctive souvenirs.

Before leaving the abbey, you might want to take a look at the **Chapter House**, entered from the east side of the cloisters. A separate admission is charged for this, which also includes the adjacent Pyx Chamber. The octagonal Chapter House was built about 1250 and used from the 13th to the 16th centuries as the meeting place for the House of Commons, thus making it a veritable cradle of representative government. It has been exceptionally well restored to its original appearance. Next door to it is the **Pyx Chamber**, which dates from the 11th century. Originally a chapel, it was used as a testing place for coinage after the Reformation and now houses an exhibition of church plate.

The **Abbey Treasure Museum** in the 11th-century Norman Undercroft, to the south of the cloisters, traces the history of the abbey through historical artifacts and features an unforgettable collection of royal funeral effigies. A realistic likeness of Lord Nelson was added in 1806 as an early tourist attraction. The museum has a separate admission fee and is closed on some major holidays.

Westminster Abbey is generally open on Mondays through Saturdays, from 8 a.m. to 6 p.m., remaining open until 7:45 p.m. on Wednesdays. On Sundays, visits to the nave and cloisters may be made between services only. The choir, transepts, and chapels can be seen on Mondays through Fridays from 9 a.m. until 4 p.m.; and on Saturdays from 9 a.m. to 2 p.m. and 3:45–5 p.m. They are closed on Sundays.

Leave the abbey through the cloisters and stroll around to the

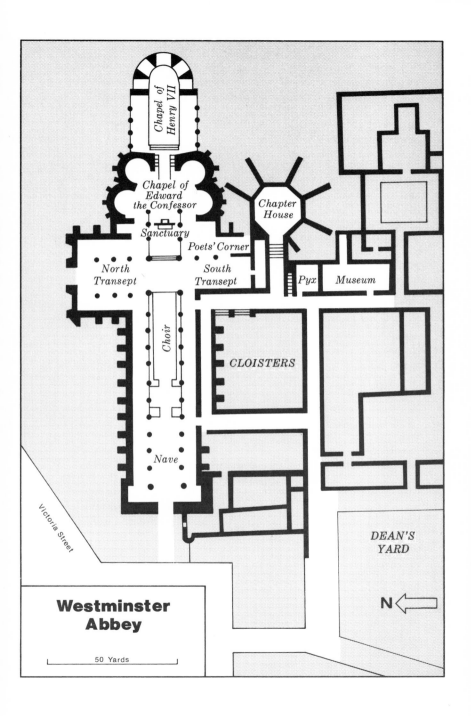

Chapel of
Henry VII

Chapel of
Edward
the Confessor

Chapter
House

Sanctuary

Poets' Corner

North
Transept

South
Transept

Pyx

Museum

Choir

CLOISTERS

Nave

Victoria Street

DEAN'S
YARD

N

**Westminster
Abbey**

50 Yards

*Houses of Parliament (8), more properly known as the **Palace of Westminster**. A royal palace was first erected here by the saint and king Edward the Confessor, or perhaps by one of his predecessors, in the early 11th century. William the Conqueror greatly enlarged it after 1066, and successive kings made major alterations. Almost from the beginning it was the meeting place for an early form of parliament, summoned occasionally to advise the monarch.

Even after Henry VIII moved his court to nearby Whitehall in 1529, the old palace, damaged by fire in 1512, continued to be the site of a parliament that grew ever stronger as the real power of the sovereigns diminished. Then, in 1834, a disastrous fire left nearly all of the palace in utter ruin, sparing only the medieval Westminster Hall, the cloisters, and the crypt, all of which are still part of the complex. The present structure, one of the most instantly recognized buildings on Earth, is in the Gothic Revival style and was erected between 1840 and 1860. Its more than 1,000 rooms, 100 staircases, and two miles of corridors cover an area of over eight acres.

Public access to the Houses of Parliament is severely limited for security reasons. Other than being the guest of a Member of Parliament (MP), your only possibility is to attend a debate of either the House of Lords or the House of Commons. Your embassy in London might be able to help, but expect to be put on a long waiting list. A few last-minute seats are usually available at St. Stephen's entrance, across from the rear of Westminster Abbey. The queues for these form early and the lucky ones are admitted around 2:30 p.m. (11 a.m. on Fridays) for the House of Lords and 4:15 p.m. (10 a.m. on Fridays) for the House of Commons. That is, when the houses are in session. Check to see if a flag is flying (by day) on Victoria Tower (at the south end) or a lantern shining (at night) in the Clock Tower (at the north end).

Just south of the abbey, opposite the south end of the Houses of Parliament, stands the 14th-century **Jewel Tower** (9). Another surviving part of the medieval Palace of Westminster, it was built by Edward III as a royal treasure house and later used as an archive, then as an assay office. You may visit it on Mondays through Saturdays, from 9:30 a.m. to 6:30 p.m. (4 p.m. in winter), but not on some major holidays.

Now follow the map through the riverside **Victoria Tower Gardens**, passing a cast of Rodin's statue of the *Burghers of Calais,* which celebrates an event in medieval English history. Continue on Millbank to the renowned ***Tate Gallery** (10), a splendid museum featuring the works of British artists from all periods along with modern foreign art. The Tate has what is surely the most comprehensive collection of British art in the world, including such illustrious names as Hogarth, Gainsborough, Reynolds, Blake, Constable, Spencer, Sutherland,

The Houses of Parliament from Westminster Bridge

Moore, and Hockney. An entire wing, the **Clore Gallery**, is devoted to an enormous collection of works by J.M.W. Turner. Modern non-British art is represented by Degas, Rodin, Matisee, Munch, Picasso, Giacometti, Pollock, Chagall, Dali, Warhol, Rauschenberg, Lichtenstein, and many, many others. There is also an exceptionally good restaurant and a cafeteria, both ideal places for lunch. The Tate Gallery is open on Mondays through Saturdays, from 10 a.m. to 5:50 p.m.; and on Sundays from 2–5:50 p.m.; but closed on a few major holidays.

From here, Vauxhall Bridge Road leads to one of London's favorite—and busiest—railway terminals, **Victoria Station** (11). Actually two adjoining stations built for two rival railways, Victoria is a confused but lively place dating in part from 1860, a pleasant survivor from the earlier days of rail. It serves an unusual mix of passengers, what with commuters from the southern counties, vacationers off to Brighton, Continentals en route to Paris or Brussels, and air travelers dashing for the Gatwick Express. The London Tourist Board has an excellent information office in the station's forecourt, opposite the bus stop.

Westminster Cathedral (12) is nearby, and well worth the slight detour down Victoria Street. In contrast with the ancient abbey, this Roman Catholic cathedral is relatively new, having been built between 1895 and 1903. Its highly unusual style is perhaps best described as being early Christian Byzantine. You can get a wonderful view of London from the top of its 284-foot **bell tower**, easily reached by elevator between April and October. The interior of the cathedral is still being decorated with mosaics, but the completed lower portions are quite impressive. Be sure to examine the **Stations of the Cross**, a series of low-relief sculptures on the main piers of the nave.

The route now leads up Buckingham Palace Road in the direction of the royal palace. On your left is the **Royal Mews** (13), one of the only parts of the palace complex that is ever open to the public. On Wednesday and Thursday afternoons, from 2–4 p.m., you can enter the mews for a small fee and see the magnificent state carriages, harness rooms, and stables. The star of the show is the **Gold State Coach**, built in 1762 for George III and still used for coronations. The Royal Mews is closed on certain ceremonial occasions and during Ascot week in June.

Continue straight ahead to **Buckingham Palace** (14) itself. The nucleus of this massive structure was a mansion built in 1703 for the Duke of Buckingham, which was purchased in 1762 by George III for use by Queen Charlotte. George IV got together with his favorite architect, John Nash, and in 1825 began expanding this into a real royal palace. Extravagant cost overruns delayed completion of the project until the time of Queen Victoria, when it became the official London residence of the sovereign, a status it has held ever since. The palace was greatly enlarged throughout the 19th century, acquiring its present uninspired façade only in 1913.

The only part of the palace proper that is open to the public is the **Queen's Gallery**, entered from Buckingham Gate along the south side. Changing exhibitions of treasures from the Royal Collection, probably the greatest private art collection in the world, may be seen here on Tuesdays through Saturdays, from 10:30 a.m. until 5 p.m.; and on Sundays from 2–5 p.m.

The famous **Changing of the Guard** ceremony is performed in the forecourt of the palace, usually at 11:30 a.m., daily from early April through mid-August and on alternate days the rest of the year, subject to weather and affairs of state. You may want to come back for this on another day, when you should arrive early to get a good vantage point.

Cross the vast open space in front of the palace, passing the enormous white marble **Queen Victoria Memorial** in its center. This is an excellent spot for viewing the Changing-of-the-Guard ceremony. ***St. James's Park** (15), opening to the east, is the oldest royal park in London. It was laid out over drained marshland for Henry VIII in 1532 and opened to the public in 1662 by Charles II. Once rather formal, its attractive present-day landscaping was designed in 1828 by John Nash, who also gave the lake its natural contours. In a city full of parks, this is among the loveliest. Amble through it leisurely, then cross **The Mall**, a processional way leading from Trafalgar Square to the palace. This was originally used for playing the game of Pall Mall, an early form of croquet.

St. James's Palace (16), on the north side of The Mall, was built in 1532 by Henry VIII and became the official residence of the sovereign from 1698, when the Palace of Whitehall burned down, until Queen Victoria moved into Buckingham Palace. Although no longer used by the Royal Family, St. James's still retains ceremonial significance and ambassadors are still accredited to the Court of St. James's.

Return to The Mall or St. James's Park and stroll back up to **Trafalgar Square** (1), where this walk began. There are three outstanding attractions there that you might have time for today, or perhaps see at another time.

The ***National Gallery** (17), dominating the north side of the square, is easily one of the greatest art museums in the world. Even though it is not particularly large by European standards, the astonishingly high quality of its collections makes a visit here an absolute must for all art lovers, and a pleasurable experience as well. Covering a vast scope of European painting from the 13th century until the beginning of the 20th, it is especially strong in works of the Italian, Dutch, Flemish, French, and Spanish schools. British art is better represented at the Tate Gallery, but the National does have some of the very best masterpieces. Visits may be made on Mondays through Saturdays, from 10 a.m. to 6 p.m.; and on Sundays from 2–6 p.m. It is closed on a few major holidays.

The same complex also houses the **National Portrait Gallery** (18), whose entrance is around the corner on St. Martin's Place. Not an art museum in the conventional sense, this is a collection of portraits—good and bad—of just about every famous British personality who ever lived, from kings to commoners, from ancient times to the present. A veritable lesson in British history, it contains not only paintings, drawings, and sculptures, but also photos and even cartoons. All of these are arranged chronologically, starting on the top floor, which can be reached by elevator. The gallery is open on Mondays through Fridays, from 10 a.m. to 5 p.m.; on Saturdays from 10 a.m. to 6 p.m.; and on Sundays from 2–6 p.m. It is closed on some major holidays.

Also facing Trafalgar Square is the celebrated **Church of St. Martin-in-the-Fields** (19), an elegant Classical structure of 1726 by the noted architect James Gibbs. It is perhaps most famous for its activities in social work, theater, and music. The world-renowned Academy of St. Martin-in-the-Fields Orchestra got its start here, and there are frequent concerts by other musical groups. The crypt contains a visitors' center and a restaurant, as well as the **London Brass Rubbing Centre**, where you can make your own souvenirs.

London

Chelsea, Kensington, Knightsbridge and Belgravia

Put on your most comfortable walking shoes for this delightful if somewhat lengthy tour through the charming neighborhoods of Chelsea, Kensington, Knightsbridge, and Belgravia. If you should happen to get tired along the way, you can always cut the distance by using either of the two suggested shortcuts without missing too many of the sights, or sacrificing much of the area's flavor.

Among the leading attractions along the route are the 17th-century Royal Hospital, the home of Thomas Carlyle, the fashionable King's Road, a visit to Kensington Palace (where several members of the Royal Family still live), the intriguing Science Museum, the engaging Victoria and Albert Museum, and a possible bankrupting shopping spree at Harrods.

Most of the walk is within the confines of the Royal Borough of Kensington and Chelsea, one of the entities that make up Greater London. These two dissimilar areas were politically combined in 1965, and each still retains its own distinctive character. The village-like ambiance of Chelsea, quite pronounced in its southwestern reaches, results from its long association with artists and writers, although rising prices have replaced many of the creative types with trendy young stockbrokers. Kensington is largely residential, but it boasts a major shopping street, a wonderful park, and some of the very best museums in London. The Knightsbridge area is noted for its fine shopping, while adjacent Belgravia—actually a part of Westminster—fairly reeks of old money.

GETTING THERE:

The Sloane Square **Underground** Station, served by the Circle and District lines, is right at the beginning (and end) of the suggested walk. By **bus**, just take routes 11, 19, 22, 137, 219, or C-1 to Sloane Square, or come by **taxi**. The nearest **British Rail** station is Victoria, about three-quarters of a mile to the east.

PRACTICALITIES:

Most of the attractions are closed on major holidays and Sunday mornings. Carlyle's House is open form April through October, on Wednesdays through Sundays only. Fine weather will make this largely outdoor tour much more enjoyable. The **London Tourist Board** office in the forecourt of Victoria Station, phone (071) 730–3488, is your best source of local information. They also have a branch in the basement of Harrods department store.

FOOD AND DRINK:

This fashionable area abounds in good restaurants and pubs, just a few of which are:

La Tante Claire (68 Royal Hospital Rd., 2 blocks southwest of the Army Museum) Creative French cuisine at its very best, in an elegant setting with flawless service. Proper dress expected, reservations essential, phone (071) 352–6045. X: Sat., Sun., late Aug.-early Sept., late Dec., around Easter. $$$+

English Garden (10 Lincoln St., 2 blocks southwest of Sloane Sq.) A modern adaptation of traditional English cuisine in the most pleasant of surroundings. Proper dress expected, reservations needed, phone (071) 584–7272. X: holidays. $$$

Gavvers (61 Lwr. Sloane St., 2 blocks south of Sloane Sq.) Classical French cuisine with excellent wines. Reservations advised, phone (071) 730–5983. X: Sun., holidays. $$$

St. Quentin (243 Brompton Rd., a block east of the Victoria and Albert Museum) A fashionable brasserie with traditional French cuisine. Quite popular, so reserve by phoning (071) 589–8005. $$

Sloane's Wine Bar (51 Sloane Sq.) This comfortable wine bar has good home-cooked lunches and dinners. $ and $$

Grenadier (18 Wilton Row, 2 blocks north of Belgrave Sq.) Well hidden behind vines in a mews, this former officers' mess was a favorite of the Duke of Wellington, who lived nearby. It is now a popular pub and restaurant. $ and $$

Henry J. Bean's (195 King's Rd., a block northeast of the Chelsea Antique Market) America's *haute cuisine*—burgers, chili, ribs, salads and the like served with American beer and wine. $

King's Head and Eight Bells (50 Cheyne Walk, near Carlyle's House) A popular riverside pub with good light meals. $

Victoria and Albert Museum Restaurant (in the museum) A pleasant, cheerful cafeteria for light meals, snacks, or drinks. $

SUGGESTED TOUR:

Sloane Square (1) forms the most natural entrance into Chelsea. Its tree-lined center separates the Royal Court Theatre of 1870, noted for its controversial productions, from the handsome Peter Jones department store of the 1930s. The King's Road, now a stylish shopping street leading to the west, remained a private royal path for the king's journeys to Hampton Court until 1829.

Leave the square at its south end and follow Lower Sloane Street, making a right turn on Royal Hospital Road. The **Royal Hospital** (2) was designed by Sir Christopher Wren in 1682 for Charles II as a retirement home for aged and disabled soldiers. Its inspiration, both socially and architecturally, was the Invalides in Paris, founded in 1670 by Louis XIV. Some 420 pensioners live in the Royal Hospital, where they wear traditional old-style uniforms of scarlet in summer and blue in winter. One of these veterans will be happy to show you the **Chapel**, virtually unchanged since Wren's time, and the **Great Hall**, with its large mural of Charles II on horseback and captured American flags from the War of 1812. Both rooms are open on Mondays through Saturdays, from 10 a.m. to noon and 2–4 p.m.; and on Sundays from 2–4 p.m. between April and September. There is also a small museum of memorabilia near the eastern end of the hospital.

Continue down the street to the **National Army Museum** (3), which might be of interest to you. Its modern displays trace the history of the British Army from the 15th century up to the present, and include weapons, uniforms, models, dioramas, audio-visual presentations, and even an art gallery. It is open on Mondays through Saturdays, from 10 a.m. to 5:30 p.m.; and on Sundays from 2–5 p.m.; but closed on a few major holidays.

Many famous people have lived in the neighborhood beyond this, including the American painters J.S. Sargent and J. M. Whistler, the writers Oscar Wilde and Mark Twain, and even—more recently—Margaret Thatcher. Be on the lookout for plaques identifying former residents.

The **Chelsea Physic Garden** (4) was founded in 1673 by the Worshipful Company of Apothecaries for the purpose of growing herbs and botanicals, and was the birthplace (so to speak) of several important species including the cotton seed first used in America, the tea grown in India, and the rubber used in Malaysia. It may be visited between mid-April and mid-October, on Wednesdays and Sundays, from 2–5 p.m.

Cheyne Walk is separated from the Chelsea Embankment along the Thames by lovely gardens. Near it is the fanciful **Albert Bridge** of 1873, whose strange suspension system and outlandish colors, along with the quaint notices requesting troops to break step, make it easily the most picturesque span on the river. Continue west to the **Chelsea Old Church** (5), which has been evolving since Norman times. It has a fine old set of chained books, the only examples of these curiosities in any London church. The 14th-century chapel was rebuilt by Sir Thomas More in 1528. More, the leader of the 16th-century Chelsea intellectuals, was Lord Chancellor of England until he opposed Henry VIII's divorce, after which he was beheaded.

Retrace your steps and turn north on Cheyne Row to **Carlyle's House** (6), where the Scottish historian and philosopher lived for 47 years until his death in 1881. It has been preserved almost exactly as he left it, with the Carlyles' own furniture, books, manuscripts, portraits, and memorabilia. One of the oldest private houses still standing in Chelsea, it is open from April through October, on Wednesdays through Sundays, from 11 a.m. to 5 p.m.

Now follow the map to the **King's Road** and the **Chelsea Antique Market** (7), a rambling indoor maze of dealers' stalls where all sorts of antiquities and assorted junk can be found. The King's Road remains as fashionable as it was in the 1960s, a vital place lined with boutiques, restaurants, and especially with colorful pubs.

Beyond this, the sights get farther apart until you reach South Kensington, although the walk is quite pleasant. It is possible to take a **shortcut** there by turning right on Old Church Street and following the map to the museum complex, thus saving a few miles while missing only three attractions.

Those energetic souls going the longer distance should amble down the King's Road and turn right on Park Walk. Becoming Gilston Road, it leads past The Boltons, a wooded oval in the center of the street, lined with fine homes. Continue following the map through a prosperous area of mostly 19th-century town houses. Another **shortcut** can be made at Courtfield Road, leading past the Gloucester Road Underground Station to the museum area. Otherwise, stick to the route on the map, passing the Earl's Court Underground Station and Cromwell Road. This brings you into Kensington proper.

The **Commonwealth Institute** (8), with its bizarre green copper roof and strange peaks, houses changing displays and permanent exhibitions from the 40-odd nations of the Commonwealth, mostly former British colonies. There are frequent cultural events as well, along with films, an art gallery, and a restaurant—all celebrating the ethnic diversity that was once the Empire. Visits may be made on Mondays through Saturdays, from 10 a.m. to 5 p.m.; and on Sundays from 2–5 p.m.; but not on a few major holidays.

Kensington High Street is another main shopping district. Follow it as far as Palace Avenue and turn left to **Kensington Palace** (9), a royal residence ever since William III purchased it in 1689. Alterations

London
Chelsea, Kensington, and Belgravia

U = Underground Station

1,000 Yards

The Albert Memorial

and additions made by Sir Christopher Wren and Nicholas Hawksmoor have left the exterior largely as you see it today, although there were interior changes in the 18th century. In general, its unpretentious design reflects the simple tastes of the Dutch-born William III, who with his wife and co-sovereign Queen Mary II moved here to escape the foul riverside air at Whitehall. Queen Victoria was born in this palace in 1819, but moved to Buckingham upon accession to the throne in 1837. Kensington Palace is still the London residence for several members of the Royal Family, including Prince Charles and Princess Diana.

Most of the palace is private, but you can visit the **State Apartments** and the **Exhibition of Court Dress** on Mondays through Saturdays, from 9 a.m. to 5 p.m.; and on Sundays from 1–5 p.m.; except for a very few major holidays.

Stroll through **Kensington Gardens**, once the private gardens of the palace and now a westward extension of Hyde Park. Lovely paths lead to the extravagant **Albert Memorial** (10), a neo-Gothic monstrosity that has to be seen to be believed. Epitomizing the sentimental tastes of the Victorian period, it is a monument to the memory of Queen Victoria's beloved consort, Prince Albert, who died in 1861. A careful examination of its ornate base will reveal many fascinating details.

In the Aeronautics Hall of the Science Museum

The statue of the prince looks across the way to the huge **Royal Albert Hall** of 1871, a circular auditorium capable of holding 8,000 people. It is used for all kinds of events, and is especially noted for its concerts.

Continue down Exhibition Road and into the world-famous museum complex of South Kensington. On your right is the utterly fascinating ***Science Museum** (11), one of the best of its kind anywhere and a long-time favorite for children and adults alike. Anyone who loves steam engines, cars, airplanes, space exploration, computers, photography, or technology of any sort will go wild in this place, where you can watch myriad devices in action and push buttons to your heart's content. Its six floors of displays are open on Mondays through Saturdays, from 10 a.m. to 6 p.m.; and on Sundays form 11 a.m. to 6 p.m.; except on a few major holidays. Just south of it is the **Geological Museum** with its magnificent gemstones, fossils, earthquake simulator, and an audio-visual exhibit called The Story of the Earth. Its opening times are the same as those of the Natural History Museum, described below.

Around the corner on Cromwell Road stands the immense **Natural History Museum** (12), an impressive neo-Romanesque edifice of 1880. Besides the dinosaurs, whales, birds, and other examples of animal life you will find outstanding exhibitions of human biology, Man's place in evolution, and on the origin of species. In addition, there are superb collections devoted to plant ecology as well as to minerals and meteorites. The museum is open on Mondays through Saturdays, from 10 a.m. to 6 p.m.; and on Sundays form 1–6 p.m.; but not on a few major holidays.

The *Victoria and Albert Museum (13), known to generations of Londoners simply as the "V & A," has what is probably the world's greatest collection of the decorative and applied arts. It is also a lively and highly enjoyable place to visit, making it one of the most popular attractions in London. There is something here for everyone, regardless of their tastes and interests, whether these run to period room settings, Oriental art, medieval artifacts, tapestries, costumes, musical instruments, or whatever. The fine arts are not overlooked either, and are especially well represented by the Raphael cartoons and the *Constable Collection. You will most likely get lost in the four-storied labyrinth of rooms and passageways, but that's part of the fun. A full day could easily be spent just sampling the countless treasures, so you might want to plan on coming back later, perhaps having lunch in the cafeteria. The V & A is open on Mondays through Saturdays, from 10 a.m. to 5:50 p.m.; and on Sundays form 2:30–5:50 p.m.; but not on a few main holidays.

The route now leads down Brompton Road, a major shopping thoroughfare. Beauchamp Place, to the right, is noted for its exceptionally fine shops and boutiques. Just a bit beyond this is **Harrods** (14), one of the largest and most famous department stores in the world, where you can buy nearly anything your heart desires, or enjoy yourself by simply browsing around. Its **Food Hall**, lined with Art Nouveau tiling, is especially attractive, and there are several restaurants and places for afternoon tea throughout the store, along with a branch of the London Tourist Board office in the basement.

From here you can return to the start of the walk by following Sloane Street to Sloane Square (1), or use the nearby Knightsbridge Underground Station to get to wherever you're going. Those with energy to spare may want to take a short stroll through Belgravia, an elegant 19th-century residential area slightly to the east. Many of the finest homes, some now used as embassies, are on **Belgrave Square** (15). The route on the map will return you from here to Sloane Square.

London
The West End

You probably won't find the West End identified on any map of London, but the term usually refers to an area more or less centered on Piccadilly Circus, taking in portions of the City of Westminster along with the southeast corner of the Borough of Camden. However you define them, the neighborhoods covered by this walking tour include some of the most varied attractions in town, such as Piccadilly Circus, Covent Garden, Lincoln's Inn, the British Museum, Regent's Park, Madame Tussaud's, Baker Street, and the exquisite shops of Mayfair. Along the way, you will be treated to several of London's less famous but equally intriguing sights, including the fascinating Transport Museum, the delightful Theatre Museum, the strangely eccentric Sir John Soane's Museum, the magnificent Wallace Collection, Selfridges department store, the Museum of Mankind, the Burlington Arcade, and the Royal Academy of Arts.

The actual walking distance can be covered comfortably in under two hours, but be sure to allow plenty of time for museum visits, lunch, shopping, and perhaps a pub stop or two.

GETTING THERE:

The suggested walk starts and ends at the Piccadilly Circus **Underground** Station, served by the Piccadilly and Bakerloo lines. By **bus**, take routes 3, 6, 9, 12, 13, 14, 15, 19, 22, 22B, 38, 53, 53X, 88, 159, or 509 to Piccadilly Circus, or come by **taxi**. The nearest **British Rail** station is Charing Cross, about one-half mile to the southeast.

PRACTICALITIES:

This walk can be taken at any time in good weather, but note that the Theatre Museum is closed on Mondays, and Sir John Soane's Museum is closed on both Sundays and Mondays. Some of the other attractions are closed on a few major holidays, and also on Sunday mornings. The **British Travel Centre** at 12 Regent Street, phone (071) 730–3400, is just a few steps south of Piccadilly Circus. They can answer your questions on both London and the rest of Britain. There is also a branch office of the **London Tourist Board**, phone (071) 730–3488, in the basement of Selfridges department store on Oxford Street.

FOOD AND DRINK:
You'll pass hundreds of good restaurants and pubs along the route of this walking tour. Just a few of the better choices are:

Inigo Jones (14 Garrick St., 2 blocks west of Covent Garden) *Nouvelle* French cuisine at its best, with service to match. Proper dress expected, reservations advised, phone (071) 836–6456. X: Sat. lunch, Sun. $$$

Boulestin (1a Henrietta St., facing Covent Garden) Classic French cuisine in the grand manner. Dress appropriately and make reservations by phoning (071) 836–7061. X: Sat. lunch, Sun., Aug. $$$

Poons (4 Leicester St., a block northwest of Leicester Sq.) Noted for its excellent Cantonese cooking, and especially for its wind-dried meats. X: Sun. $$

Chez Solange (35 Cranbourn St., a block northeast of Leicester Sq.) An old-time favorite for French provincial cooking, with plenty of traditional atmosphere. X: Sun. $$

Porter's (17 Henrietta St., a block southwest of Covent Garden) All kinds of meat pies, roast beef, and other traditional English dishes in an old-fashioned setting. X: Sun. lunch. $

L.S. Grunts Chicago Pizza Co. (12 Maiden Lane, 2 blocks southwest of Covent Garden) Deep-dish pizzas, salads, cheesecakes, and other goodies in a lively environment. $

The Fountain (in Fortnum and Mason's store at 181 Piccadilly) Time stands still in this wonderfully old-fashioned tea room of a restaurant with its refined light meals, salads, and sandwiches. X: Sun. $

My Old Dutch (131 High Holborn, 4 blocks northwest of Sir John Soane's Museum) Enormous Dutch pancakes with a huge variety of meat, cheese, vegetable, and other fillings. $

Justin de Blank's (54 Duke St., 2 blocks south of Selfridges) A sophisticated cafeteria with exceptionally good light meals. X: Sat, eve., Sun., holidays. $

SUGGESTED TOUR:
Piccadilly Circus (1) isn't much to look at in the morning, so it is best to save its attractions for later in the day, when you'll be returning. Near its center stands a famous statue that is supposed to represent the Angel of Christian Charity, but is commonly known as **Eros.** Cast in aluminum in 1893 as a memorial to the Victorian philanthropist Lord Shaftesbury, its design was so severely criticized that the artist fled the country. Since then, however, the public has taken the figure to its heart, and Piccadilly Circus just wouldn't be the same without it.

A short amble down Coventry Street leads to **Leicester Square** (2),

Inside the London Transport Museum

an entertainment center since the 18th century. Pronounced as *LES-ter*, this small spot of urban greenery is surrounded by theaters and restaurants. In its center is a statue of Shakespeare, and in the southwest corner a recent one of Charlie Chaplin. The **Half Price Ticket Booth** sells bargain tickets for same-day performances at West End theaters, but don't expect to find really big hits here. It is open on Mondays through Saturdays, from noon to 2 p.m. for matinees and 2:30–6:30 p.m. for evening shows.

Now follow the map to **Covent Garden** (3), a large open Italian-style piazza developed by the famed architect Inigo Jones in the 17th century on the site of a medieval vegetable garden belonging to a convent. The area's association with food was continued by the construction in 1830 of a huge **Central Market Building**, which served as London's main wholesale fruit and vegetable market until 1974, when its function was transferred south of the river. A battle then raged between developers and preservationists, with the end result being that this historic district was saved and the market buildings converted into trendy shops and restaurants.

St. Paul's Church, on the west side of the piazza, was built in 1633 by Inigo Jones as the "handsomest barn in Europe." Well known as an actors' church, it gained fame as the setting for the opening scene in Bernard Shaw's *Pygmalion* and the ensuing musical, *My Fair Lady*.

The 19th-century Flower Market Hall, in the southeast corner of the piazza, now houses two exceptionally interesting museums. The largest of these is the **London Transport Museum** (4), where a superb

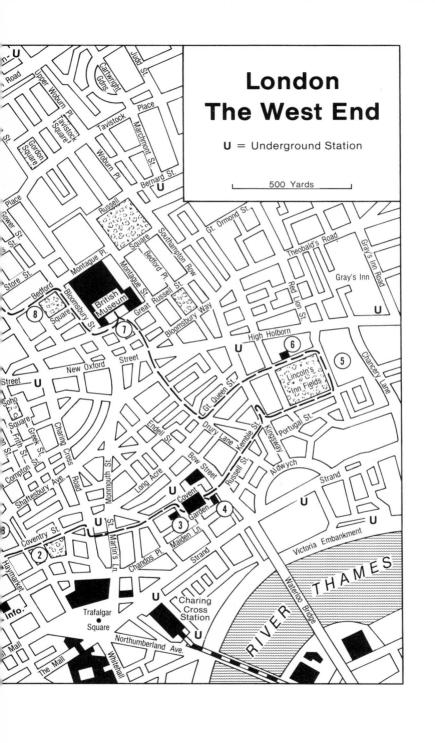

London
The West End

U = Underground Station

500 Yards

Cartwright Gdns
Judd St.
Upper Woburn Pl.
Tavistock Square
Tavistock Place
Marchmont St.
Woburn Pl.
Gordon Square
Bernard St.
Russell Square
Gt. Ormond St.
Theobald's Road
Gray's Inn Road
Gray's Inn
Southampton Row
Montague Pl.
Bedford Pl.
Store St.
Montague St.
Bloomsbury St.
British Museum
Great Russell St.
Russell St.
Bloomsbury Way
Red Lion St.
Chancery Lane
Bedford Square
High Holborn
Lincoln's Inn Fields
New Oxford Street
Portugal St.
Gt. Queen St.
Kingsway
Kemble St.
Endell St.
Drury Lane
Russell St.
Aldwych
Soho Square
Greek St.
Frith St.
Compton St.
Shaftesbury Ave.
Charing Cross Road
Monmouth St.
Long Acre
Bow Street
Strand
Covent Garden
Coventry St.
St. Martin's Ln.
Maiden Ln.
Chandos Pl.
Strand
Victoria Embankment
Haymarket
info.
Trafalgar Square
Charing Cross Station
Northumberland Ave.
The Mall
Whitehall
Waterloo Bridge
RIVER THAMES

8
7
6
5
2
3
4

collection of old trams, buses, and Underground trains (including steam engines!) are exhibited along with displays celebrating nearly two centuries of public transportation in London. You can sit in the darkened cab of an Underground train and actually "drive" it, an unusual experience complete with simulated sights through the windows, sounds, and vibrations. A treat for children and adults alike, this thoroughly enjoyable museum is open daily from 10 a.m. to 6 p.m. Adjacent to it is the **Theatre Museum**, whose collections of theatrical memorabilia are displayed amid preserved sections of old theaters. There is also a small auditorium for special events and an atmospheric cafeteria. An outpost of the Victoria and Albert Museum, it is open on Tuesdays through Sundays, from 11 a.m. to 7 p.m.

Leave the square on Russell Street, crossing Bow Street, where the famous Bow Street Runners—precursor of today's Metropolitan Police—began capturing muggers in the mid-18th century. This was once one of the worst slums in London. Just to the north stands the imposing portico of the **Royal Opera House**, which was built in 1860 and is now being extended towards the Covent Garden piazza.

Continue straight ahead past the **Theatre Royal**, Drury Lane, dating form 1812 and said to be haunted. Previous theaters have stood on this site since 1663, the first being where Charles II met his mistress, the actress Nell Gwynn. Kemble Street leads across busy, divided Kingsway, which requires a slight detour to the north. Near the southwest corner of **Lincoln's Inn Fields**, on Portsmouth Street, is the 16th-century half-timbered **Old Curiosity Shop**, possibly the oldest shop in London.

Lincoln's Inn (5) is one of the four great Inns of Court that have the right of admitting people to practice as barristers. Two of these, the Middle and Inner Temples, are described on page 25, while the other, Gray's Inn, is two blocks to the north. Lincoln's Inn, with its 15th-to-17th-century buildings, is the best preserved. Its grounds and chapel may usually be visited by asking at the porter's lodge.

On the north side of Lincoln's Inn Fields, at Number 13, is one of the most eccentric interior spaces in London. Although it is fairly well known, too many visitors completely overlook ***Sir John Soane's Museum** (6) and never realize what they have missed. A classical architect of great distinction, Soane arranged the interiors of these three adjoining houses as his personal residence and as a setting for his private collection of art and antiquities. When he died in 1837 he left them to the nation with the stipulation that nothing could ever be changed. Ever. The small rooms and basement are fairly crammed with fascinating treasures displayed in a unique manner, with mirrors creating the illusion of space. Be sure to see the wonderful series of ***paintings by Hogarth**, *The Rake's Progress* and *The Election;* as well

Inside Sir John Soane's Museum

as the alabaster **sarcophagus of Seti I,** an Egyptian pharaoh who died in 1290 B.C. The museum is open on Tuesdays through Saturdays, from 10 a.m. to 5 p.m.

Now follow the map to the ***British Museum** (7), arguably the greatest institution of its type on Earth and a not-to-be-missed attraction for all visitors to London. Only an empire the size and scope of Britain's could possibly have amassed such an unparalleled collection of treasures. At least an entire day is needed to merely sample them, but even the most time-pressed tourist can enjoy a cursory look at a few of the highlights in an hour or so.

Pick up a museum plan leaflet at the entrance and make your way to Room 8, where the renowned ***Elgin Marbles,** the 5th-century-B.C. sculptures rescued from the Parthenon in Athens in 1803, are displayed. While on the ground floor of the west wing, you should not miss the ***Rosetta Stone** in Room 25. Discovered by the French near the mouth of the Nile in 1799, this inscribed stone from the 2nd century B.C. bears the same message in hieroglyphs, later Egyptian characters, and Greek; thus providing the key to understanding ancient Egyptian writing.

Among the most important sights on the upper floor are the **Egyptian mummies** in rooms 60 and 61, some of which are rather macabre. Continue around to the east wing, where the **Mildenhall Treasure** of decorated Romano-British tableware from the 4th century is exhibited in Room 40. Next to this, in Room 41, is the fabulous **Sutton Hoo Treasure**, a 7th-century burial ship of an East Anglian king, whose rich contents shed new light on the "Dark Ages." You may also be interested in the antique **clocks and watches** displayed in nearby Room 44.

The **British Library**, which is contained within the British Museum, is scheduled to move into its own building in the future. Until then, you can see some of its holdings, including two of the four existing original copies of the **Magna Carta**, the 7th-century **Lindisfarne Gospels**, and numerous manuscripts and autographs of great historical interest. These are exhibited in rooms 29 through 33, on the ground floor. The library's famous **Reading Room** can only be visited on hourly guided tours or by special permission. If you do get in, take a peek at seat number G-7, which is where Karl Marx worked on *Das Kapital* in the mid-19th century.

This quick tour has covered only a very few of the greatest treasures in the museum, so you might want to come back on another day when you can devote more time to it. Happily, there is both a cafeteria and a restaurant in the west wing. The museum is open on Mondays through Saturdays, from 10 a.m. to 5 p.m.; and on Sundays from 2:30–6 p.m.; except for a few major holidays.

Leave the museum and follow Bloomsbury Street to the very lovely and also very private **Bedford Square** (8). Except for the traffic, this has hardly changed since it was first laid out in 1775. Take a look at the fine houses bordering it, once residential but now mostly the offices of architects and publishers. You are standing in the very heart of **Bloomsbury**, a neighborhood that was famous (or infamous) in the early 1900s for the many intellectuals and artists who lived there, including Virginia Woolf, Lytton Strachey, John Maynard Keynes, E.M. Forster, T.S. Eliot, Bertrand Russell, and D.H. Lawrence. Today, much of the area is occupied by the ever-growing **University of London**, and by numerous small hotels catering to tourists.

The route leads up Tottenham Court Road and turns left on Goodge Street. Follow Charlotte Street, noted for its restaurants, north past the imposing but functionally-designed **British Telecom Tower** (9), a major London landmark since 1964. Reaching a height of 619 feet, it was then the tallest structure in town and was designed solely for TV and telecommunications use. Fitzroy Square, just beyond this, still displays a certain elegance.

A left turn on busy Euston Road takes you past the south entrance of **Regent's Park** (10), an excellent spot for a rest. Once a royal hunting preserve, it started to become a luxurious residential estate after 1811, but the plan was never fully developed and most of it is today a public park. **Queen Mary's Gardens**, near the southern end, is an exceptionally attractive place and well worth a visit. If you have enough time, or perhaps on another day, you might want to stroll less than a mile north on Broad Walk to the **London Zoo,** described on page 94.

Continue west on Marylebone Road to one of London's most popular—and crowded—commercial tourist attractions, **Madame Tussaud's** (11). This world-famous waxworks museum had its origins in pre-Revolutionary France, where Madame's uncle first opened his establishment in Paris in 1770. She learned her trade there, and during the Terror was obliged to make death masks of the guillotine's victims. Escaping to England in 1802, she traveled the country with her creations until settling down on Baker Street in 1835. In 1850, Madame died at the age of 89. Her grandsons built the present museum, which has been entertaining folks since 1884. The exhibition is continually changing to keep up with who's in the news, and also includes a section of historical personalities, all modeled in wax and set in appropriate surroundings. The popular **Chamber of Horrors** features blood-chilling scenes enlivened with realistic instruments of torture and execution. Madame Tussaud's is open daily from 10 a.m. to 5:30 p.m. A joint ticket that includes the adjacent **Planetarium** is available on request.

Turn left on **Baker Street,** a lively thoroughfare that Sherlock Holmes would scarcely recognize today. Yes, there is a Number 221B, but the street was renumbered since Victorian times, and the "actual" lodgings of the great fictional detective are thought to be at what is now Number 31.

A left turn on Fitzhardinge Street, opposite Portman Square, leads to the somewhat secluded Manchester Square and the fabulous ***Wallace Collection** (12). Installed in the 18th-century Hertford House, this is possibly the greatest private art collection ever bequeathed to a nation. It is extraordinarily rich in French paintings of the 18th century, especially in works by Watteau, Boucher, and Fragonard. French artists from other centuries are also well represented, including Claude Lorrain, Poussin, and Delacroix. Among the Dutch and Flemish paintings are those by Rembrandt, Rubens, Frans Hals, and Van Dyck. The Italians include Titian, Guardi, and Canaletto; while there are also works by Reynolds, Gainsborough, and Velazquez. All of these are magnificently displayed in elegant surroundings filled with 18th-century French furniture and various art objects. If you love art from this era, you will love the Wallace Collection, which is open on Mondays through Saturdays, from 10 a.m. to 5 p.m.; and on Sundays from 2–5 p.m.; but closed on a few major holidays.

Now follow the map to Oxford Street, one of the main shopping areas of London. A right turn brings you to **Selfridges** (13), a massive department store in the American style that opened in 1909. An enormously wide range of goods is offered here at prices that are generally below those of Harrods. The store has several restaurants and cafeterias, along with a branch office of the London Tourist Board in the basement.

The route continues down Duke Street into what is practically American territory. **Grosvenor Square** (14), a pleasant park surrounded by offices of various U.S. government agencies, is totally dominated on its west side by the American Embassy, surmounted by a giant aluminum eagle. The square's association with the U.S.A. began as early as 1785, when John Adams, then ambassador and later president, moved into the house at Number 9. It was continued during World War II by General Eisenhower, whose headquarters were at Number 20. The statue of Franklin D. Roosevelt, near the center of the park, was paid for by small donations from ordinary British citizens in 1948.

Leave the square via Grosvenor Street and turn right onto **Bond Street**, here called New Bond Street. Its lower portion is known as Old Bond Street. Together, they constitute one of the most exclusive luxury shopping areas in the world. Check your bank balance before heading south past its elegant displays—you never know when temptation may strike!

A left turn on Burlington Gardens brings you to the **Museum of Mankind** (15), which you might want to visit. A branch of the British Museum, it specializes in changing exhibitions on non-Western societies and cultures, both past and present. The museum is open on Mondays through Saturdays, from 10 a.m. to 5 p.m.; and on Sundays from 2:30–6 p.m.; but not on a few major holidays.

The **Burlington Arcade** (16), a long covered passageway built in 1819, is lined with exquisite little shops of the highest quality. It is patrolled by uniformed beadles, who preserve a gracious atmosphere and lock it up at night and on Sundays. A stroll through this Regency gem brings you out on Piccadilly—the street, not the circus.

Just east of the arcade is the impressive façade of Burlington House, first built in the 17th century and remodeled several times since. It is home to the **Royal Academy of Arts** (17), founded in 1768 to promote British art. The painter Sir Joshua Reynolds was its first president. Changing exhibitions are on view here daily, from 10 a.m. to 6 p.m., and you might be able to see some of its interesting permanent collection as well.

Walk up Piccadilly, passing the famous, fashionable, and very luxurious **Fortnum and Mason** department store, founded in 1705. Its food department is world renowned, and this is one of the best places in London to enjoy an afternoon tea. The store's entrance is crowned by a mechanical clock on which figures of Mr. Fortnum and Mr. Ma-

In the Burlington Arcade

son greet other on the hour.

In just a few more steps you will be back at Piccadilly Circus (1), where this walk began. One final attraction, the **Trocadero Centre** (18), offers a variety of commercial entertainments that might interest you, as well as several restaurants that stay open until late evening. Among its exhibitions are an audio-visual presentation of the **Guinness World of Records** and a multi-screen spectacular called the **London Experience**. Have fun!

London
Greenwich

The lovely little Thames-side town of Greenwich is surely among the most attractive parts of London, and has long been a favorite destination for short excursions. Exceptionally rich in history, beauty, and engaging sights, it is located barely five miles east of Trafalgar Square in the ancient Borough of Greenwich, easily reached by boat, rail, bus, or car.

A great palace, once the home of royalty, stood on the green meadows by the river until the late 1600s. Henry VIII was born there, as were Mary I and Elizabeth I. For centuries, Greenwich remained the center of Britain's naval power. It is best known today, however, as the site of the Prime Meridian, that imaginary line from which all longitudinal distances on Earth are measured, and from which the world's time is reckoned using Greenwich Mean Time as the standard reference. Miraculously, Greenwich was spared the encroachment of a growing London, and it still retains much of its gracious character.

There are easily enough sights here to occupy an entire day, including the drydocked *Cutty Sark* clipper ship, the Old Royal Observatory, the National Maritime Museum, the Royal Naval College, and a host of colorful pubs. Greenwich also makes a good destination for a half-day outing, or it could be extended to include the Thames Barrier described on page 77. This is a perfect excursion for your first day in London, when jet lag makes a more demanding trip too difficult to enjoy. Depending on how you travel, just getting to Greenwich can be a large part of the fun.

GETTING THERE:

Boats depart London's Westminster Pier, just opposite Parliament, at frequent intervals for the 45-minute cruise to Greenwich. There are also departures from Charing Cross and Tower piers. Return boats operate until late afternoon. Refreshments are available on board, and there is often a running commentary on the sights.

The Docklands Light Railway provides a fast and scenic high-level trip above the revitalized Docklands area to Island Gardens, after which it's a 5-minute walk through the pedestrian tunnel under the Thames to Greenwich. Take the Underground to Tower Hill, opposite the Tower

The Cutty Sark

of London, then stroll one block to the Tower Gateway terminus of the Light Railway. Combination tickets with the Underground are available, and travel passes covering the appropriate zones are accepted. In the near future the Light Railway will be extended westward to the Bank station of the Underground. Return service operates until late evening.

British Rail trains to Greenwich leave from London's Charing Cross, Waterloo East, or London Bridge stations at frequent intervals. The trip takes between 10 to 15 minutes, and return trains run until late evening.

Buses on routes 177 and 188 connect central London with Greenwich town center.

By car, Greenwich is 5 miles east and slightly south of Trafalgar Square via local streets.

PRACTICALITIES:

The Maritime Museum and the Old Royal Observatory do not open on Sundays until 2 p.m., and are closed on some major holidays. The Royal Naval College is closed on Thursdays and some holidays. The **Greenwich Tourist Information Center**, phone (081) 858–6376, is at 46 Church Street, with a branch pavilion near the pier.

FOOD AND DRINK:

Greenwich is famous for its colorful pubs, and has a few restaurants, too. Some choices are:

Trafalgar Tavern (Park Row, by the Thames, just east of the Naval College) An old and celebrated combination pub and restaurant with traditional English fare. X: Restaurant only, Sat. lunch, Sun. eve. $$$ and $

Spread Eagle (2 Stockwell St., just southeast of St. Alfege's Church) French and modified English cuisine in an old coaching inn. X: Sat. lunch, Sun. eve., holidays. $$

The Yacht (5 Crane St., a block northeast of the Naval College) This colorful 17th-century riverside pub offers simple bar lunches and sandwiches. $

Plume of Feathers (19 Park Vista, 2 blocks east of the Maritime Museum, overlooking the park) An 18th-century pub, locally popular for its bar food. $

Dolphin Coffee Shop (in the west wing of the Maritime Museum) Light lunches and refreshments in a pleasant setting. $

SUGGESTED TOUR:

Those coming by British Rail will begin at **Greenwich Station** (1). Follow the map to the **Greenwich Pier area** (2), the arrival point for boats and for those coming via the Docklands Light Railway. The 19th-century clipper ship *Cutty Sark,* once the fastest ship in the world, sits in dry dock next to the *Gipsy Moth IV,* a 53-foot ketch in which Sir Francis Chichester single-handedly circumnavigated the globe in 1967. A few yards away stands the tourist office and the entrance to the pedestrian tunnel under the Thames.

A tour aboard the **Cutty Sark** is a must for any visitor to Greenwich. Launched in 1869 for the China Sea trade, she was later used to haul wool from Australia and served as a training ship until the end of World War II. Now honorably retired, the elegant ship is a stirring sight recalling the great days of sail. In her hold is a fascinating display of nautical items including many figureheads. The *Cutty Sark* may be visited on Mondays through Saturdays, from 10 a.m. to 6 p.m.; and on Sundays from noon to 6 p.m. It closes at 5 p.m. in winter. The **Gipsy Moth IV** may also be boarded during the same times, from Easter through September.

From here follow King William Walk to Greenwich Park and climb uphill to the **Old Royal Observatory** (3). No longer used due to London's bright lights and pollution, the observatory buildings now house an intriguing museum of astronomical and time-keeping instruments. Embedded in the courtyard pavement is a brass strip marking 0° longitude, the **Prime Meridian** that separates the eastern and western

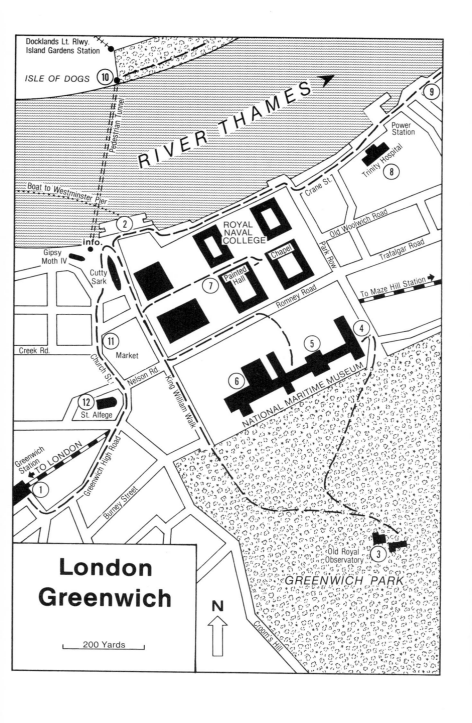

Docklands Lt. Rlwy.
Island Gardens Station

ISLE OF DOGS ⑩

RIVER THAMES

Boat to Westminster Pier

Pedestrian Tunnel

info.

②

Gipsy
Moth IV

Cutty
Sark

Creek Rd.

⑪
Market

Church St.

Nelson Rd.

⑫
St. Alfege

Greenwich
Station
◄TO LONDON

①

Greenwich High Road

Burney Street

King William Walk

ROYAL
NAVAL
COLLEGE

Chapel

Painted
Hall

⑦

Romney Road

Crane St.

Power
Station

Trinity Hospital ⑧

Old Woolwich Road

Park Row

Trafalgar Road

To Maze Hill Station ►

⑨

④

⑤

⑥

NATIONAL MARITIME MUSEUM

Old Royal
Observatory ③

GREENWICH PARK

London
Greenwich

N

↑

⊢ 200 Yards ⊣

Croom's Hill

hemispheres. Be sure to set your watch by the wonderful old clock just outside the gate, probably the most official time you'll ever get. The ornate **Flamsteed House** was built by Sir Christopher Wren in 1675 on instructions from Charles II to provide "for the Observator's habitation, and a little for Pompe." From the adjoining terrace there is a marvelous view of Greenwich, the Thames, and London. Note the time ball on a pole atop the roof, which drops at precisely 1 p.m. each day as a visual check for ships on the river. The Observatory is open during the same times as the National Maritime Museum, of which it is a part, and the same ticket covers both.

A downhill stroll through the park leads to the **East Wing** of the **National Maritime Museum** (4). This part deals with Britain's sea history during the 19th and 20th centuries, including the great migrations to the New World, the development of merchant shipping, and both world wars.

The **Queen's House** (5) is reached via a colonnade. The first Palladian villa in England, it was begun in 1616 by the famous architect Inigo Jones as a summer palace for James I's queen, Anne of Denmark. The entrance hall is an elegant 40-foot cube, from which an outstanding spiral staircase leads to the upper floor where the reconstructed Queen's Bedroom may be visited. The entire house is filled with art treasures worth a careful examination.

Continue along the colonnade to the ***Maritime Museum's West Wing** (6), its largest and most interesting part. The huge Neptune Hall contains entire boats, including a full-size paddle steamer. Several galleries are devoted to the careers of Captain Cook and Lord Nelson, while others cover the American and French revolutions. The Barge House is particularly intriguing with its collection of royal barges. Both a restaurant and a book shop are located in this wing. The entire Maritime Museum, including the Royal Observatory and the Queen's House, is open on Mondays through Saturdays, from 10 a.m. to 6 p.m.; and on Sundays from 2–6 p.m. It closes at 5 p.m. in winter, and is closed on some major holidays.

Now follow Romney Road and King William Walk to the west gate of the **Royal Naval College** (7). On this site once stood the Tudor palace of Placentia, birthplace of Henry VIII, Mary I, and Elizabeth I. Badly damaged by Cromwell's troops during the Civil War, it was torn down following the Restoration and a hospital for retired seamen erected in its place. These buildings, largely designed by Sir Christopher Wren, became the Naval College in 1873, a function they still serve today. You may visit the **Painted Hall** with its glorious ceiling, and the **Chapel**, the only parts of the college open to the public, on any day except Thursdays and some holidays, from 2:30–5 p.m.

At this point you might want to take a delightful short walk along the riverfront to Ballast Quay. A passageway just before the pier leads to the right. Follow this past the front of the Royal Naval College and continue on to the historic Trafalgar Tavern, a pub and luxury restaurant once frequented by cabinet ministers during the reign of Queen Victoria. From here stroll along narrow Crane Street. The Yacht Tavern is a more modest pub that recaptures some of the old nautical charm. In a short distance you will come to **Trinity Hospital** (8), an almshouse founded in 1614 and still the home of some 20 pensioners. The walk now passes a power station and leads to the Cutty Sark Tavern on the pleasant **Ballast Quay** (9), where you can relax at outdoor riverside tables before returning to the pier.

Another interesting walk is under the Thames through the old **pedestrian tunnel** of 1902, reached by an ancient elevator whose domed entrance is near the *Cutty Sark* ship. This brings you to the **Isle of Dogs** (10) for a classic panoramic view of Greenwich. The Tower Isle terminus of the modern Docklands Light Railway is just a few steps away, adjacent to the Island Gardens.

Some other sights back in Greenwich proper include the **Covered Market** (11) of 1831, where an arts-and-crafts market operates on Saturdays and Sundays. **St Alfege's Church** (12) was completed in 1714 by Nicholas Hawksmoor on the site of a 12th-century church, which stood on the spot where Alfege, Archbishop of Canterbury, was murdered by drunken Vikings in 1012 for quoting scriptures at them. Henry VIII was baptized in the earlier church, and the present structure has some interesting paintings and carvings.

NEARBY SIGHT:

The recently completed **Thames Barrier**, built to protect London from tidal flooding, is the world's largest movable flood barrier and may be inspected at close range from its Visitors' Centre, which also features working models and an audio-visual show. You can get there by boat, train, bus, or car. Ask for details at the Greenwich tourist office.

London
Hampstead

Although it is still in London, and only four miles from Trafalgar Square, Hampstead is a world removed with its picturesque village atmosphere, unspoiled heathland, forested hills, and secluded valleys. Famous artists and writers settled these heights shortly after it became something of a spa in the 18th century, and Hampstead is still a favored residential area for intellectuals, architects, musicians, media folk, and other creative types. Its twisted narrow lanes and attractive old houses yield gently to the natural beauty of Hampstead Heath, crowning—at 443 feet—the highest point in London, with views to match its elevation.

Along with the scenery, this walk takes you to some first-rate attractions including the 17th-century Fenton House, the exquisite art-filled Kenwood House mansion, the romantic home of the poet John Keats, and some very appealing old inns and pubs. Try to allow the better part of a day to enjoy it all at leisure, perhaps lingering over lunch and doing some shopping on the fashionable High Street.

GETTING THERE:

By Underground, take the Northern Line to Hampstead, being careful to get on the right train as this line divides along the way.

British Rail trains on the North London Link line stop frequently at the Hampstead Heath Station. Leave Euston Station on a local train first and change at Willesden Junction, or take a local from St. Pancras Station and change at West Hampstead. Return service operates until late evening.

Bus routes 24, 46, 168, and 268 connect central London with Hampstead.

By car, Hampstead is a bit under 4 miles northwest of Trafalgar Square via local streets.

PRACTICALITIES:

Good weather is essential for this outdoor walking tour. Fenton House is closed from November through February, and on weekend mornings and weekdays in March. During the rest of the year it is closed on Thursdays and Fridays. Kenwood House and Keats House are closed on some major holidays. For information on Hampstead contact any office of the **London Tourist Board**, or call them at (071) 730–3488.

FOOD AND DRINK:

There are several famous old pubs in and around Hampstead, as well as a few modest restaurants. Some choices are:

Jack Straw's Castle (North End Way, just north of Whitestone Pond) A reconstructed historic inn, once the hangout of highwaymen. Very popular today, it has a pub with bar food, garden tables, and a regular dining room. $$ and $

Spaniards Inn (Spaniards Lane, near the northwest end of the Heath) This 16th-century pub was once the home of the Spanish ambassador, later a favorite haunt of highwaymen, poets, and authors. Bar snacks and hot meals are offered. $

Kenwood House Café (in the stables of Kenwood House) A self-service restaurant with garden and indoor tables. Light lunches, pastries, and the like. $

Holly Bush (Holly Mount, off Heath St., a block northwest of the Underground station) An early-19th-century pub with good lunches and plenty of atmosphere. $

The Buttery (in the basement of the Burgh House, near the end of Flask Walk) Light lunches in the community art center. X: Mon., Tues. $

SUGGESTED TOUR:

Those coming by British Rail to the Hampstead Heath Station should start at number 7 on the map, follow it to the end, then continue from number 1.

Begin at the **Hampstead Underground Station** (1), which has the distinction of being the deepest in London. Don't worry, an elevator will lift you up the 180 feet. Cross the High Street and follow Heath Street south to **Church Row**, a thoroughly enchanting lane lined with 18th-century terrace houses. This leads to the parish **Church of St. John** (2), whose interior contains a bust of Keats and several interesting memorials. The painter John Constable is buried in the southeast corner of its graveyard.

Now take Holly Walk north past St. Mary's Catholic Church, built in 1816 by refugees from the French Revolution. The road junction known as Mount Vernon is a bit confusing, but shelters the very romantic dwelling of the 18th-century painter George Romney, marked by a plaque. Just beyond this is the delightful **Fenton House** (3) on Hampstead Grove. Built in 1693 and now owned by the National Trust, this small and simple brick mansion is set in a beautiful garden. It contains a remarkable collection of early **musical keyboard instruments**, including a harpsichord of 1612 that was once used by Handel. Most of these are kept tuned and may be played by music students. There is also a splendid collection of 18th-century furniture and porcelains. Fenton House is open on weekends during March from 2–6 p.m.; and on Saturdays through Wednesdays from April through October, from 11 a.m. to 6 p.m. Last admission is at 5 p.m.

Continue north for a few steps and turn left on Admiral's Walk, passing the early-18th-century Admiral's House with its unusual superstructure. Next to it is the house where the author John Galsworthy lived from 1918 until 1933, and where he completed the monumental *Forsyte Saga*. John Constable resided near the corner of Lower Terrace, at Number 2, from 1821 to 1825. Turn north on this to **Whitestone Pond**, the highest point in London and the site of an old signal beacon that once warned of the Spanish Armada's arrival in the Channel.

Jack Straw's Castle (4), full of historical associations, is an old weatherboarded inn and pub that was rebuilt in the 1960s. From here, Spaniards Road leads into the forests of **Hampstead Heath**. You can stroll along trails through this (and probably get momentarily lost), or take the road north to the **Spaniards Inn** (5), a 16th-century tavern once favored by highwaymen and later by artists. This is a good place to stop for lunch or just a drink.

Whichever way you go, follow the map to the magnificent 18th-century ***Kenwood House** (6), a large mansion with a sweeping panoramic view of London. Remodeled in 1764 by the noted architect Robert Adam, it was bequeathed to the nation in 1928 along with its fabulous collection of art. On view in these luxurious surroundings are major works by Rembrandt, Frans Hals, Vermeer, Reynolds, Romney, Gainsborough, and many others. Be sure to see the lovely ***Library**, one of Adam's best interiors. There is an excellent cafeteria in the adjoining Coach House, whose outdoor tables makes it a perfect spot for an inexpensive lunch. Kenwood House is open daily from 10 a.m. to 6 p.m.; closing at 4 p.m. from October until Good Friday. In the gardens just west of the mansion stands the charming **Dr. Johnson's Summerhouse**, moved here in 1968. Outdoor concerts are held by the small lake during the summer.

Now follow the map through a more open and park-like section of the immense 825-acre Hampstead Heath. Passing several ponds along the way you will exit onto Parliament Hill, which leads to the **Hampstead Heath British Rail Station** (7), the beginning of the tour for those who came by train.

Just a few steps from this is Keats Grove, a small street lined with

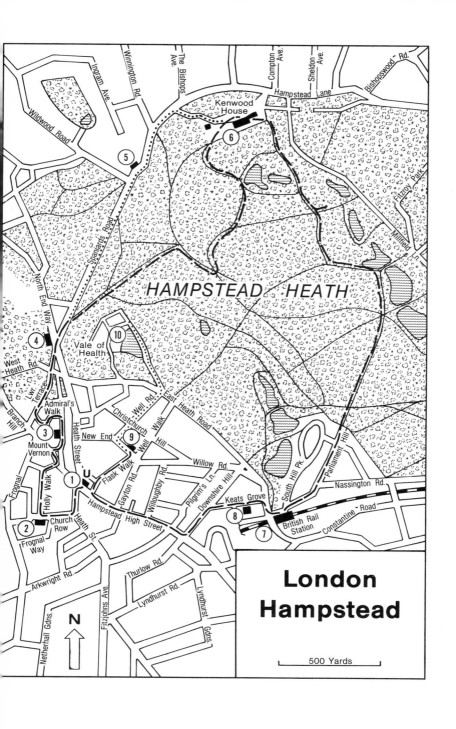

London
Hampstead

N

500 Yards

Kenwood House from the Heath

attractive detached cottages. One of these is **Keats House** (8), where from 1818 to 1820 the great poet John Keats spent the most productive two years of his short career, and where he wrote his inspired *Ode to a Nightingale* by the plum tree in the garden. The present tree is, of course, a replacement. You can visit the house, filled with memorabilia of the poet's life along with original manuscripts, on Mondays through Fridays from 2–6 p.m., on Saturdays from 10 a.m. to 1 p.m., and on Sundays from 2–5 p.m.; except for a few major holidays. The hours are slightly shorter from November through March.

Make a left turn on Downshire Hill and a right onto Hampstead High Street, one of the most attractive shopping streets in England. Some of the little alleys leading off this are interesting, particularly the **Old Brewery Mews** and **Flask Walk**. The latter leads to the early-18th-century **Burgh House** (9), now used as a museum of local history enlivened with changing exhibitions of local artists' work. It is open on Wednesdays through Sundays, from noon to 5 p.m., and has a pleasant café.

If you still need more exercise, you might want to continue up Well Walk and onto a curious enclave called the **Vale of Health** (10), whose name was probably invented by 18th-century real estate promoters anxious to sell what was then malaria-infested swamp land. Its cluster of lovely little houses has been home to various famous writers throughout the years.

London
Richmond

The London Borough of Richmond-upon-Thames, spread along the banks of the river, is the setting for this delightful stroll through the world-renowned Kew Gardens and on to the historic old town of Richmond. The Royal Botanical Gardens alone can keep you pleasantly engrossed for half a day, while other attractions include the intriguing Kew Bridge Steam Museum, the smallest royal palace in England, one of the loveliest urban greens anywhere, superb riverside views, and a great selection of colorful pubs. This is really a day for casual pleasure, an easy escape from the steady rounds of great monuments and cultural institutions.

GETTING THERE:

British Rail trains depart London's Waterloo Station frequently for the 25-minute ride to Kew Bridge, where the walk begins. Return trains from Richmond Station operate until late evening, and some services are a bit less frequent on Sundays and holidays.

By Underground, take the District Line marked for Richmond to the Kew Gardens Station, then walk north to the beginning of the tour. If you prefer to start at the Kew Royal Botanical Gardens, you can enter them more conveniently from the Victoria Gate near the Underground station. You will be returning from the Richmond Underground Station, on the same line.

Bus route 27, running via Paddington and Kensington, connects parts of London proper with Kew Gardens and Richmond.

Boats operate from Westminster Pier, opposite Parliament, to Kew Gardens ($1\frac{1}{2}$ hours) and Richmond ($2\frac{1}{2}$ hours) several times daily between April and October.

PRACTICALITIES:

Good weather is necessary for this almost totally outdoor trip. The gardens at Kew are at their peak in spring and early summer, but remain enjoyable all year round. The **Richmond Tourist Information Centre**, phone (081) 940–9125, is located in Richmond's Old Town Hall, near the river and the bridge.

83

FOOD AND DRINK:

Some good pubs and restaurants are:

Jasper's Bun in the Oven (9 Kew Green, near the entrance to the gardens) French provincial specialties in a cozy little restaurant, with garden tables in season. For reservations phone (081) 940–3987. X: Sun. $$

White Cross Inn (Cholmondeley Walk, a block west of the Old Town Hall) An old riverside pub with good bar food and a restaurant. X: Sun. eve. $$ and $

Mrs. Beeton (58 Hill Rise, just east of the Richmond Bridge) Real British home cooking in delightful surroundings. B.Y.O.B. X: Sun. eve., Mon. eve. $

Orange Tree (45 Kew Rd., opposite Richmond Station) Simple bar food upstairs, warm meals downstairs in this popular, lively pub. X: Sun. eve. $

Angel and Crown (5 Church Court, between Red Lion St. and George St., a block northeast of the Old Town Hall) Have lunch at a popular pub in the center of the old town. X: Sun. $

SUGGESTED TOUR:

Begin at Kew Bridge, next to the **Kew Bridge British Rail Station** (1). From here it is only a few steps to the **Kew Bridge Steam Museum** (2), located in a former water works pumping station that supplied London with water from 1838 until 1958. Anyone who is fascinated by Victorian steam machinery will have fun examining the old pumping engines dating from as far back as 1820, especially so on weekends when some of them are fired up and operated. There are also workshops, displays on the history of London's water supply, and a typical water works railway under restoration. The museum is open daily from 11 a.m. to 5 p.m.

Cross the bridge over the Thames and turn right into **Kew Green**, a lovely village setting with 18th-century houses built for members of George III's court. St. Anne's Church, on the green, was begun in 1710 under royal patronage. The painter Thomas Gainsborough is buried in its churchyard. At the west end of the green is the main gate leading into the fabulous *Kew Gardens (3), officially known as the **Royal Botanic Gardens**. With so much exquisite beauty spread over 300 acres of woods and gardens, it is perhaps difficult to realize that their main purpose is not aesthetic but scientific, for this is first and foremost a botanical research and training center. Plants from all corners of the Earth are grown here, many of them indoors under controlled climatic conditions.

London
Richmond

1,000 Yards

B.R. Station

① ②

Kew Bridge Rd.

Brentford High Street

Kew Bridge

London Road

RIVER THAMES

Kew Green

③

Kew Road

④ ⑤

⑥

KEW
GARDENS

⑦

Mortlake

⑨

⑧

Kew Gardens Rd.

U

Kew
Gardens
B.R. & U.
Station

Road

SYON PARK

Syon House

⑪ ⑬

Kew Road

Ennerdale Road

North Road

⑩

⑫

Sandycombe Road

Lwr. Richmond Rd.

N

Kew Road

Lower Mortlake Road

Twickenham Road

Parkshot

U

Manor Road

King's Road

Sheen Road

Richmond
B.R. & U.
Station

⑱

⑭

Church Rd.

Twickenham Bridge

Old Palace Lane

George St.

Red Lion St.

Paradise Rd.

Mount

Ararat Rd.

Queen's Road

⑮

The Vineyard

info.

⑯

Richmond
Bridge

Richmond Hill

⑰

The botanical gardens began in 1759 on nine acres of this former royal estate, and were soon extended by George III, who often stayed at Kew Palace. In 1841 they were given to the nation, and by 1904 enlarged to their present size.

Before ambling through the gardens proper, you might want to visit **Kew Palace** (4) at their northern end. Once known as the Dutch House, this is all that remains of a royal complex that occupied the site until being demolished in 1802. Built in 1631 by a rich London merchant, the house was acquired by the Crown in 1728 for use by members of the Royal Family. From 1802 until 1818 this surviving structure served as a favorite country retreat for George III and Queen Charlotte, who died there in 1818. Today, England's smallest royal residence has been restored to its appearance during the reign of George III, and contains mementos of the king and his family. The palace is open daily from April through September, from 11 a.m. to 5:30 p.m. Don't miss seeing the **Queen's Garden** at its rear, arranged in a formal 17th-century style.

Begin your tour of the Royal Botanic Gardens at the **Orangery** (5), which was built in 1761 and now houses changing exhibitions. Adjacent to this is the **Filmy Fern House**. Continue on past the **Wood Museum**, whose displays explain the various uses of timber, to the **Alpine House** (6), a modern glass structure where alpine and arctic plants are grown under refrigerated conditions. From here, stroll through the aquatic and grass gardens to Kew's latest addition, the stunning **Princess of Wales Conservatory** (7). This huge, partially underground greenhouse re-creates tropical environments from swamps to deserts, featuring such exotica as carnivorous plants and a simulation of the Mohave Desert.

The most famous building at Kew, indeed its trademark, is the magnificent ***Palm House** (8), an enormous Victorian greenhouse from 1848 that shelters a wide variety of tropical plants. Just to the north of this is the **Waterlily House** of 1852. The commercial uses of plants can be explored in the nearby **Museum**, a 19th-century house at the east side of the pond.

If the weather is exceptionally fine and you feel up to a long walk, you might want to make a side trip through the woods past the azalea and bamboo gardens to the **Rhododendron Dell** (9), which is just lovely in the spring. This route then continues along the river, with good views of Syon House, and winds around to **Queen Charlotte's Cottage** (10), built in the 1770s as a rustic summerhouse for George III's family. Its interior may be visited on weekends only, from April through September, 11 a.m. to 5:30 p.m. From here, the route on the map returns you through woods and gardens to the main route near the Palm House.

The Princess of Wales Conservatory

Continue on to the **Temperate House** (11), a gigantic late-Victorian structure housing several thousand varieties of temperate species. The **Australian House**, behind it, features plants from Down Under. Nearby, poking through the trees, is the **Japanese Gateway** left over from a 1910 exhibition, and the rather strange 10-story-high **Chinese Pagoda** (12) that was erected in 1761 as an ornamental folly.

This southern end of Kew Gardens has a few other points of interest, including the **Marianne North Gallery** (13), a Victorian building containing hundreds of botanical paintings by the 19th-century artist. Nearby (at last!) is the **Refreshment Pavilion**, where you can enjoy anything from a drink to a complete meal, cafeteria or restaurant style, indoors or out.

Kew Gardens is open daily, from 9:30 a.m. to 6:30 p.m.; closing at 6 p.m. in March, September, and October; at 5 p.m. in February; and at 4 p.m. from November through January. A free map is available at the entrance.

Leave the gardens via the Lion Gate and turn right on Kew Road, following the map into the historic old town of Richmond and its exceptionally attractive **Richmond Green** (14). In Tudor days this was a jousting ground where tournaments were held next to the former Richmond Palace, of which only traces remain. The palace itself was demolished after the 17th-century Civil War, but sporting activity on the green survives to this day in the form of cricket. All around the large open square are lovely houses from the 17th and 18th centuries, many of which now serve as antique shops, boutiques, and pubs. The **Maids of Honour Row** along the southwest side is a particularly notable set of four adjoining houses built in 1724 as residences for the ladies-in-waiting to the Princess of Wales. To the right of them is an alleyway leading to the 16th-century **Gate House**, the only intact structure from the former palace. Henry VII's coat of arms still decorates its arch. Some of the houses in the courtyard beyond incorporate portions of the original brickwork from the old palace, the third on this site, where Elizabeth I died in 1603.

Continue down Old Palace Lane, passing an inviting pub called the White Swan, to the River Thames and turn left on Cholmondeley Walk. To your left is the 18th-century **Asgill House**, once a weekend retreat for the Lord Mayor of London. Beyond it, through the trees, you can see the **Trumpeters' House**, where the exiled Austrian chancellor Metternich lived in 1848–9.

The riverside path now opens into a large terraced area. At the top of this is the **Old Town Hall** (15) of 1893, housing the local tourist office. From here you get an excellent view of **Richmond Bridge** (16), a handsome stone span completed in 1777 and now the oldest existing bridge over the Thames in Greater London.

An interesting side trip can be made beyond the bridge by following Hill Rise and the fairly steep **Richmond Hill** (17, off the map) to its top. The splendid *panoramic view from here of a sharp bend in the Thames is famous, and has been painted by such artists as Turner and Reynolds. As long as you're up there, you might want to continue into **Richmond Park**, the largest and most unspoiled royal park in London. Its 2,470 acres were enclosed by Charles I in 1637 as a royal hunting ground.

Back in town, you can wander around the narrow old streets, perhaps stopping at some shops or pubs, before heading to **Richmond Station** (18), which is used by both British Rail and the Underground.

London
Additional Attractions

This short chapter has absolutely nothing to do with daytrips, but gives a brief description of some of the more outstanding attractions in London that were not covered on the seven previous one-day walking tours. They are listed alphabetically and include the address, the name of the nearest Underground or British Rail station, and the times of opening.

Apsley House *(The Wellington Museum)*—Britain's great soldier, the Duke of Wellington, who was also a Prime Minister, lived in this grand mansion from 1817 until his death in 1852. Now a museum, it contains various memorabilia of the duke along with his remarkable art collection, especially rich in Spanish and Dutch works. Don't miss the colossal 11-foot-high statue of Napoleon in the nude, a somewhat bizarre gift from the British government after the Battle of Waterloo. Located at 149 Piccadilly by Hyde Park Corner, Apsley House is open on Tuesdays through Sundays from 11 a.m. to 5 p.m.; but closed on some major holidays. Take the Piccadilly Line of the Underground to Hyde Park Corner.

Bethnal Green Museum of Childhood—Located in the East End, this outpost of the Victoria and Albert Museum features a fabulous collection of toys along with costumes for both children and adults from 1770 to the present. Of special interest are the model trains, dolls' houses, board games, toy soldiers, and puppets. There are also displays of furniture, the decorative arts, and articles relating to childhood. You'll find it all on Cambridge Heath Road near the Bethnal Green Underground Station on the Central Line. The museum is open on Mondays through Thursdays and Saturdays, from 10 a.m. to 5:50 p.m.; and on Sundays from 2:30–5:50 p.m.; but not on a few major holidays.

Chiswick House—Admirers of Palladian architecture will love Chiswick House, arguably England's finest example of that classical 18th-century style. Loosely based on Andrea Palladio's great 16th-century Villa Rotonda near Vicenza, Italy, this beautiful country mansion is set in its own lovely park and contains elaborately decorated—although sparsely furnished—interiors. The house is open daily from Good Friday through September, 10 a.m. to 6 p.m., closing at 4 p.m.

the rest of the year. Nearby is **William Hogarth's House**, where the famed satirical artist lived during the summers from 1749 until 1764. It contains a fine selection of his socially biting engravings along with furniture from the period. Both houses are located near the Hogarth Roundabout on the Great West Road and can be reached by Underground on the District Line to Turnham Green (¾ mile walk) or by British Rail to Chiswick (¼ mile walk) from Waterloo Station.

Courtauld Institute Galleries—At last, the treasures of the Courtauld Institute have found a worthy home. These masterpieces of Impressionist, Post-Impressionist, Renaissance, Baroque, and modern art are now conveniently displayed in the elegant Somerset House on the Strand, near Waterloo Bridge. By Underground, take the Circle or District line to Temple; or the Bakerloo, Northern, or Jubilee line to Charing Cross. The galleries are open on Mondays through Saturdays from 10 a.m. to 5 p.m., and on Sundays from 2–5 p.m.; but closed on major holidays.

Dickens House—This is where the suddenly prosperous Charles Dickens lived from early 1837 until late 1839, and where he completed his *Pickwick Papers* and wrote both *Oliver Twist* and *Nickolas Nickleby*. Now a museum exhibiting manuscripts and mementos of his life, it is furnished as it would have been in his time. Dickens House is at 48 Doughty Street, 5 blocks east of the Russell Square station of the Underground's Piccadilly Line. Visits may be made on Mondays through Saturdays, from 10 a.m. to 5 p.m., but not on major holidays.

Docklands—The most exciting inner-city redevelopment plan in Europe is presently taking place in London's historic and highly atmospheric Docklands, an area along the Thames just east of Tower Bridge. From the 17th century until the 1960s this was one of the world's major ports, but since then shipping has moved closer to the mouth of the river to accommodate larger vessels. Quite a few of the old docks, basins, and warehouses have already been restored and converted to modern use. A walk along the river from St. Katherine's Dock (see page 36) to Limehouse Basin—once an unsavory district notorious for its opium dens—and the West India Docks, or Cubitt Town on the Isle of Dogs, will reveal many fascinating attractions, not the least of which are *The Prospect of Whitby* and *The Grapes*, two historic and very popular old pubs. The entire area is well served by the modern elevated **Docklands Light Railway** (see page 20), and guide brochures describing the sights are available from tourist offices.

Dulwich Picture Gallery—One of the best small art museums in England, Dulwich is situated in a delightful, nearly rural suburb some four miles south of the Tower of London. It opened in 1814 as Britain's first public art gallery, and is housed in a simple but beautiful building designed by the noted classical architect, Sir John Soane. The collec-

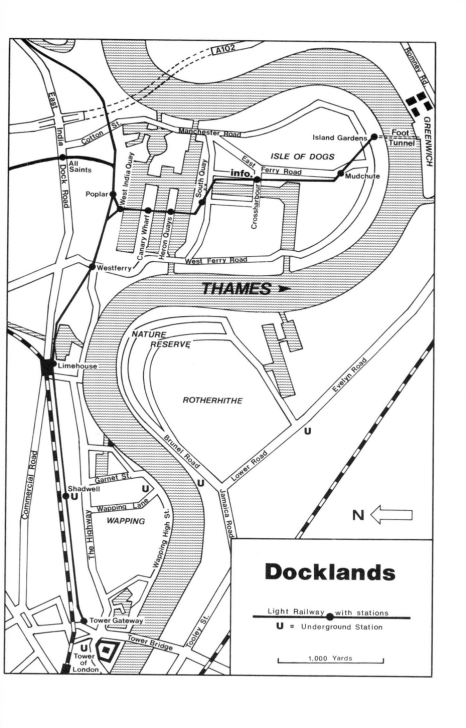

tions here are rich in Old Masters, with superb paintings by Rembrandt, Rubens, Van Dyck, Cuyp, Murillo, Claude, Poussin, Gainsborough, Reynolds, and many others. Located on College Road in Dulwich, the museum is best reached by taking British Rail from Victoria Station to West Dulwich and walking a few blocks northeast along the playing fields. It is open on Tuesdays through Saturdays, from 10 a.m. to 1 p.m. and 2–5 p.m.; and on Sundays from 2–5 p.m.; but closed on a few major holidays.

Ham House—Noted for its luxuriantly Baroque interior, this splendid 17th-century mansion is set in terraced gardens overlooking the Thames just below Richmond (see page 83). The period furnishings are of the highest quality, and a fine collection of miniature paintings adds another touch of elegance to an already exuberant scene. Among the most outstanding features are the Great Staircase, the Marble Dining Room, the Queen's Bedchamber, and the Long Gallery. Take either the Underground (District line) or British Rail (from Waterloo Station) to Richmond. From there it's bus number 65 or 71 to Ham House, or you could walk the lovely 2-mile distance. Visits may be made on Tuesdays through Sundays, from 11 a.m. to 5 p.m., but not on a few major holidays.

*Hampton Court—Henry VIII's great royal palace on the Thames is one of London's most fabulous attractions. First built in 1514 by the ostentatious Cardinal Wolsley, it was given to Henry in 1529 in a vain attempt to appease the king, who was angered by the thought of a commoner living better than himself. Succeeding monarchs (and Oliver Cromwell!) enjoyed its luxury right down to the death of George II in 1760, although William III had significant alterations made by the famed architect Sir Christopher Wren in 1689. Queen Victoria opened the palace and its magnificent gardens to the public in 1838. There is a lot to see here, including the **Great Gatehouse**, the **State Apartments**, the **Guard Chamber, William III's Bedroom**, the **Cartoon Gallery**, the **Haunted Gallery**, the **Royal Chapel**, the **Great Watching Chamber**, and the **Great Hall**. A few of the best outdoor sights are the **Orangery**, the **Fountain Court**, the **Great Vine** which still yields grapes after 200 years, and the early-18th-century **Maze** where you can get lost. Hampton Court Palace is open daily from mid-March through mid-October, 9:30 a.m. to 6 p.m.; and the rest of the year daily from 9:30 a.m. to 4:30 p.m., but closed on a few major holidays. There is both a restaurant and a cafeteria. Get there via British Rail from Waterloo Station direct to Hampton Court, a 32-minute ride. You can also come by Green Line Coach, or even by boat from Westminster Pier—a 3- or 4-hour cruise operated between April and October. This is a great little effortless trip for your first day in London, when the effects of jet lag make more complex excursions too tiring.

Imperial War Museum—Military buffs will appreciate this extensive collection of weapons, tanks, aircraft, vehicles, uniforms, documents, and art relating to all conflicts involving Britain and the Commonwealth from 1914 until the present. Ironically, it is housed in a part of the former Bedlam Insane Asylum. The emphasis, however, is not on the ''glory'' of war but on its causes and on honoring those who served. Located on Lambeth Road in Southwark, the museum can be reached by Underground (Bakerloo Line) to Lambeth North. It is open daily from 10 a.m. to 6 p.m., but closed for a few major holidays.

Little Venice—An unexpected and highly attractive corner of London is hidden away north of Paddington Station, at the junction of the Regent's and Grand Union canals. Completed in the early 19th century, these waterways link London's Limehouse Basin (see Docklands) on the Thames with cities to the north. No longer used for commercial traffic, they are maintained for pleasure boats and provide a tranquil scene where the past is still alive. The basin at Little Venice is especially lovely and well worth visiting. Trips on a colorfully-painted traditional narrowboat are offered by **Jason's Trip**, phone (071) 286-3428, from Easter through September; and to the London Zoo and other destinations by the **London Waterbus Company**, phone (071) 482-2550. It is also possible to take a delightful walk along the towpath, detouring around the Maida Hill and Islington tunnels. Little Venice is two blocks south of the Underground's Warwick Avenue Station, on the Bakerloo Line.

London Dungeon—The darker side of English history is brought chillingly to life in this scary museum of medieval horror. Its location in the dank vaults beneath the rumbling railway lines of London Bridge Station only adds to the atmosphere. Watch the plague spread! Watch heads roll! Squirm to the eerie sounds! Lots of gruesome fun for all but the squeamish. The entrance is at 34 Tooley Street, served by the Northern Line of the Underground to London Bridge, and it is open daily from 10 a.m. to 5:30 p.m., closing at 4:30 p.m. in winter. You have been warned.

London Toy and Model Museum—This wonderful world of children's toys is as much a treat for grownups as it is for kids. Room after room in a fine old house are filled with model trains, dolls and dolls' houses, teddy bears, and toys of all kinds from the 1850s to the present. There is even an outdoor garden with a working miniature railway. The museum is at 23 Craven Hill in Bayswater, and is best reached by Underground to Lancaster Gate or Queensway on the Central Line, or to Paddington on the Circle or District lines. It is open on Tuesdays through Saturdays, from 10 a.m. to 5:30 p.m., and on Sundays from 11 a.m. to 5:30 p.m.

London Zoo—Located at the northern end of Regent's Park and bisected by the Regent's Canal, the zoo was first opened in 1828. Since then, there have been a great many changes reflecting new attitudes in animal care, making the zoo of today one of the finest and most innovative in the world. Its main gate is on the Outer Circle of Regent's Park, reached by Underground (Circle, District, Jubilee, or Bakerloo lines) to Baker Street followed by a number 74 bus to the zoo. You could also take the Underground (Northern Line) to Camden Town and walk, or get there by waterbus from Little Venice (see above). The zoo is open daily from 9 a.m. (10 a.m. in winter) to 6 p.m. (7 p.m. on Sundays) or dusk if earlier.

Royal Air Force Museum—Aviation activities began in the North London suburb of Hendon as early as 1910, when its flying field was laid out. It was from here that the first non-stop London-to-Paris flight was made, and where a naval air service was established in 1914, later to become an R.A.F. station. Although the runways have long since yielded to housing developments, some of the hangars from World War I were preserved internally and given a new façade. These now house the fabulous collections and displays of the **R.A.F. Museum**, incorporating the **Battle of Britain** and **Bomber Command** museums, which together comprise some 60 military aircraft from the earliest days of flying to the present. Shown along with the planes are related equipment, reconstructed operations rooms, souvenirs of the Red Baron, and the like. Aircraft from America, Germany, and Italy are also included, and there is a restaurant and bar. Take the Underground (Northern Line bound for Edgware) to Colindale, then walk a half-mile east on Colindale Avenue and Grahame Park Way to the museum. It is open daily from 10 a.m. to 6 p.m.

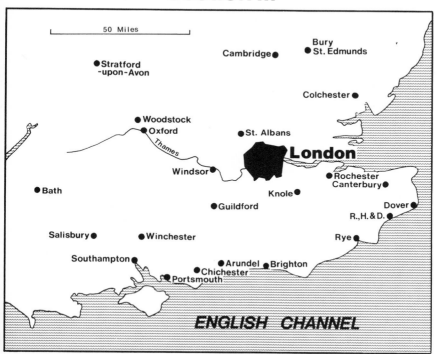

DAYTRIPS FROM LONDON

It may be surprising to realize just how many of England's best attractions are within easy daytrip range of London. The southeast corner of the nation is so compact that rail travel times to its most delightful destinations range from only 25 minutes to less than two hours, with corresponding driving distances of just 20 to about 100 miles. With so much to see this close to the capital, you can enjoy a broad variety of thoroughly English experiences without ever having to check out of your London accommodations.

   The advantages of staying in one hotel and traveling without the burden of luggage far outweigh the additional mileage involved. By departing London around 8 or 9 a.m. you will reach your daytrip des-

*The historic charms of Winchester
are only an hour from London*

tination in mid-morning, leaving nearly all of the day free for sightseeing, shopping, dining, or just relaxing before returning in time for an evening's entertainment.

A good way to add variety to your visit is to alternate between making one-day excursions and spending entire days exploring London, which also lets you sleep later on the days you choose to stay in town. Doing this has become more practical with the introduction of "flexible" railpasses that do not have to be used on consecutive days.

Should you prefer following a point-to-point itinerary instead of making daytrips, you could select whichever destinations interest you and link them together with direct road or rail routes, usually avoiding London completely. The strategy of doing this is discussed on page 102.

The 23 daytrips described in this section were chosen to cover a wide diversity of interests and experiences. Some are to world-famous destinations, while others will take you well off the beaten path to unusual adventures. Those that have most consistently pleased nearly everyone include Canterbury, Rye, Salisbury and Stonehenge, Oxford, Stratford-upon-Avon, and Cambridge—all exceptionally good choices for first-time visitors.

Getting Around
Southeastern England

Getting around southeastern England on your own is really quite easy once you know a few of the practicalities. This section discusses your transportation options, and then goes on to describe 23 of the most exciting daytrip possibilities within easy range of London. All of the excursions can be made by either train or car.

BY RAIL:

The British invented passenger trains and, on balance, their systems is probably the best in the world. While some of the trains and stations are not quite as sleek as the latest found in, say, France or Germany, **British Rail** has the decided advantage of taking you where you want to go, when you want to go, and of doing so with a minimum of fuss. With over 2,400 destinations and some 15,000 trains a day, there are few places that cannot be reached quickly and comfortably from London. BritRail stations are usually located right in the heart of towns, so close to the major tourist attractions that most of the walking tours described in this section begin right at the station. Trains have the additional advantage of neatly bypassing traffic going in and out of the metropolis, and of generally being the quickest way to cover the distances involved.

Equipment varies from the swift **InterCity 225s** (a new series of electric expresses operating at 140 mph) and the highly successful **InterCity 125s** (at 125 mph, the world's fastest diesels) to some rather quaint and colorful old commuter trains. Between these extremes are a wide variety of reliable workhorses, including the **Sprinters,** a new generation of self-propelled trains now in widespread use. All express trains and some locals carry both first- and standard (economy 2nd)-class accommodations. Most intercity runs have a buffet or dining car, serving meals, snacks, and drinks.

Seasoned travelers often consider riding trains to be one of the best ways of meeting the British people on their home ground. It is not unusual to strike up an engaging conversation that makes your trip all the more memorable. You also get a view of the passing countryside from the large windows, and have time to catch up on your reading. Then too, you are spared the worries of driving, especially after making a few pub stops.

London has many **train stations,** a legacy from the days before nationalization, when just about every route was operated by a separate company. The map opposite shows the general location of those that are likely to be used by tourists. All of these are connected to the **Underground** (subway, see page 19) and can be reached easily. Be sure you know which station you are leaving from, and allow a little extra time to orient yourself the first time you use it. All main stations have an information office where you can check the current schedules or any possible temporary variations to them. Information can also be had by calling the following phone numbers in London:

FOR TRAINS LEAVING FROM: CALL:

Charing Cross, Victoria, Waterloo, Waterloo East, Liverpool Street, Cannon Street, or London Bridge . . . . (071) 928-5100

St. Pancras, Euston, or Marylebone . . (071) 387-7070

King's Cross . . . . (071) 278-2477

Paddington . . . . (071) 262-6767

There is generally no need for **reservations** on BritRail trains, especially not for the daytrips described in this section, but you might consider making them for possible long-distance trips such as London to Edinburgh. A very few departures (shown on schedules with a boxed letter "R") require reservations during peak periods.

The system-wide **British Rail Passenger Map** is highly detailed and very useful in planning your trips. It is available free of charge from the North American offices of BritRail Travel International or can be purchased from the Transportation Centres in the larger train stations in Britain. Although you really don't need it, a **Timetable Book** of the entire system can also be bought at major stations, or you might want to use the handy but somewhat less comprehensive **Thomas Cook European Timetable,** covering all of Europe and sold at Thomas Cook travel offices throughout Britain. It is also available at some travel bookstores in America or by mail from the Forsyth Travel Library, P.O. Box 2975, Shawnee Mission KS 66201-1375, phone 1-800-FORSYTH for credit-card orders.

You should be aware that train service is often reduced on Sundays and holidays, and that travel at those times might involve delays or diversions due to track maintenance work. Check for announcements at the station.

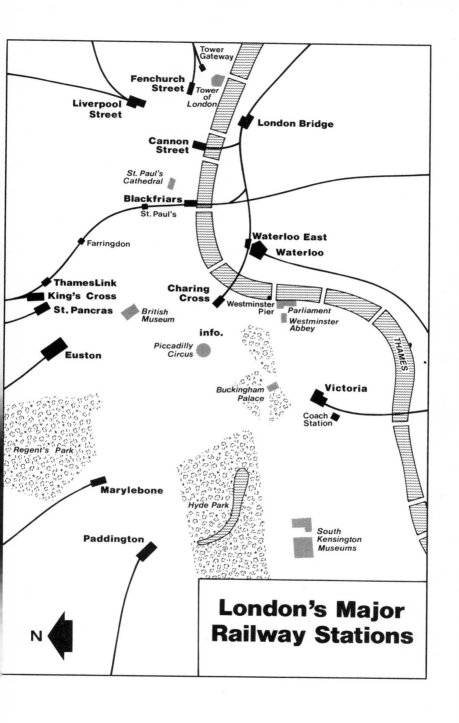

Tower
Gateway

Fenchurch
Street

Tower
of
London

London Bridge

Liverpool
Street

Cannon
Street

St. Paul's
Cathedral

Blackfriars

St. Paul's

Waterloo East

Waterloo

Farringdon

ThamesLink

King's Cross

Charing
Cross

St. Pancras

Westminster
Pier

Parliament

British
Museum

Westminster
Abbey

info.

Euston

Piccadilly
Circus

THAMES

Buckingham
Palace

Victoria

Coach
Station

Regent's Park

Marylebone

Hyde Park

Paddington

South
Kensington
Museums

N

London's Major
Railway Stations

RAILPASSES can be a terrific bargain if you intend to do extensive train travel, but they must be obtained before going to Britain as they cannot be purchased once there. British Rail accepts the following passes:

BRITRAIL PASS—The original railpass for Britain allows unlimited train travel throughout the entire British Rail system (all of England, Wales, and Scotland) for periods of 8, 15, or 22 consecutive days, or for one month; and is available in both first- and standard (economy second)-class versions for adults. The pass is also sold at a reduced price for children from 5 to 15 years of age, for youths between 16 and 25 (second class only), and for senior citizens 60 and over.

BRITRAIL FLEXIPASS—This handy version of the BritRail Pass offers the same unlimited train travel on any 4 days during an 8-day period, on any 8 days during a 15-day period, or on any 15 days during one month. Again, both first- and second-class versions are available, and there are special deals for children, youths, and senior citizens. Although it costs a bit more, the Flexipass allows you to take time out between your daytrips, and might in the long run be the greater bargain.

BRITRAIL/DRIVE—A package deal that combines the BritRail Flexipass with car-rental vouchers valid at over 100 Hertz locations throughout Britain, many of which are in BritRail stations. This plan could be very useful on some longer and more complex trips, where you can take a train most of the way and complete your trip by rental car, thus getting better acquainted with the countryside while avoiding city traffic.

BRITFRANCE RAILPASS—Allows unlimited rail travel throughout both Britain and France on any 5 days within a 15-day period; or on any 10 days in a one-month period. It is offered in both first- and second-class versions, and includes a round-trip crossing of the Channel by Hovercraft. Although rather expensive, it affords great flexibility and could be a good deal for those visiting both countries on the same trip, especially if you're traveling from Scotland to the Riviera and back with time-out periods in both London and Paris. A cheaper second-class version is available to those between the ages of 12 and 25.

LONDON EXTRA—This is a convenient and economical arrangement for visitors to London who are also making some of the daytrips. The low-cost package includes a 3-, 4-, or 7-consecutive-day first- or second-class **railpass** valid throughout the "Network Southeast" area (which includes all of the destinations in this book *EXCEPT* Bath, Stratford-upon-Avon, and Bury St. Edmunds) with a 3-, 4-, or 7-consecutive-day **London Visitor Travelcard** valid for unlimited travel on London Transport's Underground and buses. The two elements do not have to be used at the same time, so you can explore London with the Travelcard, then make daytrips with the railpass.

Railpasses will probably save you a considerable amount of money if you travel extensively by train throughout Britain. Be sure to analyse the different prices and arrangements carefully in light of your plans and the amount of flexibility that you *really* need. Some of the passes cost up to three times as much *per day* as others, even for the same class of travel! If it fits your needs, the London Extra is definitely the least expensive option, while the BritFrance Railpass is the costliest.

Even if the savings over regular fares is not great, a pass should still be considered for the convenience it offers in not having to line up for tickets, and for the freedom of just hopping aboard almost any train at whim. Possession of a pass will also encourage you to become more adventurous, to seek out distant and offbeat destinations. And, should you ever manage to get on the wrong train by mistake (or change your plans en route), your only cost will be your time—not an extra fare back!

The various railpasses **must** be obtained **before** going to Britain. Current details about prices and conditions of use, as well as the passes themselves, are available from most travel agents, by mail from the Forsyth Travel Library mentioned above, or from the nearest offices of BritRail Travel International—located in New York, Los Angeles, Dallas, Toronto, and Vancouver. Written or phone inquiries can be made to:

BritRail Travel International
1500 Broadway
New York, NY 10036-4015
Phone (212) 382-3737—FAX (212) 575-2542

Railpasses must be **validated** before use. They provide transportation only and do not cover possible additional charges such as reservations, sleeping accommodations, or meals. If you have decided against a pass—or live in Britain and cannot buy one—you still have several money-saving options. Before purchasing a full-fare ticket you should always ask about special fares that might be applicable to your journey, including same-day returns, called "Awayday" tickets.

BY CAR:

Making your daytrips by car can be an attractive proposition *if* several people are traveling together and *if* you can cope with the hassles of London traffic. It is actually the preferred way to travel for the Knole, Romney Hythe & Dymchurch, Brighton, Chichester & Bosham, Salisbury & Stonehenge, Woodstock, and Stratford-upon-Avon trips, which involve more complex transportation than do the other excursions.

If you prefer to follow an itinerary rather than make daytrips, you'll find that a car is certainly more convenient for hopping directly from one destination to another without returning to London, particularly if you stay at country inns. This strategy is discussed below under the heading "Links."

It is possible to economically combine both car and rail travel, riding trains through congested areas and driving rental cars in the countryside, by using the **BritRail/Drive** package described on page 100. The various money-saving **Fly/Drive** deals offered by **British Airways** and other carriers in conjunction with their transatlantic flights are another good way to cut your car-rental expenses. Ask you travel agent about both of these plans, as well as regular car rentals, as far in advance as possible.

Other than getting used to driving on the left, you should have no trouble adapting to English roads, which are usually quite excellent. Routes prefixed with the letter "M" are Motorways (toll-free superhighways with speed limits up to 70 mph), those with an "A" are regular highways (sometimes divided), while those marked with a "B" or no letter are rural routes. Among the many excellent **road maps** of this region is the Michelin number 404 "Midlands and Southeast England." American and Canadian driver's licenses are valid, although there are usually minimum age and experience restrictions for rentals.

LINKS:

Although this book is about daytrips, it can just as well be used for conventional point-to-point itinerary travel. Just select the destinations that interest you most, locate them on the map opposite, and note the linkage routes that tie them directly together without returning to London. Each chapter has a paragraph labeled "Links" that will help clarify this. Those traveling by train will find a rail map and timetable book (see page 98) to be especially useful.

Overnight accommodations, often in charming country inns, are easily arranged through the local **Tourist Information Centres,** who can also make instant reservations for the next stop on your trip through the handy "Book-A-Bed-Ahead" facility. These information offices are usually closed on Sundays and sometimes on Saturdays, so try to anticipate your needs before the weekends.

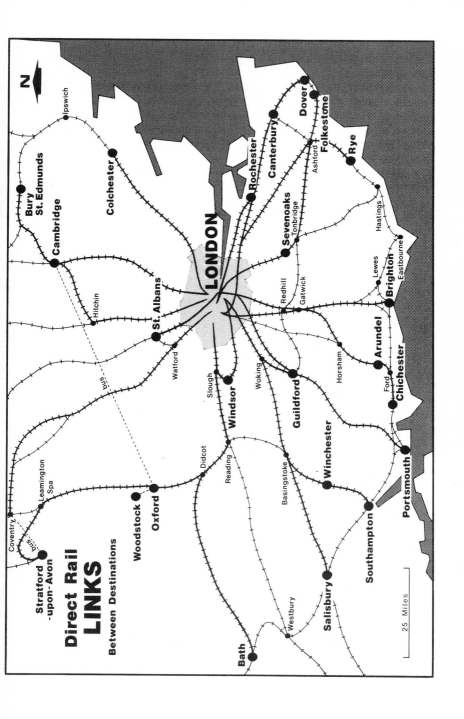

Direct Rail LINKS

Between Destinations

N

25 Miles

LONDON

Ipswich
Bury St. Edmunds
Colchester
Cambridge
Hitchin
St. Albans
Watford
Slough
Windsor
Woking
Guildford
Winchester
Didcot
Reading
Basingstoke
Horsham
Woodstock
Oxford
Leamington Spa
Coventry
Stratford-upon-Avon
bus
bus
Salisbury
Westbury
Bath
Southampton
Portsmouth
Ford
Chichester
Arundel
Brighton
Eastbourne
Lewes
Hastings
Gatwick
Redhill
Rye
Folkestone
Dover
Ashford
Canterbury
Rochester
Sevenoaks
Tonbridge

Rochester

The ancient cathedral town of Rochester is most famous for its close association with Charles Dickens, who spent much of his life nearby and used the town as a locale for many of his stories. A marvelous museum that explores his life and works in stunning audio-visual terms has been opened and is reason enough for the visit. There are several other attractions as well, including a massive Norman castle, a 12th-century cathedral, remains of a Roman wall, the excellent Guildhall Museum, several buildings of historic importance, and an exceptionally attractive main street.

No one knows just how old Rochester is, but it probably dates from prehistoric times. The early Britons called it *Doubris,* which the Romans changed to *Durobrivae* after they built their bridge across the River Medway. The present name derives from the Anglo-Saxon *Hrofesceaster.* In A.D. 604 the second-oldest bishopric in England was established here, becoming the foundation for the present Norman cathedral.

GETTING THERE:

Trains to Rochester depart at about half-hour intervals from London's Victoria, Charing Cross, and Waterloo East stations, with a journey time of about an hour. Return service operates until late evening.

By car, Rochester is 30 miles southeast of London via the A-2 road. There are convenient parking lots along Corporation Street.

LINKS:

Rochester has good direct rail service to **Canterbury** and **Dover** for those following an itinerary rather than making daytrips. By changing trains you could also ride to Folkestone Central for the **Romney, Hythe & Dymchurch** trip, Sevenoaks for the **Knole** trip, or Ashford for connections to **Rye**. All of these destinations are described later in this section, and all can be easily reached by car as well.

PRACTICALITIES:

The important sights in Rochester are open daily throughout the year, except on a few major holidays. A general outdoor market is held on Fridays, and a flea market on Saturdays. Some shops close early on Wednesdays. The local **Tourist Information Centre,** phone (0634) 43-666, is in Eastgate Cottage, next to the Charles Dickens Centre. Rochester is in the county of **Kent,** and has a **population** of about 24,000.

Miss Havisham in the Charles Dickens Centre
(Photo courtesy of Rochester Tourist Office)

FOOD AND DRINK:

There are several good restaurants and pubs along High Street, a few choices being:

Royal Victoria and Bull (16 High St., opposite the Guildhall) A 400-year-old inn used as a locale by Dickens. $$

King's Head (58 High St., a block south of the Guildhall) Serving traditional fare for over four centuries. $$

Castle Tea Rooms (151 High St., near Dickens Centre) Light lunches in a comfortable setting. $

SUGGESTED TOUR:

Leaving **Rochester Station** (1), turn right and follow High Street to the ***Charles Dickens Centre** in **Eastgate House** (2). The 16th-century house itself was mentioned in Dickens' novel *Pickwick Papers* as the

"Westgate House," and in *The Mystery of Edwin Drood* as the "Nun's House." Inside, two floors are filled with life-size models of his characters, reconstructions of scenes from his books, and mementos of his life. All of this is brought to life through the clever use of sound and light, a theatrical experience that is absolutely first rate. The museum is open daily from 10 a.m. to 5:30 p.m. Upon leaving, be sure to take a look at Dickens' tiny Swiss Chalet in the garden, which was moved here from his home at nearby Gad's Hill. The gabled house on the other side of High Street is Uncle Pumblechook's house in *Great Expectations*.

Continue along High Street to the **Six Poor Travellers' House** (3), otherwise known as the Watts Charity. Founded in 1579, it provided lodging for impoverished travelers until 1947. You may visit the little Elizabethan bedrooms from April through October, Tuesdays through Saturdays, from 2–5 p.m. Dickens changed its name to "The Seven Poor Travellers" in his *Christmas Tale* of 1854.

A further stroll down High Street leads to the Corn Exchange of 1706 with its extraordinary moon-faced clock projecting over the street. This was mentioned in Dickens' novel *The Uncommercial Traveller*. Just beyond is the **Guildhall** (4), built in 1687, which now houses a town museum dealing with regional history from the Stone Age onward. The collection of **Victorian toys** is especially interesting and should not be missed. The museum is open daily except for a few major holidays, from 10 a.m. to 12:30 p.m. and 2–5 p.m. Across the street is the Royal Victoria and Bull Hotel, which appears as "The Bull" in *Pickwick Papers* and as the "Blue Boar" in *Great Expectations*. Queen Victoria stayed there when she was still a princess.

Now return on High Street to Chertsey's Gate, also known as College Gate, a 15th-century structure featured in Dickens' *The Mystery of Edwin Drood*. Pass through it and look to the left. The tombstones in the graveyard of St. Nicholas' Church provided Dickens with names for many of his characters!

You are now at **Rochester Cathedral** (5). An almost perfect example of early Norman architecture, it resembles Canterbury Cathedral and has several of the same features, including double transepts, an elevated choir, and an extensive **crypt**. The **west front**, with a magnificent doorway, is among the finest in England. Built on the site of an early-7th-century church, the cathedral was begun in 1080 and consecrated in 1130. Many additions were made through the centuries, making the mixture of styles particularly interesting.

Stroll over to **Rochester Castle** (6). The Romans had a fortress here to guard their bridge, and in later centuries Saxons fought Vikings on this hill. Of the great castle begun in 1087 by William the Conqueror, only the massive 12th-century keep remains. One of the finest ex-

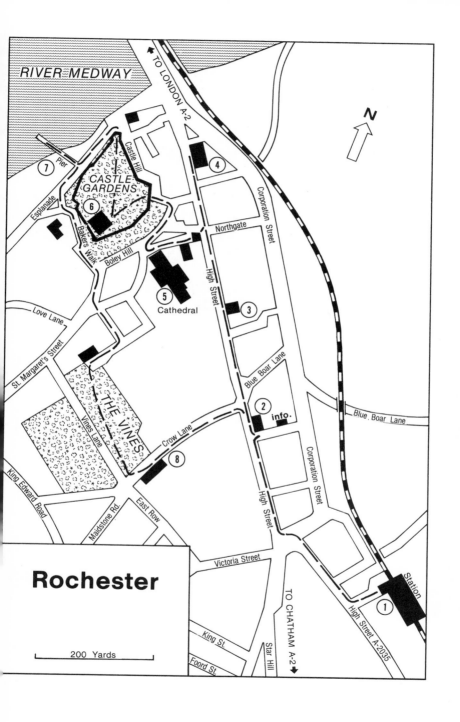

RIVER MEDWAY

TO LONDON A·2

N

⑦ Pier

Esplanade

Castle Hill

CASTLE GARDENS

⑥

Bakers Walk

Boley Hill

④

Northgate

Corporation Street

High Street

⑤
Cathedral

③

Love Lane

St. Margaret's Street

THE VINES

Vines Lane

Blue Boar Lane

Blue Boar Lane

② info.

Crow Lane

⑧

King Edward Road

Maidstone Rd.

East Row

Corporation Street

High Street

Victoria Street

Rochester

⊢———— 200 Yards ————⊣

King St.

Foord St.

Star Hill

TO CHATHAM A·2

High Street A-2035

Station

①

Inside Rochester Castle

amples of Norman military architecture, it is 113 feet high and has
walls that are 12 feet thick. A climb to the top will reward you with a
superb **panorama** of the town and the Medway estuary. The castle is
open on Mondays through Saturdays, from 9:30 a.m. to 6:30 p.m.;
and on Sundays from 2:30–5:30 p.m.. It closes at 4 p.m. in winter.

Descend through the park to the Bridge Warden's Chapel of 1387
and turn left to **Rochester Pier** (7). From here you will get a good view
of activities on the river. Follow the map past the Satis House, where
Queen Elizabeth I was entertained in 1573, and the Old Hall, an early
Tudor building. Continue on past Minor Canon Row, mentioned in
Dickens' *Edwin Drood;* the King's School, founded in 1542 by Henry
VIII; and the Archdeaconry of 1661.

Pass through The Vines, a park where monks once had their vineyard. Parts of the old Roman city wall can be seen on the north side.
The **Restoration House** (8) on Crow Lane was the home of Miss Havisham in Dickens' *Great Expectations*. Its name derives from the tradition that Charles II stayed here in 1660 on his way to be crowned
king following the end of the Commonwealth. A few steps down Crow
Lane will return you to High Street and the end of the tour.

*Canterbury

Over two thousand years of history have left their mark on Canterbury, a magnet for countless pilgrimages since the 12th century. St. Augustine established the Christian Church in England here as far back as A.D. 597, and in 1170 the martyr Thomas à Becket was murdered in its cathedral. As a convenient place to ford the River Stour, Canterbury was a strategic settlement ever since the Iron Age. Under the name *Durovernum,* the Romans made it an important center of trade in the 1st century A.D. This status increased during Anglo-Saxon times, when the name was changed to *Cantwarabyrig,* and it became the capital of the Kingdom of Kent. Much of Canterbury's colorful past remains intact today, despite the ravages of Cromwell's troops and the bombs of World War II.

GETTING THERE:

Trains to Canterbury East Station depart from Victoria Station in London at hourly intervals. The journey takes about 80 minutes. Be sure to get on the right car, as some trains split en route. Return service operates until late evening.

By car, Canterbury is 58 miles southeast of London via the A-2 and M-2 highways.

LINKS:

For those following an itinerary rather than making daytrips, Canterbury East Station offers good direct rail service to both **Rochester** and **Dover.** By changing trains at Dover you can easily get to Folkestone for the **Romney, Hythe & Dymchurch** trip. Trains from Canterbury West Station go to Sevenoaks for the **Knole** trip, or connect at Ashford for **Rye.** All of these destinations are featured elsewhere in this section, and all can easily be reached by car as well.

PRACTICALITIES:

Any day is a good day to visit Canterbury, bearing in mind that some minor sights are closed on Sundays. The local **Tourist Information Centre**, phone (0227) 766-567, is at 34 St. Margaret's Street, three blocks southwest of the cathedral. You might ask there about renting a **bicycle** in town as this is good cycling country. Canterbury is in the county of **Kent,** and has a **population** of about 35,000.

FOOD AND DRINK:

Having attracted pilgrims and their modern counterparts since the Middle Ages, Canterbury has no shortage of restaurants and pubs in all price ranges. Some particularly good choices are:

Michael's (74 Wincheap, 2 blocks southwest of East Station) Regarded as the best restaurant in Canterbury, in a 16th-century house outside the town center. For reservations phone (0227) 767-411. X: Sat. lunch, Sun. $$$

Waterfield's (5a Best Lane, just northeast of the Weavers' House) In an old house with a view of the river. X: Sun. $$

George's Brasserie (71 Castle St., 2 blocks northeast of the Norman Castle) Mostly traditional French bistro food. X: Sun. $$

Caesar's (46 St. Peter's St., between the Weavers' House and Westgate) A favorite with the young crowd for its salads and burgers. $

SUGGESTED TOUR:

Leaving **Canterbury East Station** (1), cross the footbridge over the A-2 highway and turn right on the ancient city walls. Dating from the 13th and 14th centuries, these were built on Roman foundations. To your left is **Dane John Gardens** (2), a pleasant 18th-century park with a strange mound of unexplained but probably prehistoric origin. Continue atop the walls and turn left by the bus station onto St. George's Street. The tower on the right is all that remains of St. George's Church, where Christopher Marlowe was baptized in 1564.

St. George's Street soon becomes High Street. Stroll down this and make a right into narrow **Mercery Lane**, the traditional pilgrim's approach to the cathedral. During medieval days this was lined with stalls selling healing water from Becket's Well, medallions of St. Thomas, and other mementos of the pilgrimage. At its far end is the Butter Market, an ancient center of trade. The magnificent **Christchurch Gate** (3), opposite, dates from the early 16th century and is the main entrance to the cathedral grounds.

Pass through the gate and enter the grounds of *****Canterbury Cathedral** (4), the mother church of the Anglican faith throughout the world. For centuries it has been a center of pilgrimage and in a sense still is, although today's visitors are more likely to be tourists. Neither the largest, the tallest, nor the most beautiful of English cathedrals, it nevertheless has an attraction that is second to none.

A cathedral was built on this site by St. Augustine, the first Archbishop of Canterbury, in 602. This lasted until 1067, when it burned down. The present structure was begun in 1070 and completed in 1503, although little of the earlier work remains.

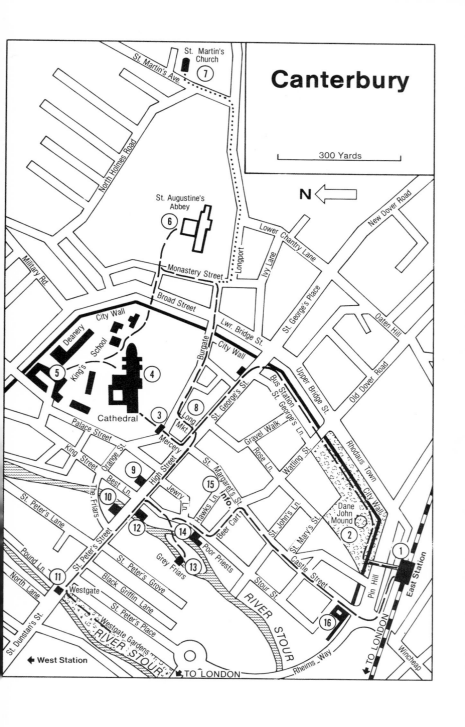

Canterbury

300 Yards

N

St. Martin's Church
7

St. Martin's Ave.

North Holmes Road

St. Augustine's Abbey
6

Military Rd

New Dover Road

Oaten Hill

Lower Chantry Lane

Ivy Lane

Longport

Monastery Street

St. George's Place

Broad Street

City Wall

Deanery

King's School

Lwr. Bridge St.

City Wall

Burgate

Old Dover Road

5

4

Cathedral

3

8

Long Mkt.

Palace Street

King Street

Orange St.

Mercery

St. George's St.

St. George's St.

Bus Station

Upper Bridge St.

Gravel Walk

St. George's Ln.

Rhodaus Town

City Wall

9

Best Ln.

High Street

Jewry

St. Margaret's St.

Rose Ln.

Watling St.

The Friars

10

St. Peter's Lane

12

14

Hawks Ln.

15

Bear Cart

St. John's Ln.

Dane John Mound

2

Pound Ln.

North Lane

11

Westgate

St. Peter's Street

St. Peter's Grove

Grey Friars

13

Poor Priests

St. Mary's St.

Castle Street

Stour St.

1

East Station

TO LONDON

Pin Hill

Winchead

Black Griffin Lane

St. Peter's Place

Westgate Gardens

16

St. Dunstan's St.

RIVER STOUR

◄ West Station

RIVER STOUR

↓ TO LONDON

RIVER STOUR

Rheims Way

Rhodaus Town

Canterbury Cathedral from the King's School

Enter the cathedral by way of the southwest porch. The lofty nave was built in the Perpendicular style during the 14th century, replacing an inadequate Norman original. Above the crossing you can see up the entire height of the magnificent **Bell Harry Tower**, whose bell is rung every evening for curfew and tolled on the death of a sovereign or an archbishop. A flight of steps to the right of the screen leads to the elevated **Choir**, one of the longest in England.

Behind the High Altar is the **Trinity Chapel**, which held Becket's tomb until Henry VIII had it demolished and the bones scattered in 1538. The tomb of the only king to be buried at Canterbury, Henry IV, and that of Edward, the Black Prince, are also in this chapel. At the extreme east end is a circular chapel known as the **Corona**, or Becket's Crown. The marble chair in its center is used for the enthronement of every archbishop.

The north aisle leads past the choir to the northwest transept, the scene of the martyrdom. It was here that Archbishop Thomas à Becket was murdered on December 29, 1170. The four knights who committed the deed thought they were carrying out the desire of their king, Henry II, although his part in it is disputed by historians. Henry certainly had reason to get rid of "this turbulent priest," his former friend and ally who had challenged the power of the State. Whatever the rationale behind the killing, it led to the canonization of Becket, the chastisement of Henry II, the role of Canterbury as a place of pilgrimage, and helped further the cause of individual freedom.

In the Choir of Canterbury Cathedral

The spacious **Crypt** is the oldest part of the cathedral, dating from Norman times. Along its south aisle there is a Huguenot chapel where services in French are still held. Becket was first buried at the east end, which was also the scene of Henry II's penance.

Stroll into the early-15th-century **Cloisters** by way of the northwest transept. Adjoining it is the Chapter House and Library. Follow the passageway and turn left into the grounds of the **King's School** (5). Although it was refounded by Henry VIII, the school claims an ancestry going back to the time of St. Augustine, which would make it the oldest in England. The 12th-century Norman staircase near the northwest corner of the Green Court is truly magnificent, as are the views of the cathedral from this point.

Returning, bear left and walk around the rear of the cathedral to the Kent War Memorial Gardens. Go through the gate in the far corner and follow the map to the ruins of **St. Augustine's Abbey** (6). Originally founded in 598 and rebuilt several times since, it was destroyed by Henry VIII following the Reformation. Excavations have revealed the layout of several buildings including the church, monk's dormitory, kitchen, refectory, and cloisters. The abbey is open on Mondays through Saturdays, from 9:30 a.m. to 6:30 p.m.; and on Sundays from 2–6:30 p.m. It closes at 4 p.m. in winter.

From here you might want to make a little side trip to an interesting old church. To do this, walk back around St. Augustine's and turn left on Monastery Street, then left again on Longport. Just past the jail make another left to **St. Martin's Church** (7), said to be the oldest church in England that is still in use. Parts of it date from before the time of St. Augustine and were used by Queen Bertha, Christian wife of King Ethelbert. Explore the interior, noting in particular the Saxon font, then stroll through the tranquil graveyard.

Returning to town via Longport and Church Street, walk down Burgate and turn left into Butchery Lane. In a basement below a modern shopping center is an excavated **Roman Pavement** (8), once part of a large villa erected around A.D. 100. It may be seen on Mondays through Saturdays, from 10 a.m. to 1 p.m. and 2–5 p.m., with shorter hours in winter.

Continuing along High Street, you will pass Queen Elizabeth's Guest Chamber, a Tudor house on the left in which the queen entertained her French suitor, the Duke of Alençon. It is now a restaurant. Farther along on the right is the **Royal Museum and Art Gallery** (9), otherwise known as the Beaney Institute. It has a fine collection of Roman and other antiquities as well as local art, and may be visited on Mondays through Saturdays, from 10 a.m. to 5 p.m. The famous **Weavers' House** (10) on the edge of the River Stour was occupied by Huguenot weavers who settled in Canterbury after fleeing France in the 17th century. Now a gift shop, it is open to visitors, who may inspect the old looms and ducking stool, or even take a boat ride on the river.

Walk along St. Peter's Street to the **Westgate** (11). Built in the late 14th century, this imposing fortification once guarded the western approach to Canterbury. Its upper floor served as the city jail until 1829. Now a museum of arms and torture instruments, it is open daily except on Sundays, from 10 a.m. to 1 p.m. and 2–5 p.m.; with winter hours being 2–4 p.m. There is a superb view from the top.

A stroll through Westgate Gardens is very inviting. Return to St. Peter's and turn right. Opposite the Weavers' is the **Eastbridge Hospital** (12), a well-preserved 12th-century hostel for poor pilgrims. Its crypt, chapel, and hall are open to visitors daily, from 10 a.m. (11 on Sundays) to 1 p.m. and 2–5 p.m.

Turn right on Stour Street and then right again into a tiny lane marked "to Greyfriars." Follow the path onto a small island. The extremely picturesque 13th-century **Greyfriars** (13) is all that remains of the first Franciscan friary in England. From inside you can get a feeling of what monastic life in medieval Canterbury was like.

Just beyond this, also on Stour Street, is the **Poor Priests' Hospital** (14). This 14th-century hostel now houses the **Canterbury Heritage Museum**, where the latest techniques are used to re-create the city's

The Weavers' House

past, from Roman times to the near present. It is open on Mondays through Saturdays, from 10:30 a.m. to 4 p.m., and on summer Sundays from 1:30–4 p.m.

Turn left on Beer Cart and left again on St. Margaret's Street to Canterbury's latest attraction, the ***Pilgrims' Way** (15), a magnificent exhibition based on Chaucer's *Canterbury Tales*. Live actors are used along with moving sets and the latest audio-visual techniques to bring this classic story to life. Located in a former church, it is open daily, from 9:30 a.m. to 5 p.m.

You can head back to the station via Castle Street. At its end, opposite the city wall, are the ruins of an 11th-century **Norman Castle** (16). Never very effective as a defensive bastion, it was later used as a jail, a coal dump, and a water tank.

Dover

The White Cliffs of Dover have marked the gateway to England for over two thousand years. Iron Age men settled on these shores, and so did the Romans, who built their port of *Dubris* in A.D. 43. Strategically, Dover is of paramount importance to Britain, being the closest point to the Continent and only 22 miles from France. It was inevitable that a great fortress would rise here, one that has defended the island nation down to our own times. Today, this massive 12th-century castle is a major tourist attraction, while the harbor it overlooks is the busiest passenger port in England.

GETTING THERE:

Trains to Dover's Priory Station leave at least hourly from either Victoria or Charing Cross stations in London. The journey time is about 90 minutes. Be sure to board the correct car as some trains split en route. Return service operates until mid-evening.

By car, Dover is 74 miles southeast of London by way of either the A-2 and M-2 highways, or the A-20 and M-20 highways.

LINKS:

For those following a continuous itinerary, Dover offers good direct rail service to **Canterbury** and **Rochester**; and also to Folkestone Central for the **Romney, Hythe & Dymchurch** trip or Sevenoaks for the **Knole** trip. A change at Ashford takes you directly to **Rye**, while changing at both Tonbridge and Redhill lets you ride to **Brighton** without returning to London. All of these destinations are described elsewhere in this section of the book, and all can be easily reached by car as well.

PRACTICALITIES:

Good weather is essential for this largely outdoor trip, especially for the maritime views for which you might want to bring along binoculars. The castle is open every day except on Christmas and New Year's, but the Roman Painted House is closed in winter and on Mondays in April, September, and October. The local **Tourist Information Centre**, phone (0304) 205-108, is on Townwall Street, just inland from Marine Parade. Dover is in the county of **Kent**, and has a **population** of about 34,000.

Medieval Games by the Castle Keep

FOOD AND DRINK:

There is a fairly good selection of restaurants and pubs in all price ranges, including:

Dover Moat House (Townwall St., near the tourist office) A modern restaurant in a large hotel. $$

White Cliffs (Marine Parade, on the seafront below the castle) In a pleasant old hotel with a good view of the port. $$

Britannia (Townwall St., near the tourist office) Both a downstairs pub and an upstairs restaurant. $ and $$

Dino's (58 Castle St., near the Market Square) Good Italian cooking at modest prices. X: Mon. $

SUGGESTED TOUR:

Leave **Priory Station** (1) and walk down St. Martin's Hill to the busy traffic circle. A crosswalk to the right of this brings you to Pencester Road, which leads to the **Bus Station** (2). Here you can get a ride up to the castle, perched dramatically atop a nearby hill. It is also possible to get there by taxi or car, or even on foot if you don't mind the stiff climb.

*Dover Castle is by far the finest and most fascinating military structure in England. While essentially of Norman construction, parts of it date from Saxon and even Roman times. Brutally strong, its 20-foot-thick walls have withstood sieges during its entire history. Begin your visit with the mighty Keep (3), surrounded by a defensive curtain wall. Built in 1180 by Henry II to replace earlier structures, the keep has been continually modified down through the centuries. You can easily spend hours exploring the many rooms and passageways, and examining the Battle of Waterloo Model along with an exhibition of military history called All the Queen's Men. Be sure to get up to the roof, from which there is a fabulous *view extending all the way to France in clear weather. A visit to the Underground Works beneath the castle is well worth the effort, although it involves some steep climbs. The entry to this tunnel system is just outside the keep, and an audio guided tour is available.

Stroll over to the Pharos (4), a Roman lighthouse erected in the 2nd century A.D. to guide the Imperial Navy into port. This is the tallest surviving Roman structure in Britain. Directly adjacent to it is the Saxon Church of St. Mary de Castro, which was heavily restored during the 19th century. Although its exact age is unknown, parts of it may date from as far back at the 7th century. Still used as a garrison church, it is open to visitors and a guide leaflet is available. From here you might want to amble around the outer ramparts before leaving the precincts. Dover Castle is open every day except Christmas and New Year's, from 10 a.m. to 6 p.m.; closing at 4 p.m. from October through March. The last entry is 45 minutes before closing time.

Return to the town by bus or, since it is downhill, on foot. Just follow the path opposite the bus stop, which leads through Victoria Park. Laureston Place and Castle Hill Road will bring you to Castle Street, at the end of which is the Market.Square, built over the site of the ancient Roman harbor. From there take King and Bench streets to Marine Parade. Along the way you will pass Townwall Street, where the tourist office is located.

There are splendid views of the harbor from Marine Parade (5), but for an even better look you should walk out on the Prince of Wales Pier (6), which offers wonderful panoramas of the famous White Cliffs of Dover. From here you can also watch the comings and goings of the speedy hovercrafts, those strange seagoing contraptions that look like boats topped with windmills.

Return to Market Square and visit the nearby Roman Painted House (7) on New Street. Britain's answer to Pompeii, this excavated 2nd-century town house has lovely painted walls and an intact underfloor heating system. Well preserved and beautifully presented, it is open daily from May through August, from 10 a.m. to 6 p.m.; and on Tues-

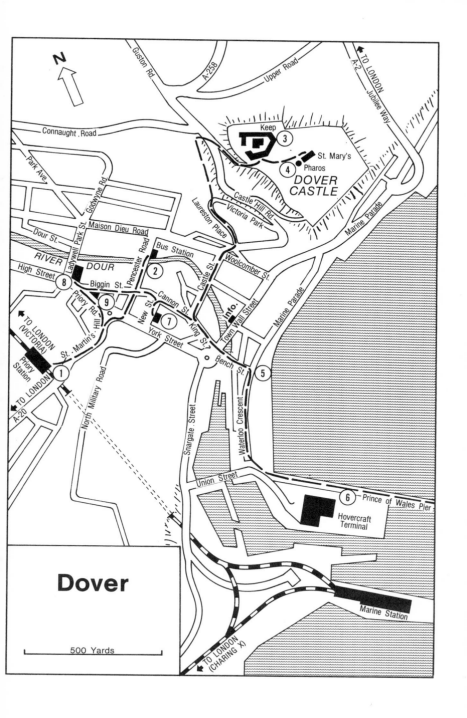

N

Guston Rd.

A-258

Upper Road

TO LONDON
A-2

Jubilee Way

Connaught Road

Keep ③

St. Mary's
Pharos ④

DOVER
CASTLE

Park Ave.

Godwyne Rd.

Maison Dieu Road

Laureston Place

Castle Hill Rd.

Victoria Park

Marine Parade

Dour St.

Ladywell Park St.

Pencester Road

Bus Station

River DOUR

High Street

②

Biggin St.

⑧

Castle St.

Woolcomber St.

Priory Rd.

⑨

Cannon St.

info.

Town Wall Street

Marine Parade

TO LONDON
(VICTORIA)

New St.

⑦

King St.

St. Martin's Hill

York Street

Bench St.

⑤

Priory
Station

①

TO LONDON
A-20

North Military Road

Snargate Street

Waterloo Crescent

Union Street

⑥ Prince of Wales Pier

Hovercraft
Terminal

Dover

TO LONDON
(CHARING X)

Marine Station

500 Yards

View from the Castle Keep

days through Sundays during April, September, and October, from 10 a.m. to 5 p.m.

Now follow Cannon Street and Biggin Street to the **Maison Dieu** (8), a 13th-century Pilgrims' hostel that is now part of the Town Hall. It contains some interesting weapons, armor, and stained-glass windows depicting the town's history. Attached to it is the **Dover Museum**, displaying ancient coins, archaeological finds, and bits of Victoriana. Visits may be made on Mondays through Saturdays, except Wednesdays, from 10 a.m. to 4:45 p.m.

St. Edmund's Chapel (9) on Priory Road is on the way back to the train station. Dating from the 13th century, it ceased religious services in 1544 and was later used as a forge. In 1968 the tiny wayside chapel was re-consecrated and is thought to be the smallest in England in regular use.

Knole

Knole ranks as one of the largest and most famous of England's stately homes. It is also among the oldest. The building as it stands today was largely begun by Thomas Bouchier, Archbishop of Canterbury, in the mid-15th century. It remained a palace for the archbishops until being appropriated by Henry VIII for the Crown. In 1566 Queen Elizabeth I presented the estate to her cousin, Thomas Sackville, whose descendants have lived there ever since. One of these was the famous writer Victoria Sackville-West, whose close friend Virginia Woolf immortalized Knole in her 1928 novel, *Orlando.*

Sometimes called the "Calendar House," Knole is said to have 365 rooms, 52 staircases, and seven courtyards. Those parts that are open to the public contain a large number of paintings by various artists, including some good ones by Gainsborough and Reynolds, magnificent tapestries, and furnishings dating from Elizabethan times. The surrounding park covers a thousand acres of pleasant countryside where tame deer roam freely.

As a bonus to this trip, a short side excursion can be made to nearby Ightham Mote, a very different and thoroughly enchanting early-14th-century moated manor house. Alternatively, you can visit Chartwell, the home of Sir Winston Churchill for over 40 years. If you plan to take either of these options, please note the opening times carefully. Minibus tours to two or three of the·attractions are operated out of Sevenoaks between late spring and early fall. For details and reservations contact the Sevenoaks tourist office.

GETTING THERE:

Trains leave London's Charing Cross Station frequently for Sevenoaks, the town in which Knole is located. The journey takes about 32 minutes, with returns until late evening. There is also good service from King's Cross ThamesLink and other stations in northern London.

By car, Sevenoaks is about 25 miles southeast of London via the A-20 and A-225 roads.

LINKS:

For those following an itinerary rather than making daytrips, Sevenoaks has good direct rail service to **Canterbury** (West) and **Dover**; and to Folkestone Central for the **Romney, Hythe & Dymchurch** trip. A simple connection can be made at Ashford for **Rye**, or at Hastings for **Brighton** via Lewes. These destinations are described elsewhere in this book, and can be reached easily by car as well.

PRACTICALITIES:

Knole is open from April through October; on Wednesdays through Saturdays plus bank holiday Mondays, from 11 a.m. to 5 p.m.; and on Sundays from 2–5 p.m.

Ightham Mote is open from April through October; on Mondays, Wednesdays, Thursdays, and Fridays from noon to 5:30 p.m., and on Sundays from 11 a.m. to 5:30 p.m.

Chartwell is open from Easter through October; on Tuesdays through Thursdays from noon to 5 p.m., and on weekends and holidays from 11 a.m. to 5 p.m. During March and November it is open on weekends and Wednesdays from 11 a.m. to 4 p.m.

The above times should be confirmed with the **Sevenoaks Tourist Information Centre**, phone (0732) 450-305. They are located on Buckhurst Lane, just off High Street, between the train station and Knole Park. Sevenoaks is in the county of **Kent**, and has a **population** of about 25,000.

FOOD AND DRINK:

No food is available at either Knole or Ightham Mote, but you could bring along a picnic lunch. There is a restaurant at Chartwell, and also a few restaurants and pubs in Sevenoaks, including:

Royal Oak (Upper High St., just beyond the turn into Knole Park) Intimate dining, with French cuisine. X: Sat. lunch, Sun. eve. $$

SUGGESTED TOUR:

Leaving the **Sevenoaks Train Station** (1), you can either walk or take a taxi the one-mile distance to ***Knole**. If you walk, just turn right and continue straight ahead until you come to a sign pointing to Knole Park on the left. Go through the park to the **manor house** (2) and take the guided tour. A leisurely stroll in the surrounding deer park and gardens is absolutely delightful.

Those wanting to visit **Ightham Mote** (3) can get there by walking the four-mile distance, which is completely over pleasant country lanes, or by returning to Sevenoaks and taking a bus or taxi. If you go by bus, take one that follows route A-25 and get off at Ightham Common,

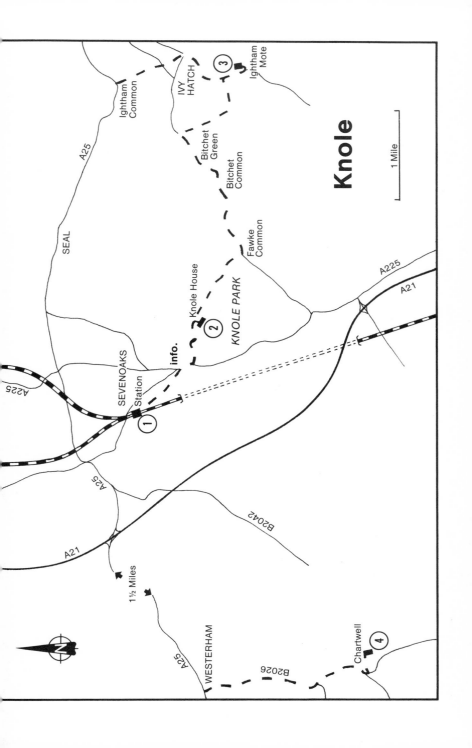

Knole

1 Mile

N

A25

SEAL

Ightham Common

IVY HATCH

Bitchet Green

Bitchet Common

Fawke Common

③ Ightham Mote

Knole House

② KNOLE PARK

A225

info.

SEVENOAKS Station

①

A225

A25

A21

A25

1½ Miles

WESTERHAM

B2042

B2026

Chartwell ④

A21

A225

Knole House

then walk the remaining mile-and-a-half. The map shows the way on foot or by bus.

If you would rather see **Chartwell** (4), take bus number 483 from Sevenoaks to Westerham, then walk one-and-a-half miles to the estate by following the map. You could, of course, take a taxi all the way. The house contains many personal mementos of the great prime minister in rooms that remain as he left them. There is also a good selection of Churchill's paintings in his garden studio, and you can examine the famous brick walls that he laid with his own hands.

Romney, Hythe & Dymchurch

A ride on the Romney, Hythe & Dymchurch Railway is a pure delight. There are no famous sights along its 14-mile length, just the exhilarating joy of being hauled across the Romney Marshes aboard a miniature steam train. This fun-filled daytrip is the perfect antidote to a steady diet of cathedrals, castles, and stately homes.

Opened in 1927, the railway is one of the most popular attractions in southern England. Its one-third-scale locomotives are faithful replicas of famous engines that once served on the main lines. Over 300,000 passengers, not all of them children by any means, are carried each year in the diminutive coaches. Join them in the fun and you'll be glad you did.

GETTING THERE:

Trains leave twice an hour from London's Charing Cross Station for Folkestone Central Station. The journey time is about 80 minutes, and service is reduced on Sundays. Some trains split en route. Return trains run until mid-evening. From Folkestone you can travel the five miles by bus or taxi to Hythe, where the steam line begins.

By car, take the A-20 and M-20 roads to Newingreen/Stanford, then the A-261 to Hythe. The total distance is about 68 miles southeast of London.

LINKS:

If you're following an itinerary, Folkestone Central Station offers direct rail service to **Dover**, and to Sevenoaks for the **Knole** trip. You can change at Dover for **Canterbury**, at Ashford for **Rye**, or at Tonbridge for **Brighton, Arundel**, or **Chichester** via Redhill. All of these destinations are featured elsewhere in this book, and can be just as easily reached by car.

PRACTICALITIES:

Good weather is necessary to really enjoy this trip. The Romney, Hythe & Dymchurch Railway operates daily from Easter to the end of September, and on weekends in March and October. Service is more frequent during the peak summer months. For more information about the steam railway call their offices in New Romney at (0679) 62-353. The local **Tourist Information Centre** in Folkestone, phone (0303) 58-594, is near the harbor, with a branch on Sandgate Road, phone (0303) 53-840. This entire trip is in the county of **Kent**.

Steaming Along on the R, H & D
(Photo courtesy of R, H & D Railway)

FOOD AND DRINK:

Snacks are available at the Hythe and New Romney stations, and drinks are served on the miniature bar car attached to some of the trains. A few nearby restaurants and pubs are:

Butt of Sherry (5 Theatre St., Hythe) A wine bar with traditional English fare. X: Sun., Mon. eve. $

Country Kitchen (18 High St., New Romney) Light lunches not far from the station. X: Sun. $

The Pilot (on the beach at Dungeness) An unusual pub noted for fish and chips. $

La Tavernetta (Leaside Court, Clifton Gardens, near Castle Hill Ave. and The Leas in Folkestone) Italian cuisine. X: Sun. $$

Emilio's Portofino (124a Sandgate Rd., 3 blocks southwest of the bus station in Folkestone) Another Italian restaurant. X: Mon. $$

SUGGESTED TOUR:

Those coming by train will begin their trip at **Folkestone Central Station** (1). From here follow the map to the **Folkestone Bus Station** (2), a few blocks away. Board a bus for Hythe and ask to be let off at the Light Railway Station. You could, of course, take a taxi directly from Folkestone Central to Hythe, a distance of about five miles.

The Romney, Hythe & Dymchurch Light Railway Station in **Hythe**

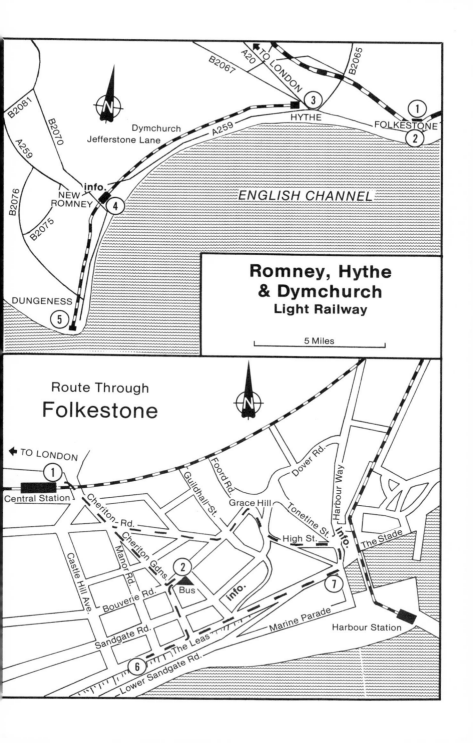

A Locomotive being Serviced at New Romney
(Photo courtesy of R, H & D Railway)

(3) is next to the Royal Military Canal, which was built as a defense during the Napoleonic Wars. A short walk along its banks is a pleasant way to while away some time if you have a wait before the next train departure. Take a careful look at the posted schedule and decide whether you want to go just to New Romney, or make a stop there and then continue on all the way to Dungeness. Note that a very few of the miniature trains are hauled by diesel traction, in which case you might want to wait for steam.

The ride from Hythe to New Romney takes about 35 minutes, stopping at Dymchurch and Jefferstone Lane along the way. **New Romney** (4) is the headquarters of the railway and has several interesting things to see, including yards, engine shops, and a fascinating exhibition of model trains. There is also a snack bar with hot meals, and a gift shop.

Continuing on to **Dungeness** (5), the rails follow very close to the sea. This is a lovely and sparsely inhabited region, a perfect spot for the nuclear power plant at the end of the line. Getting off there, you may visit the lifeboat station and perhaps climb to the top of the old lighthouse.

Those traveling back to London via Folkestone will probably want to see a bit of that town before they leave. From the bus station it is an easy walk to **The Leas** (6), a promenade with magnificent maritime views. The **harbor** (7) is in the oldest part of town. Return via the quaint and narrow High Street, then head back to Central Station by bus, taxi, or on foot.

*Rye

A relic from the Middle Ages, the once-great seaport of Rye has been stranded ever since its harbor silted up in the 16th century. Today, only small craft can sail the two miles up the River Rother to the town's docks. In a way this is fortunate, as it left England with a well-preserved medieval port that still clings to its salty past. Rye is alive with the smell of the sea, and working fishermen still walk its ancient streets, side by side with their many visitors. It easily ranks among the prettiest towns in Britain, and is one of the most enjoyable for tourists.

GETTING THERE:

Trains depart London's Charing Cross or Victoria stations frequently for Ashford, where you change to a local for Rye. The total journey takes less than two hours. Return trains run until mid-evening. Service is reduced on Sundays and holidays.

By car, the shortest route is to take the A-21 from London to Flimwell and change to the A-268. Rye is 63 miles southeast of London.

LINKS:

Those following an itinerary instead of making daytrips can change trains at Ashford for another train to Folkestone Central for the **Romney, Hythe & Dymchurch** trip, to Sevenoaks for the **Knole** trip, or to **Dover.** By changing at Hastings instead, you can reach **Brighton** via Lewes. These destinations are described elsewhere in this book, and can also be easily reached by car.

PRACTICALITIES:

Rye may be savored on a fine day in any season. The local **Tourist Information Centre,** phone (0797) 222-293, is at 48 Cinque Ports Street. Rye is in the county of **East Sussex,** and has a **population** of 4,000.

FOOD AND DRINK:

Rye has plenty of quaint old inns, tea shops, and pubs. Some choices are:

> **Flushing Inn** (Market St., near the Town Hall) A 15th-century inn noted for its seafood. X: Mon. eve., Tues., Jan. $$ and $$$

> **Mermaid Inn** (Mermaid St.) An old smugglers' haunt from the 15th century. $$

Fletcher's House (Lion St., just north of St. Mary's Church) Light meals in an historic medieval house. $$

Elizabethan Restaurant (Cinque Ports St., near the tourist office) A Tudor setting for lunch and teas. X: Sun. $

Standard Inn (The Mint, near Needles Passage) A delightful pub with meals. $

SUGGESTED TOUR:

Leaving the **train station** (1), walk straight ahead and turn left on Cinque Ports Street. In a few yards you will pass the tourist office and, on the right, remnants of the original 14th-century towns walls, just behind a parking lot. The **Land Gate** (2) is the only remaining town gate of the three that once protected Rye. It was probably constructed about 1340 and originally contained machinery for a drawbridge over the town ditch.

Walk uphill along Hilder's Cliff, with its marvelous views across the Romney Marsh. Much of this lowland was once an open ocean, but that was before the sea receded as the River Rother silted up and the tides washed countless pebbles onto the shore.

Make a right down Conduit hill to the **Augustine Friary** (3), commonly known as The Monastery. Originally built in 1379, it was used in the 16th century as a refuge for persecuted French Huguenots. Today it houses a pottery that you can visit. Now return to High Street and follow it to the Old Grammar School, erected in 1636 and immortalized by Thackeray. Opposite this is the 400-year-old George Hotel.

A left onto Lion Street leads past Fletcher's House, once a vicarage and now a tea shop. The dramatist John Fletcher was born here in 1579. At the corner of Market Street stands the **Town Hall** (4), which contains some interesting artifacts, including the gruesome gibbet cage with the remains of a notorious 18th-century murderer who was executed in the town. Ask to be shown these.

In a few more steps you will come to ***St. Mary's Church** (5), first erected between 1150 and 1300. Facing the top of Lion Street is the ***church clock**, the oldest in England still functioning with its original works. Two figures above the clockface strike the quarter hours but not the hours. Between them is a plaque that proclaims, "For our time is a very shadow that passeth away." A climb to the top of the ***tower** is well worth the effort. The extremely narrow stairway leads to the bell-ringing room where various combinations of changes are posted. In the same room is the venerable clock mechanism, from which hangs an 18-foot-long pendulum. A ladder goes to the bell room itself, and another to the roof. From here there is an unsurpassed view of the entire area. A visit to the church interior is also worthwhile.

Across from the churchyard there is a curious oval-shaped brick

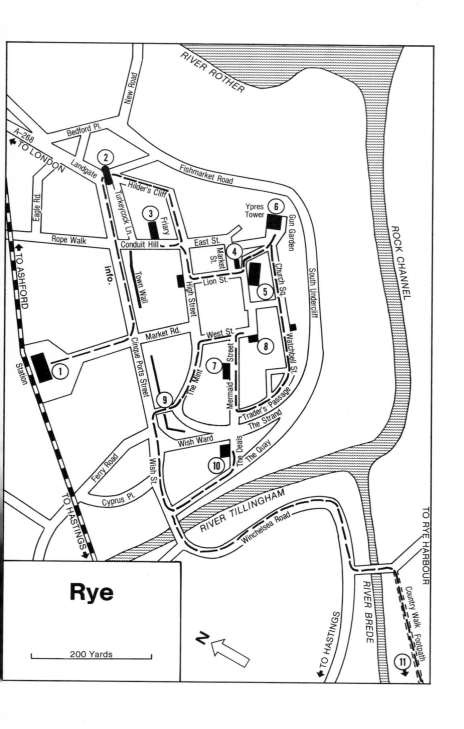

RIVER ROTHER

New Road

A-268
TO LONDON

Bedford Pl.

Landgate

②

Hilder's Cliff

Fishmarket Road

Turkeycock Ln.

③ Friary

Ypres
Tower

⑥

Gun Garden

ROCK CHANNEL

Eagle Rd

Rope Walk

Conduit Hill

East St.

④

Church Sq.

South Undercliff

Info.

Town Wall

High Street

Market
St.

Lion St.

⑤

TO ASHFORD

Market Rd.

West St.

Watchbell St.

⑧

Cinque Ports Street

The Mint

⑦

Mermaid
Street

Trader's Passage

The Strand

Station

①

⑨

Wish Ward

Ferry Road

The Deals

The Quay

Wish St.

⑩

TO HASTINGS

Cyprus Pl.

RIVER TILLINGHAM

Winchelsea Road

TO RYE HARBOUR

TO HASTINGS

RIVER BREDE

Country Walk Footpath

⑪

Rye

N

200 Yards

Along Church Square

water reservoir, built in 1735 but no longer used. Bear right and stroll down to **Ypres Tower** (6). Pronounced *Wipers*, this is the oldest existing structure in town. Largely unchanged since it was first constructed as a defensive fortification around 1249, it ceased to have any military value in later years and was sold to one John de Ypres as a private habitation. The town bought it back in 1513 for use as a jail, a function it served until 1865, when it became a mortuary. The tower is now the **Rye Museum**, housing artifacts of the town's history. A visit to its various rooms and cells is very interesting and may be made between Easter and mid-October, daily from 10:30 a.m. to 1 p.m. and 2:15–5:30 p.m. Just below this is the **Gun Garden**, an emplacement for artillery pieces that once helped defend England's shores.

Walk down Church Square, an exceptionally lovely cobbled street. This becomes Watchbell Street, whose name derives from the warning bell once housed there. Along the way you will pass a Spanish-style Catholic church. At the end is the **lookout**, overseeing the harbor.

Traders Passage leads to ***Mermaid Street**, quite possibly the most picturesque thoroughfare in all England. Go uphill to the **Mermaid Inn** (7), a famous hiding place for smugglers and highwaymen, first built in the late 15th century and much altered over the years. It is now a hotel and restaurant, the perfect spot for a refreshment break. Walk through a passage into the courtyard for a look.

Mermaid Street

Continue up Mermaid Street and turn right on West Street. Here, where the street bends, you will find the **Lamb House** (8), formerly the residence of the Lamb family, which for a long time provided many of the mayors of Rye. Henry James lived in this house from 1897 until 1916, writing many of his best-known novels there. It is now owned by the National Trust and receives visitors on Wednesdays and Saturdays, April through October, from 2–5:30 p.m.

Stroll back down West Street to High Street and turn left to The Mint, then make a right into **Needles Passage** (9). This narrow path takes you through a gap in the old town wall and down a few steps to Cinque Ports Street. Turn left and follow Wish Street.

Another left, just before the bridge, leads onto The Strand, where you will find an interesting group of 19th-century **warehouses** (10) that bear testament to the town's past as a trading port. The **Rye Town Model**, a highly entertaining sound-and-light show, is held in one of these every half-hour, daily from 10:30 a.m. to 5 p.m.

Before leaving Rye, you might want to take a delightful walk in the countryside. From the bridge at the foot of Wish Street it is only 1½ miles to **Camber Castle** (11), built by Henry VIII in the 16th century. To get there just follow the map to the public footpath along the River Brede. This trail leads through some pleasant sheep-grazing land and is well marked.

Brighton

Londoners have been tripping down to Brighton in search of amusement since the mid-18th century, when a local doctor first promoted his famous sea cure. What made the town fashionable, though, was the frequent presence of naughty George IV, then the pleasure-loving, womanizing Prince of Wales, who began construction on his Royal Pavilion in 1787. Brighton remained an aristocratic resort until the coming of the railway turned it into the immensely popular "London-by-the-Sea" that it is today.

The town itself is actually very old, dating from at least Roman times. It was mentioned in the famous *Domesday Book* of 1086 as *Brighthelmstone,* then a tiny fishing village. Traces of what Brighton looked like before becoming a resort can still be found in the area of The Lanes, a colorful district between the Pavilion and the sea.

Brighton has no equal as an easy and fun-filled daytrip from London. Here you will mix with every sort of Englishman, from aristocrats to cockneys, and visit elegant places as well as popular amusements.

GETTING THERE:

Trains leave London's Victoria Station at least hourly for Brighton, a ride of about one hour. There are also direct hourly trains from London's King's Cross ThamesLink and Blackfriars stations, a 90-minute ride. Return service operates until late evening.

By car, Brighton is 54 miles south of London via the A-23, bypassing Gatwick on the M-23.

LINKS:

For those following a point-to-point itinerary, Brighton offers good direct rail service to **Chichester** and **Portsmouth.** By making a change or two, it is also relatively easy to get to **Rye**, **Arundel**, or **Guildford**. All of these are described elsewhere in this book, and can be just as easily reached by car.

The Royal Pavilion

PRACTICALITIES:

Most of the major sites are open daily, but the art museum is closed on Mondays and some major holidays. A bright, warm day will add to your enjoyment. The local **Tourist Information Centre**, phone (0273) 237-55, is in the Marlborough House at 54 Old Steine, with a branch kiosk at the foot of West Street during the summer. You might ask them about local **bicycle** rentals or buses to nearby attractions. Brighton has a **population** of about 200,000 and is in the county of **East Sussex**.

FOOD AND DRINK:

Brighton offers the widest range of restaurants this side of London. Some good choices are:

> **English's Oyster Bar** (29 East St., in The Lanes) Considered to have the best seafood in town. $$$

> **Wheeler's Restaurant** (64 King's Rd., in the Sheridan Hotel, near The Lanes) Renowned for its seafood. $$$

> **Le Grandgousier** (15 Western St., north of King's Rd., between Montpelier and Waterloo streets) French cuisine in a casual setting. X: Sat. lunch, Sun. $$

> **Stubbs** (14 Ship St., in The Lanes) A popular place in the middle of an historic district. X: Mon. lunch, Sat. lunch. $$

> **Brown's Café** (3–4 Duke St., in The Lanes) Steaks, grills, chili, and the like. $

Food for Friends (17 Prince Albert St., in The Lanes) Vegetarian food in a simple atmosphere. $

Cricketers (15 Black Lion St., in The Lanes) A friendly old pub with good food. $

SUGGESTED TOUR:

Leaving the marvelously Victorian **train station** (1), follow the map to **Old Steine** (2), an easy stroll of about ten minutes. Along the way you will pass the Royal Pavilion, a treat best saved for the end of the tour. The Old Steine (pronounced *Steen*) is the center of activity in Brighton and is probably named after a stone on which fishermen dried their nets in those quiet centuries before the town became London's playground.

Continue straight ahead to the **Palace Pier** (3), a gaudy Victorian structure dating from 1899 that juts some 1,717 feet, nearly a third of a mile, into the English Channel. On it you will find a fantastic variety of fun houses, rides, shows, shops, and people from all over Britain, with accents ranging from pure North Country to London Cockney.

The best way to explore the beach is to take a ride on **Volk's Railway** (4). This quaint, open train has been operating since 1883, the first in Britain to run on electricity. It follows right along the edge of the beach from near Palace Pier to the marina at Black Rock, a distance of about a mile. Volk's Railway operates from April through September.

Brighton Marina (5, off the map) is the largest in Europe and can accommodate over 2,000 yachts. Just west of this is the "naturist" beach, where—as the tourist office so tactfully puts it—clothes need not be worn.

Return by walking along Marine Parade with its attractive 19th-century terraces, squares, and crescents. The distance is only a bit over a mile, but you could, of course, take a bus or Volk's Railway. At the end, near the Palace Pier, is the **Aquarium** (6), which features performing dolphins and over 10,000 fish from all over the world. Opened in 1872, this is Britain's largest aquarium. Its subterranean galleries alone are worth the visit, and are open daily.

Just beyond Old Steine lies the original Brighton, now known as **The Lanes** (7). No longer inhabited by fishermen, this warren of narrow traffic-free alleyways has become a fashionable center of boutiques, antique shops, pubs, and restaurants. The Lanes are a good spot for aimless strolling, although you should not miss Brighton Square and Duke's Lane, the most attractive of the tiny byways. This is also a great place to stop for a refreshment break.

Walk out onto **King's Road** and turn right along the beach. This is the main promenade of Brighton, a stretch of seaside lined with the

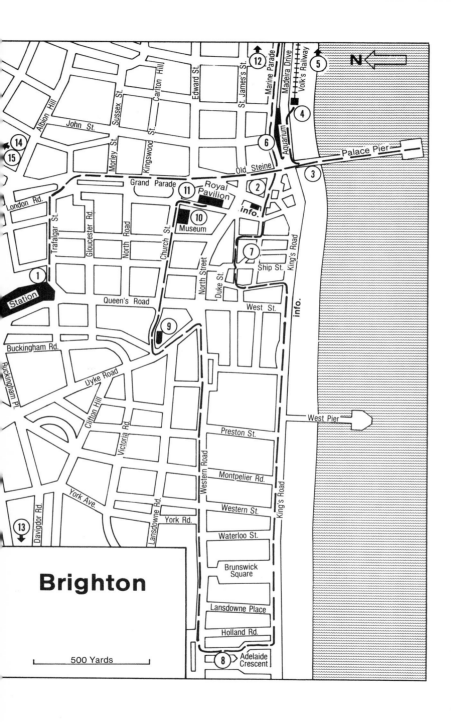

Brighton

N

Albion Hill

John St.

Sussex St.

Carlton Hill

Kingswood St.

Morley St.

Edward St.

St. James's St.

Marine Parade

Madeira Drive

Volk's Railway

(12)

(5)

(4)

(14)
(15)

(6)

Aquarium

Palace Pier

London Rd.

Grand Parade

Royal Pavilion

Old Steine

(3)

(2)

info.

(11)

Trafalgar St.

Gloucester Rd.

North Road

Church St.

(10)
Museum

(7)

(1)

Station

Queen's Road

North Street

Duke St.

Ship St.

King's Road

West St.

info.

Buckingham Rd.

Buckingham Pl.

Dyke Road

(9)

Clifton Hill

Victoria Rd.

Preston St.

West Pier

Western Road

Montpelier Rd.

York Ave.

Lansdowne Rd.

Western St.

King's Road

(13)

Davigdor Rd.

York Rd.

Waterloo St.

Brunswick
Square

Lansdowne Place

Holland Rd.

(8) Adelaide
Crescent

500 Yards

traditional entertainments. Fish-and-chips shops, ice cream stands, the famous Brighton rock candy—it's all here. As you approach the adjoining town of Hove the atmosphere changes to one of sedate elegance.

Make a right at **Adelaide Crescent** (8), a beautiful open area of green surrounded by Regency town houses from the early 19th century. From here you can either return along King's Road or take Western Road back to Brighton. Your next stop should be the **Church of St. Nicholas** (9) on Dyke Road. Originally built in 1380 and reconstructed in 1853, it has a remarkable 12th-century Norman font. The churchyard is a perfect spot to rest before passing on.

A short stroll down Church Street leads to the **Art Gallery and Museum** (10), a very worthwhile stop. Its collection of Art Nouveau and Art Deco pieces is probably the best in Britain. In addition, there are several Old Masters, superb porcelains, silver, furniture, and a fascinating display of local history—along with a gallery of fashion history. The museum is open on Tuesdays through Saturdays, from 10 a.m. to 5:45 p.m.; and on Sundays from 2–5 p.m.; but not on Mondays or some major holidays.

Brighton's stellar attraction, the ***Royal Pavilion** (11), is just around the corner. King George IV, known as "Prinny," began this hedonistic pleasure palace when he was still Prince of Wales, and over the years from 1787 to 1822 it evolved from a classical structure into the bizarre pseudo-Oriental fantasy that it is today. The final design, from 1815 on, was the work of John Nash, the greatest architect of the Regency period. Before entering the pavilion you should stroll around it as the best views face Pavilion Parade.

The **interior** of the palace, every bit as extravagant as the outside, may be visited on any day except Christmas and Boxing Day, from 10 a.m. to 6 p.m. (until 5 p.m. from October through May). The king used the pavilion until 1827, and it was also used by his brother, King William IV and, in turn, by Queen Victoria. Its end as a royal residence came in 1850 when Victoria, not amused by the theatricality of it all, sold the pavilion to the town for a fraction of its value. Another century passed before the palace was fully restored to its former splendor as a result of a permanent loan, made by Queen Elizabeth II, of original furnishings.

NEARBY SIGHTS:

Brighton has several other interesting attractions that may be reached by local bus, car, or rented bike. Ask for directions at the tourist office on Old Steine. The best of these are:

Rottingdean Village (12), a picturesque spot four miles east of Brighton on a cliff overlooking the sea. Rudyard Kipling lived here and

On the Palace Pier

mementos of his life can be seen at **The Grange**, a former vicarage that is now a museum.

British Engineerium (13), located in a former pumping station on the edge of Hove Park on Nevill Road, has a magnificent collection of stationary steam engines and mechanical inventions from the Victorian era.

Preston Manor (14), two miles from Old Steine on London Road, is an 18th-century Georgian mansion in a lovely setting. The manor is open on Tuesdays through Sundays, from 10 a.m. to 5 p.m., except on some major holidays.

Stanmer Village (15) preserves a turn-of-the-century atmosphere of rural England and is located four miles from central Brighton along Lewes Road.

Arundel

Like a vision from a fairy tale, the picture-book town of Arundel nestles snugly at the base of its massive castle. Both date from the time of the Norman Conquest, and possibly even earlier. Arundel was mentioned in the *Domesday Book* of 1086 as a port of some consequence, which it remained throughout the Middle Ages. There is still a good deal of boating activity on its river, the Arun, which flows into the sea at nearby Littlehampton. Delightful country walks can be made along its banks and to the Wildfowl Reserve, or through peaceful Arundel Park. Those preferring more sedentary activities will find excellent antique and crafts shops, charming pubs, and a pair of small museums. The main attraction remains, of course, the castle—one of the finest in all England.

GETTING THERE:
   Trains to Arundel leave hourly from London's Victoria Station. The journey takes about 80 minutes, with return service until mid-evening.
   By car, Arundel is 56 miles south of London via the A-24 and A-29 roads.

LINKS:
   If you're following an itinerary instead of taking daytrips, Arundel has direct rail service to **Chichester** and **Portsmouth**; as well as fairly easy connections to **Brighton**, **Guildford**, and **Southampton**. These destinations are featured elsewhere in this book, and can just as easily be reached by car.

PRACTICALITIES:
   Avoid coming on a Saturday or between late October and the end of March, when the castle is closed. The local **Tourist Information Centre**, phone (0903) 882-268, is at 61 High Street, below the castle. Arundel is in the county of **West Sussex**, and has a **population** of about 2,500.

Arundel Castle

FOOD AND DRINK:

Among the many restaurants, pubs, and tea rooms are:

Norfolk Arms (22 High St., near the tourist office) Traditional English dishes in an old coaching inn. $$

Belinda's (13 Tarrant St., just southwest of High St.) A 16th-century coffee house with old-fashioned home-cooked lunches. X: Mon., Jan. $

Swan (29 High St., near the bridge) A popular old pub with homemade daily specials. $

General Abercrombie (Queen St., near the river) A 16th-century pub with atmosphere and good food. $

SUGGESTED TOUR:

Leaving the **train station** (1), turn left and follow The Causeway and Queen Street to the River Arun. Because the castle is not open in the mornings, you might want to begin with a short **country walk** of a bit over one mile.

To do this, cross the bridge and turn right on Mill Road, passing a parking lot. Continue on until you come to a recreation ground on the right. Just beyond this turn right on a well-defined track that leads to the river, then turn right and follow the embankment with its gorgeous views of town and castle. Back near the bridge are the ruins of the **Maison Dieu** (2), an almshouse for poor men founded in 1395. It was disbanded in 1532 during the Reformation and destroyed in the Civil War of the 17th century.

*Arundel Castle (3) is everything a great fortress should be. Built in the late 11th century, it was besieged by Henry I in 1102 and again by King Stephen in 1139. After severe damage caused by Parliamentary forces during the Civil War in 1643, it fell into a dilapidated state until restoration began in the 18th century. What you see today is mostly a romantic Victorian vision, a stately home with all the trappings of a medieval stronghold. Throughout most of its history, the castle has been the seat of the dukes of Norfolk and their ancestors, the Fitzalans. This family, among the highest nobility in England, has always remained Roman Catholic despite centuries of persecution, a fact that explains much of what you will see in Arundel.

Enter the castle grounds and walk around to the **Barbican Tower** of 1295. Once inside, turn hard right and follow the marked route to the 11th-century keep, which was occupied only during a siege. A banner is flown from its top when the duke is in residence. Return and enter the living quarters by way of the chapel. The immense **Barons' Hall** features some interesting paintings, including a double portrait by Van Dyck. The route leads past the dining room and the drawing room, which has an appealing lived-in quality and several fine portraits by Gainsborough, Reynolds, and Van Dyck. The elaborate bed in the **Victoria Room** was made for the queen's visit in 1846. From here you go through the handsome library and several smaller rooms to an exit near the keep. Arundel Castle is open from April 1st until the last Friday in October, on Sundays through Fridays, from 1–5 p.m. During June, July, and August it opens at 12 noon. The last admission is always at 4 p.m., and it is always closed on Saturdays.

Before leaving the castle grounds, take a walk over to the 14th-century **Fitzalan Chapel** (4). Many of the earls of Arundel and dukes of Norfolk are buried here. A wrought-iron grill and glass wall separates this Catholic chapel from the Anglican parish church, another part of the same building.

Exit through the gate and stroll up London Road. On your right is the Protestant part of the church, which makes an interesting contrast and should be visited.

Just beyond this is the Roman Catholic **Cathedral** (5), built in a grandiose Gothic style in 1869 as a parish church. It became a cathedral only in 1965, when a new bishopric was created for the region.

Follow the map to the **Arundel Museum and Heritage Centre** (6), in the same building as the tourist office. Its interesting displays of bygone times may be seen daily from June through August, from 10:30 a.m. to 12:30 p.m. and 2–5 p.m.; and on weekends during March, April, May, and September at the same times.

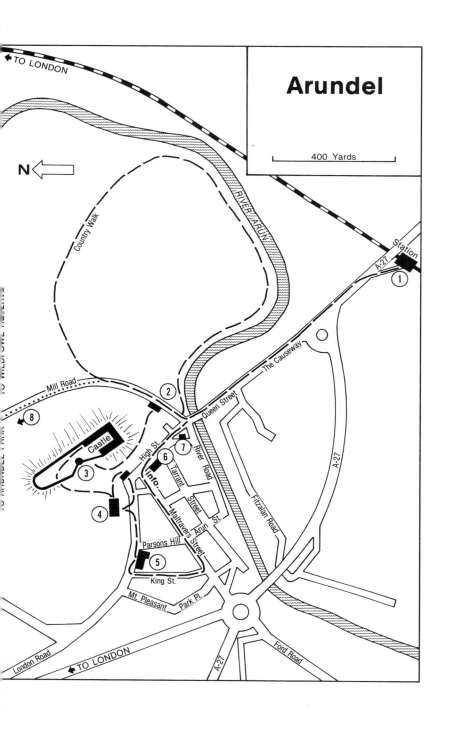

Arundel

400 Yards

TO LONDON

N

RIVER ARUN

Station

A-27

①

The Causeway

Country Walk

Mill Road

②

Queen Street

⑧

Castle

High St.

⑦

River Road

③

Info.

⑥

Tarrant Street

Fitzalan Road

A-27

④

Arun St.

Maltravers Street

Parsons Hill

⑤

King St.

Mt. Pleasant

Park Pl.

London Road

TO LONDON

A-27

Ford Road

Entrance to the Castle

The **Toy and Military Museum** (7), just down the street, features antique toys, tin soldiers, stuffed animals, and the like. It is usually open daily from Easter through October, and on weekends the rest of the year.

Two other places in Arundel may interest you, both just off the map but within easy walking distance along **Mill Road** (8). They are **Arundel Park**, a gorgeous 1,100-acre spread of natural beauty beginning at Swanbourne Lake, and the **Wildfowl Reserve** where you can observe a great variety of waterfowl from hidden vantage points. It is open daily from 9:30 a.m. to 6:30 p.m., or until dusk if that is earlier.

Chichester and Bosham

The coastal region of West Sussex is unusually rich in history as well as natural beauty. Its location on the English Channel has long made it the doorstep to the Continent, a place where battles were fought and trade flourished. Three aspects of its character are explored in this delightful daytrip—the medieval town of Chichester, the Roman Ruins at Fishbourne, and the Saxon hamlet of Bosham.

For hundreds of years the Celts had occupied this territory. One of their tribes had a king named Cogidubnus, who ruled the area near what is now Chichester. When the Romans invaded Britain in A.D. 43, Cogidubnus—no fool—submitted without a fight, became a Roman citizen, and retained his local power. The palace at Fishbourne was probably built for him as a reward. The invaders also built him a proper Roman capital, *Noviomagus,* later to become Chichester. Cogidubnus played a pivotal role in English history, for it was his defection that allowed the legions of Claudius to conquer Britain so swiftly and easily.

With the departure of the Romans about A.D. 410, the region was overrun by barbaric Saxons. Their conversion to Christianity first occurred at Bosham in the 7th century. Bosham also figured in the Norman Conquest of 1066, its church being pictured on the famous Bayeux Tapestry.

William the Conqueror brought peace and unity to Britain, and Sussex prospered as a trading center. By medieval times, Chichester had become an important town. Many of its fine structures still survive, side by side with those of later eras. Bosham, now a yachting center, preserves the feeling of bygone days in a sublimely beautiful setting, the perfect place to end this day's outing.

GETTING THERE:

Trains leave London's Victoria Station hourly for Chichester, arriving there about 90 minutes later. Be careful to board the correct car, as some trains split en route. Return service operates until mid-evening.

By car, Chichester is 63 miles southwest of London. Take the A-3 to Guildford and then switch to the A-286.

LINKS:

For those traveling an itinerary route rather than making daytrips, Chichester offers direct rail service to **Arundel** and **Portsmouth**. Easy connections can be made to **Brighton, Guildford,** and **Southampton**; and less easily to **Winchester** and **Salisbury**. These destinations are described elsewhere in this book, and can be reached just as readily by car.

PRACTICALITIES:

Good weather is essential for this largely outdoor trip. Most of the attractions are open daily, except that a few museums close on Sundays and Mondays, and during winter the Roman Palace at Fishbourne is open only on Sundays. The local **Tourist Information Centre**, phone (0243) 775-888, is in St. Peter's Market on West Street, near the cathedral. Chichester is in the county of **West Sussex**, and has a **population** of about 26,000.

FOOD AND DRINK:

Being a festival town, Chichester has an unusually good selection of restaurants and pubs in every price category, including:

> **Hole in the Wall** (1 St. Martin's St., near St. Mary's Hospital) A casual place with a loyal clientele. $$
>
> **The Noble Rot** (41 Little London, near the District Museum) A wine bistro and restaurant in the old wine vaults. $ and $$
>
> **Clinch's Salad House** (14 Southgate, near the station) Healthy food, mostly vegetarian. X: Sun. $
>
> **Carter's** (South St., near Canon Lane) Light lunches in an ancient crypt. X: Sun. $
>
> **Royal Arms** (East St., by the Market Cross) A popular pub with good food. $

And in Bosham, you may want to try:

> **Millstream Restaurant** (Bosham Lane) A lovely place for French and English cuisine. $$ and $$$
>
> **Berkeley Arms** (near Bosham Lane) A friendly local pub with meals. $

SUGGESTED TOUR:

Leaving the **train station** (1), walk up Southgate and South Street to the **Market Cross** (2). This medieval shelter, the most elaborate in England, was erected in 1501 by a local bishop. The town's Roman origins become obvious at this point, with the four main streets meeting at right angles in the center.

Stroll down West Street to the tourist office and turn left at the cathedral's detached **Bell Tower**, the only one of its kind in the coun-

The Market Cross

try. The ***Cathedral** (3) itself, predominantly Norman, was consecrated in 1108. Its 277-foot spire collapsed in 1861 and was rebuilt in 1866. Inside, it has a remarkably comfortable, almost cozy atmosphere. For nearly 900 years this has been the repository of a vast collection of art objects. The nave has two aisles, an unusual arrangement, separated from the choir by a carved stone screen from 1475. Note the modern pulpit, installed in 1966. The beautifully carved **misericords** and Bishop's Throne in the choir are outstanding, but the best works here are the two ***Romanesque wall carvings** just opposite them in the south aisle. These depict the *Raising of Lazarus* and *Christ at the Gate of Bethany,* and are the finest of their kind in England.

A visually exciting point of focus is provided by the vivid tapestry of abstract design behind the contemporary **High Altar**. Roman floor **mosaics** from a much earlier structure on the same spot can be seen in the south aisle near the retro-choir. Not to be missed is the ***stained-glass window** by Marc Chagall and the modern Graham Sutherland painting.

Leave by the main entrance and turn left into the **Cloisters**. Their irregular 15th-century walls enclose a garden known as the Paradise. From here follow St. Richard's Walk, a narrow and very charming passage, to Canon Lane. To the right, a 14th-century gateway leads to the Bishop's Palace and the public gardens. Return on quiet Canon Lane,

lined with intriguing old houses, to South Street and turn left. In a few
yards make a right onto West Pallant. The **Pallants** are a miniature
version of the town itself, reflecting a distinctly Roman layout. Once
a special preserve of the bishop, these four streets are lined with outstanding 18th- and 19th-century buildings. The most notable of these
is the **Pallant House** of 1712 at the intersection with North Pallant,
now home to an interesting public art gallery with mostly changing
exhibitions. This is open on Tuesdays through Saturdays, from 10 a.m.
to 5:30 p.m.

Continue along East Pallant and turn left at Baffin's Lane. Once
across East Street this becomes Little London. The **District Museum**
(4) at the corner of East Row is housed in an 18th-century corn store.
Its collections include objects relating to the district that date from
prehistoric to modern times, including Roman armor. The museum is
open on Tuesdays through Saturdays, from 10 a.m. to 5:30 p.m.

Now follow Little London into **Priory Park** (5). A shady footpath
runs along the top of the medieval city walls, built on original Roman
foundations. The 13th-century Greyfriars Church in the middle of the
lawn houses the **Guildhall Museum**, featuring archaeological finds,
which is open on summer afternoons, on Tuesdays through Saturdays.

Walk down Priory Lane and turn left on North Street. A few blocks
to the north lies the Festival Theatre, built in 1962 for the world-famous Chichester Festival, held annually from April to September. Stop
at the intersection of Lion Street and visit the elegant **Council House**
(6) of 1731. On its outer wall is mounted a Roman stone, found nearby,
which reads: *By the Authority of Tiberius Claudius, Cogidubnus, King
Legate of Augustus in Britain.* Inside, there is a fine assembly room
and council chamber, which may be inspected.

Lion Street leads to St. Martin's Square and **St. Mary's Hospital** (7),
built in 1290. Since 1528 it has been an almshouse for the aged, a
function it still serves. Its well-preserved medieval interior can be seen
on Tuesdays through Fridays, from 11 a.m. to noon and 2–5 p.m.

Follow St. Martin's Street and turn right on East Street, passing the
Market Cross. Continue along West Street to Westgate. From here it
is about 1½ miles to Fishbourne following the route on the map. You
can also get there by a number 700, 276, or 266 bus; or by hourly train
from the station to Fishbourne Halt.

The ***Roman Palace at Fishbourne** (8), the largest building of that
era in Britain, was discovered in 1960 by workmen laying a water main.
Those parts of it that survived the centuries of destruction and burial
can only hint at the grandeur it must have had in the time of Cogidubnus. A museum and protective structure has been erected over a large
part of the remains. In order to understand these it is helpful to first

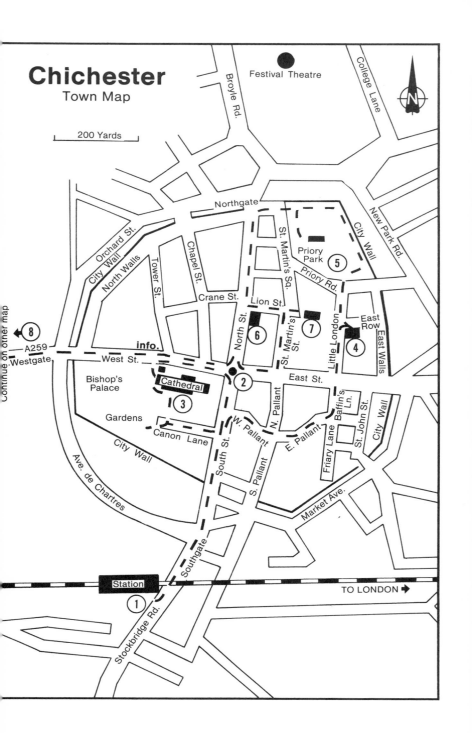

Chichester
Town Map

200 Yards

Festival Theatre

Broyle Rd.

College Lane

N

Northgate

Orchard St.

City Wall

North Walls

Tower St.

Chapel St.

Crane St.

St. Martin's Sq.

Priory Park

5

City Wall

New Park Rd.

Lion St.

North St.

St. Martin's St.

6

7

East Row

Little London

East Walls

4

Continue on other map

8

A259

Westgate

West St.

info.

2

East St.

Bishop's Palace

Cathedral

3

Gardens

Canon Lane

South St.

W. Pallant

N. Pallant

E. Pallant

Friary Lane

Baffin's Ln.

St. John St.

City Wall

City Wall

Ave. de Chartres

S. Pallant

Market Ave.

Southgate

Station

1

Stockbridge Rd.

TO LONDON ➜

see the short film shown frequently in the museum's theater, and to study the scale model. A **Roman dining room** has been reconstructed, and there is a **farming display** outside with live Roman-type animals and crops. The palace is open daily from March through November, from 10 a.m. to 6 p.m.; and on Sundays the rest of the year. It closes at 5 p.m. in March, April, and October; and at 4 p.m. from November through February. There is a cafeteria on the site.

From here you can either return to Chichester or continue on to Bosham via bus from the intersection of Portsmouth Road (A-27) and Salthill Road. Walking the 2-mile distance, however, is much more adventurous. To do that, turn right on Portsmouth Road until you get to a pub called the Black Boy, then bear left on Old Park Lane. At the end of this you will find a public footpath going straight ahead, which follows a row of trees to the left. Walk along this until you cross a private road. Climb over a stile and continue on the footpath, which soon runs into a paved road. Walk straight ahead, ignoring the sign to Bosham Hoe, and pass the Berkeley Arms Inn. The street now becomes Bosham Lane, which makes a left and leads to the harbor.

It was from ***Bosham** (pronounced *Boz-zum*) that Harold set sail in 1064 on that fateful journey that ended in the Norman Conquest. This delightfully dreamy village is, however, much older than that, going back at least as far as the Romans. Turn right on High Street and follow it to **Bosham Church** (9). Begun around 1020, it incorporates parts of a Roman basilica of A.D. 350. The young daughter of King Canute, an 11th-century ruler of England and Denmark, is believed to be buried here.

Wander past the old mill, then return along the water's edge to Bosham Lane. A stroll along **The Trippet** to the opposite bank reveals the full nautical flavor of Bosham, while a visit to **Bosham Walk**, a local arts and crafts center, is a pleasant diversion. At the post office on High Street you can get information concerning bus service back to Chichester. If you prefer to take the train, just follow the map to the **station** (10), about a mile away. Trains to Chichester leave hourly from the platform on the far side of the tracks.

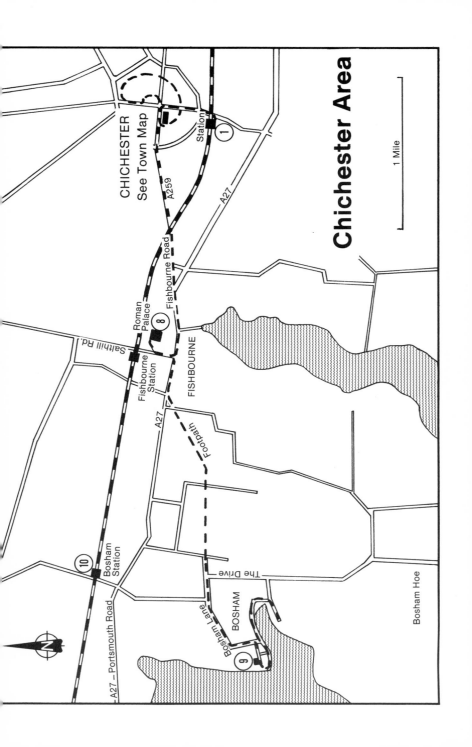

Guildford

Dating back at least a thousand years, Guildford is an unusually attractive old town with a rich architectural heritage. The Saxons named it *Gyldeford*—the ford of the golden flowers—after its strategic position on the River Wey. A Norman castle was built here, which remained a favorite royal residence for centuries. During medieval times, Guildford was made the county town of Surrey, a status it still holds. Throughout the Middle Ages the peaceful and prosperous town had a thriving woolen industry that died out in the 17th century, only to be replaced by another source of wealth, the shipping of goods by barge along its newly navigable river.

Guildford today is a remarkable blend of past and present. While it has done a good job of preserving the old, it also has some first-rate modern structures. The town is particularly rich in parks, gardens, and open spaces.

GETTING THERE:

Trains to Guildford leave London's Waterloo Station at least every half-hour, with a journey time of well under an hour. On Mondays through Saturdays there are also trains every half-hour from London's King's Cross ThamesLink and Blackfriars stations. Return service operates until late evening.

By car, Guildford is 33 miles southwest of London via the A-3 road.

LINKS:

If you're following a point-to-point itinerary, Guildford offers good direct rail service to **Portsmouth**, along with easy connections to **Arundel**, **Winchester**, **Southampton**, and **Salisbury**; and less simple connections to **Brighton**. All of these destinations are featured elsewhere in this book, and all can be easily reached by car as well.

PRACTICALITIES:

Guildford may be visited at any time, but note that the museums are closed on Sundays and the castle is closed from October through March. The local **Tourist Information Centre**, phone (0483) 444-007, is in the Guildford House at 155 High Street. Guildford is the county seat of **Surrey**, and has a **population** of about 62,000.

High Street in Guildford

FOOD AND DRINK:

Some of the better restaurants and pubs are:

Café de Paris (35 Castle St., near the castle) Exceptional French cuisine in a combined bistro and restaurant. X: Sun., Mon. eve., Sat. lunch. $$

Angel Inn (High St., opposite Chapel St.) A 16th-century coaching inn with traditional English fare. $$

Rumwong (16 London Rd., 2 blocks northeast of the Royal Grammar School) The tasty cuisine of Thailand in a colorful restaurant. X: Mon. $$

Rat's Castle (80 Sydenham Rd., 2 blocks northeast of the castle) A stylish pub noted for its traditional dishes. X: Sun. eve. $

Star (Quarry St. at High St.) Have lunch in a very old pub, alleged to be haunted.

SUGGESTED TOUR:

Leaving the **train station** (1), follow Park Street and Millmead to the River Wey, which was converted into a navigable waterway as early as 1653. Through a series of canals and locks it is joined with the Thames to the north, and at one time was open all the way to the south coast.

Now owned by the National Trust, The Wey Navigation is very popular with pleasure boaters, who have replaced the commercial barges of old.

Cross the footbridge to Millmead Lock. From here you can stroll down along the water past the **Guildford Boathouse** (2), which offers river cruises and boat rentals. To reach it, use the footbridge and return via Millbrook.

The **Yvonne Arnaud Theatre** (3), delightfully located by Millmead Lock, is a modern circular structure that often previews productions before they open in London's West End. Just beyond it is the town mill, built over the millrace and now used as a scenery workshop for the theater.

Cross Millbrook and follow Mill Lane to **St. Mary's Church** (4), the oldest building in Guildford. Its Saxon tower dates from about 1050, with the rest being completed by the 13th century.

Continuing along Quarry Street, take a look down Rosemary Alley, a steep medieval path to the river. Just beyond it is the **Guildford Museum** (5), which has exhibits of local archaeology and history as well as items connected with Lewis Carroll, author of *Alice in Wonderland*, who spent a great deal of his time in Guildford. It is open on Mondays through Saturdays, from 11 a.m. to 5 p.m.

Pass through the adjacent Castle Arch, which dates from 1265. To the right, on Castle Hill, is a private house called The Chestnuts that was leased by Lewis Carroll as a home for his six spinster sisters. This is where he died in 1898.

A path leads up to the **Castle Keep** (6). Built in 1170 on an earlier mound, this is all that remains of the great Norman castle that was once a favorite royal residence until it fell into neglect in the 15th century. Later used as a jail, the keep is open to visitors daily from April through September, from 10:30 a.m. to 6 p.m. There is a marvelous **view** from the top.

Leave the grounds and follow the map to Milk House Gate, a quaint narrow passageway just before the multi-story parking facility. This leads to High Street, across which to the left is the **Guildhall** (7) with its protruding clock, easily the most photographed sight in Guildford. Its dramatic façade was erected in 1683, but the main structure is Elizabethan.

Turn right on High Street and visit the **Guildford House** (8) at number 155. Now used for art exhibitions, it was built in 1660 and is worth seeing for its beautifully molded plaster ceilings and carved wooden staircases alone. Open on Mondays through Saturdays, from 10:30 a.m. to 4:30 p.m., it is also home to the tourist office.

Just beyond this is **Abbot's Hospital** (9), or Hospital of the Blessed Trinity, an old almshouse with an interesting history. It was founded

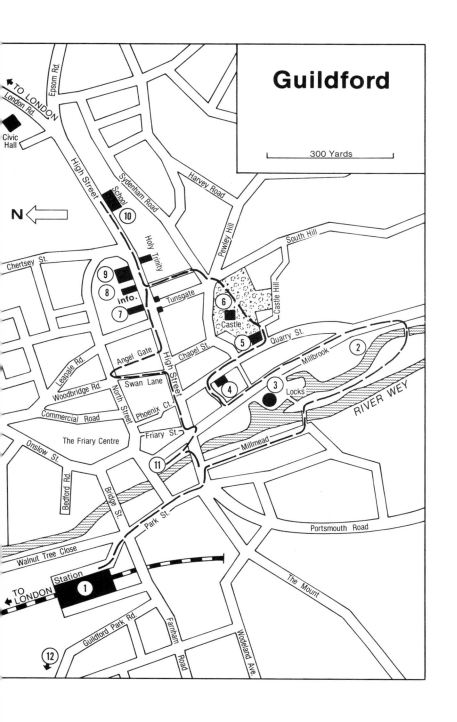

Guildford

300 Yards

TO LONDON
London Rd.

Civic Hall

N

Epsom Rd.

High Street

Sydenham Road

Harvey Road

Pewley Hill

South Hill

Chertsey St.

School

Holy Trinity

Castle Hill

10

9

8

info.

7

Tunsgate

6

Castle

5

Quarry St.

2

Leapale Rd.

Angel Gate

Chapel St.

Millbrook

Woodbridge Rd.

Swan Lane

North Street

High Street

4

3

Locks

Commercial Road

Phoenix Ct.

RIVER WEY

The Friary Centre

Friary St.

Millmead

Onslow St.

11

Bedford Rd.

Bridge St.

Park St.

Millmead

Portsmouth Road

Walnut Tree Close

TO LONDON

Station

1

The Mount

Guildford Park Rd.

Farnham Road

Wodeland Ave.

12

in 1619 by George Abbot, a poor local boy who was given a free education by the town. He rose to become the Archbishop of Canterbury and repaid the people of Guildford by building this home for their elderly poor, which is still used for that purpose. A guided tour of its splendid interior is available at stated times.

The **Royal Grammar School** (10) is a little farther up High Street. Its modern buildings are on the left side, but those on the right date from 1586. Enter the old courtyard and look around. Visitors are occasionally admitted to the library, which contains priceless old chained books.

Return down High Street, passing Holy Trinity Church on the left. This classical building was erected in 1763 on the site of the medieval church that collapsed in 1740. It was used as a cathedral from 1927 to 1961. Another classical structure, the **Tunsgate Arch**, directly opposite the Guildhall, fronted the former Corn Exchange when it was built in 1818. A road now passes beneath it.

Turn right on Angel Gate, a narrow lane by the side of the ancient Angel Inn. This leads to North Street, scene of a colorful farmers' market held on Fridays and Saturdays. Make a left and return by Swan Lane to High Street, which you follow to the river.

Use the underpass to reach the restored late-17th-century **Treadwheel Crane** (11) on the old town wharf, a relic of the former Wey Navigation. Up to ten men were needed to work it, unloading the barges that were the backbone of Guildford's prosperity. From here you can stroll back to the station via Friary Bridge or through the Friary Shopping Centre, a well-designed enclosed mall.

There is one more sight in Guildford that may interest you. It is the modern **Cathedral of the Holy Spirit** (12) on Stag Hill, reached via Guildford Park Road and Ridgemount, about one mile from the station. The first Anglican cathedral to be built on a new site in the south of England since the Reformation, it was begun in 1936 and consecrated in 1961.

Portsmouth

There is one very compelling reason to visit Portsmouth, and that is to go aboard H.M.S. *Victory*, Nelson's flagship at Trafalgar. Here you can relive one of the proudest moments in British history. Located on a naval base, the ship has been perfectly restored to the condition she was in on October 21, 1805, when she won the most decisive battle ever fought at sea.

Portsmouth, long known to sailors as "Pompey," has many other attractions as well, including the *Mary Rose*, a Tudor warship sunk in 1545, and H.M.S. *Warrior*, the sole survivor from the Royal Navy's ironclad era. There are also forts and fortifications, splendid harbor views, several museums, a cathedral, and best of all, Old Portsmouth, which retains much of its nautical atmosphere despite heavy bombing during World War II.

The town was originally founded in 1194 by Richard the Lion-hearted but did not achieve real importance until 1495, when the first dry dock in the world was established there by Henry VII. Since then, Portsmouth has grown to become one of the major naval bases in the world, a position it still holds.

GETTING THERE:

Trains to Portsmouth Harbour Station, the end of the line, leave frequently from London's Waterloo Station. The journey takes about 90 minutes, with returns operating until mid-evening.

By car, Portsmouth is 71 miles southwest of London via the A-3 road. You may want to drive around the town instead of walking or taking buses.

LINKS:

For those following an itinerary rather than taking daytrips, Portsmouth has good direct rail service to **Guildford, Brighton, Arundel, Chichester, Southampton, Salisbury**, and **Bath**; along with easy connections to **Winchester**. These destinations are described elsewhere in this book, and are just as easily reached by car.

PRACTICALITIES:

Portsmouth may be visited at any time except during the Christmas holidays. Most of the sights are open daily. The local **Tourist Information Centre**, phone (0705) 826-722, is on The Hard, near the entrance to the naval base. Portsmouth is in the county of **Hampshire**, and has a **population** of about 175,000.

FOOD AND DRINK:

Some good choices of pubs and restaurants are:

Le Talisman (123 High St., Old Portsmouth, near the cathedral) Excellent meals in the Old Town. X: Sat. Lunch, Sun., Mon. $$$

Bistro Montparnasse (103 Palmerston Rd., 2 blocks north of Southsea Castle) A popular French-style restaurant. X: Sun. $$$

Pendragon (Clarence Parade, 2 blocks northeast of Southsea Castle) Fine dining in a small hotel. $$

George (84 Queen St., near the naval base) A colorful old pub serving lunches. $

Pembroke (Pembroke Rd., Old Portsmouth, near the cathedral) A pub with meals in a nautical ambiance. $

The Lone Yachtsman (at The Point in Old Portsmouth) A pub restaurant with traditional fare. $

SUGGESTED TOUR:

Leaving **Portsmouth Harbour Station** (1), turn left on The Hard and enter the main gate of the naval base. Continue straight ahead to ***H.M.S. Victory** (2), where you join the queue for guided tours aboard the ship. Each group is escorted through the entire vessel by a sailor who is well versed in its history. Built in 1759, H.M.S. *Victory* has been in continuous commission since 1778, and is still manned by serving officers and men. Visits may be made on any day except Christmas, from 10:30 a.m. to 5 p.m., but not before 1 p.m. on Sundays.

The **Royal Naval Museum**, occupying three old storehouses just a few steps away, is an interesting place to visit after the tour. In addition to the expected material relating to Lord Nelson and the Battle of Trafalgar, there are exhibits of more contemporary naval matters, including a mock-up of a modern frigate's operations room. The museum is open daily, except for one week at Christmas, from 10:30 a.m. to 5 p.m.; closing at 4:30 p.m. in winter.

The **Mary Rose** was the flower of Henry VIII's fleet, a revolutionary warship lost while defending Portsmouth in 1545. Long forgotten, its oaken hull lay preserved in the seabed mud for four centuries. In 1979, a team led by Prince Charles began recovery work and in 1982

H.M.S. Victory

the remains of the ship were raised. These are now on display in a covered dry dock next to H.M.S. *Victory*. There is also a fascinating exhibition of *Mary Rose* artifacts in a boathouse close to the naval base entrance. Both may be seen daily except on Christmas, from 10:30 a.m. to 5 p.m.

A new addition to the naval base, just west of the entrance gate, is **H.M.S. Warrior**. This iron-hulled warship was built in 1860 as the world's fastest and best protected. She is the only remaining 19th-century capital ship in existence, the sole survivor of the Royal Navy's ironclad era. Visits may be made daily, from 10:30 a.m. to 5 p.m. An inexpensive **cafeteria** next to the museum offers lunches, snacks, and refreshments.

Follow the map to High Street in Old Portsmouth. The **Cathedral of St. Thomas** (3) is a rather odd structure. It was begun in 1188 as a chapel, became a parish church in 1320, and a cathedral only in 1927. The old church now forms the choir and sanctuary, with a new, still unfinished nave having been started in 1935. Although not a great cathedral by any standard, it is certainly interesting and deserves a visit.

At the end of High Street, next to the sea, is the 15th-century **Square Tower** (4), one of the first forts specially designed for cannon warfare. On its side is a gilded bust of Charles I that mysteriously survived the Civil War.

Turn right on Broad Street and pass the **Sally Port**, the traditional point of embarkation for Britain's naval heroes. Just beyond this is the **Round Tower** (5). Begun in 1415, it was the first permanent defensive work to be built in Portsmouth. You can climb up on it for a good view. An iron chain ran across the harbor from here to prevent unfriendly ships from entering.

The Point (6) still retains some of the flavor of Old Portsmouth. Once known as Spice Island, this small peninsula fairly teemed with bawdy pubs and brothels. To this day it remains a colorful place for eating and drinking, and the perfect spot for a **refreshment break**.

Return on Broad Street and continue to the **Garrison Church** (7). Now in ruinous condition, it was founded in 1212 as a hospice but was disbanded in 1540. It then became an armory and later a residence for the military governors. Charles II was married here in 1622. The building was restored as a church in the 19th century and badly damaged during World War II. It may be visited.

Stroll down to **Clarence Pier** (8), a popular amusement area with the usual seaside amenities. From here you can walk or take a bus past the beautiful gardens of Southsea Common to **Southsea Castle** (9), built in 1545 by Henry VIII. Inside the fort is a museum of local military history and archaeology, which may be visited daily from 10:30 a.m. to 5:30 p.m. Nearby is the **D-Day Museum**, featuring the 272-foot-long Overlord Embroidery, audio-visual shows, vehicles, weapons, and the like. The only museum in Britain devoted solely to the Normandy Invasions, it is open daily from 10:30 a.m. to 5:30 p.m.

Return to Pier Road and follow it to Museum Road. You can also take a bus from the front of Southsea Castle if you're tired. The **City Museum** (10) displays decorative and fine arts from the 16th century to the present, and is open daily from 10:30 a.m. to 5:30 p.m. At this point you could return directly to Portsmouth Harbour Station (1), or follow Cambridge Road to the **Civic Centre** (11). The Guildhall there is an outstanding Victorian structure flanked by modern glass buildings. Another tourist office is in one of these. To the north is the main shopping area along Commercial Road. This street leads, off the map, to the **Charles Dickens Birthplace Museum** at 393 Old Commercial Road. It is open from March through October, daily from 10:30 a.m. to 5:30 p.m. The **Portsmouth and Southsea Station** (12) is a convenient place to get a train back to London.

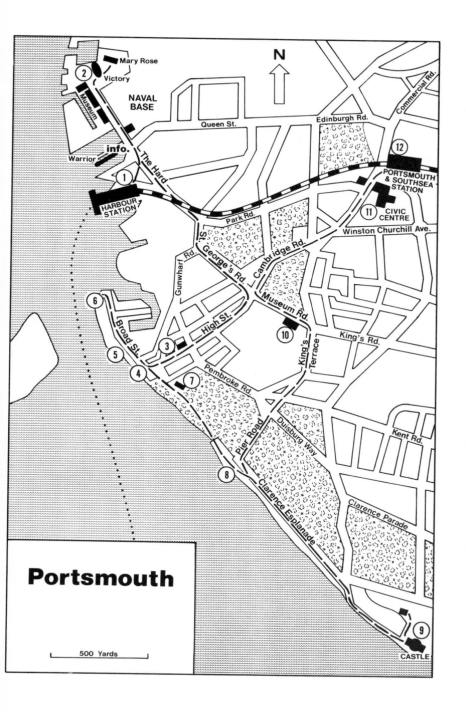

Portsmouth

500 Yards

Winchester

Winchester wears its history gracefully. The first "capital" of England, it was an important town from Roman times until the 12th century, when it lost out to rival London. Despite this decline, it remained a major religious and educational center, a role it still plays today. There are few places in England where the past has survived to delight the present quite so well.

The history of Winchester goes back to the Iron Age, when the Belgae, a Celtic tribe, settled in the valley of the River Itchen. This became the Roman town of *Venta Belgarum,* the fifth-largest in Britain. Following the collapse of the Roman Empire, the Anglo-Saxons took over and, changing the name to *Wintanceaster,* made it the capital of their kingdom of Wessex. Threats from marauding Danes caused the rival kingdoms of England to unite behind Egbert, the king of Wessex, in the mid-9th century; an act that made Winchester the effective capital of all England. A few decades later, under Alfred the Great, the town reached its peak of importance, and afterwards became the seat of such kings as Canute, Edward the Confessor, and William the Conqueror. Winchester's time had passed, however, and during the Norman era the center of power was gradually transferred to London.

GETTING THERE:

Trains leave London's Waterloo Station hourly for the one-hour ride to Winchester, with returns until late evening.

By car, Winchester is 72 miles southwest of London via the M-3 highway.

LINKS:

For those following a point-to-point itinerary, Winchester offers direct rail service to **Southampton** or **Oxford**, along with easy connections to **Guildford**, **Portsmouth**, **Salisbury**, and **Bath**. By making two changes you can reach **Chichester** or **Windsor**. All of these are featured elsewhere in this book, and can just as easily be reached by car.

Winchester Cathedral

PRACTICALITIES:

This trip can be made at any time, although some sights are closed on Sundays, and sometimes on Mondays. The local **Tourist Information Centre**, phone (0962) 840-500, is in the Guildhall on The Broadway. Winchester is the county seat of **Hampshire**, and has a **population** of about 34,000.

FOOD AND DRINK:

Winchester has a wide selection of restaurants and pubs in all price ranges. A few good choices are:

Old Chesil Rectory (1 Chesil St., near the City Mill) Traditional English food in a 14th-century rectory. X: Sun. eve., Mon. $$

The Elizabethan (18 Jewry St., near High St.) A Tudor house with traditional English fare. $$

Mr. Pitkin's (4 Jewry St., near High St.) Buffet meals in the wine bar and full meals in the restaurant. $ and $$

Spys (9 Great Minster St., near the City Cross) A wine bar for snacks and a restaurant for full meals. X: Sun. $ and $$

Wykeham Arms (75 Kingsgate St., near Winchester College) An 18th-century inn, now a pub with excellent meals. X for food: Sun., Mon. eve. $

Royal Oak (Royal Oak Passage, just off High St.) Lunch in an ancient pub with plenty of atmosphere. X for food: Sun. $

SUGGESTED TOUR:

From the **train station** (1), follow Sussex Street to the **Westgate** (2), one of Winchester's two remaining medieval gatehouses. Built in the 12th century, its upper floor was added in 1380 and later served as a debtors' prison. It is now a small museum with an interesting collection of ancient armor and related objects. The view from its roof is excellent. Visits may be made on Mondays through Saturdays, from 10 a.m. to 5 p.m.; and on Sundays from 2–5 p.m. From October through March it is closed on Mondays, and closes on Sundays at 4 p.m.

Strolling down High Street, you will pass the **Old Guildhall** on the right. Its projecting clock and figure of Queen Anne were given to the town to commemorate the Treaty of Utrecht in 1713. On the roof is a wooden tower that houses the curfew bell, still rung each evening at eight. The 16th-century **God Begot House**, opposite, occupies the site of a manor given by Ethelred the Unready to his Queen Emma in 1012.

A few more steps brings you to the **City Cross** (3). Also known as the Butter Cross, it was erected in the 15th century. Make a right through the small passageway leading to The Square. William the Conqueror's palace once stood here. The **City Museum** (4) has fascinating displays of local archaeological finds, including Celtic pottery, a Roman mosaic floor, and painted walls. It is open during the same times as the Westgate, above.

*Winchester Cathedral (5), among the largest in Europe, was begun in 1079 on the site of earlier Saxon churches. During the 14th century the cathedral was altered with a new Gothic nave, resulting in a mixture of styles ranging from robust Norman to graceful Perpendicular. Several of England's earliest kings are buried here, including Ethelwulf, Egbert, Canute, and William II Rufus, son of the Norman conqueror.

Enter the nave through the west doorway. The windows retain some of the original 14th-century stained glass, most of which was destroyed by Puritan zealots during the Civil War. About halfway down the nave, on the right, is the magnificent **Wykeham's Chantry**, dedicated to Bishop William of Wykeham, who was also the founder of Winchester College and New College at Oxford, as well as a noted statesman. Almost opposite this, on the north aisle, is an outstanding 12th-century **font**, carved with the story of St. Nicholas. The tomb of the authoress Jane Austen is nearby in the north aisle.

The massive transepts are almost unchanged since Norman times. Near the southeast corner is a chapel containing the tomb of Izaak Walton, author of *The Compleat Angler*, who died here in 1683. A doorway in the south wall leads to the **Library**, which has a 10th-century copy of the Venerable Bede's *Ecclesiastical History* as well as a rare 12th-century illuminated Bible. During the summer it is open every

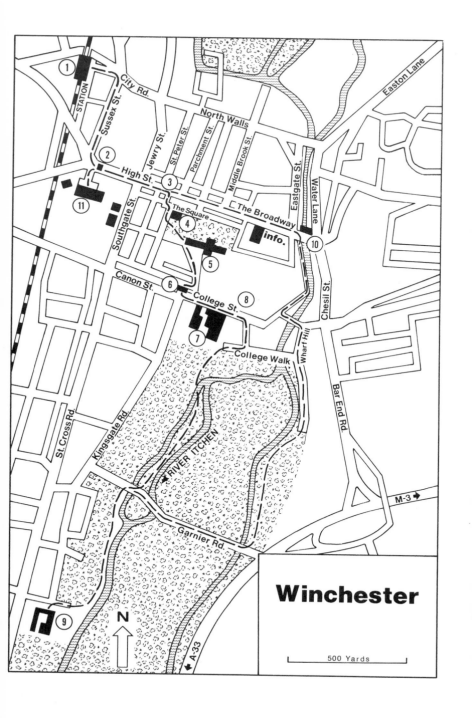

Winchester

500 Yards

day except on Sundays; and in winter on Saturdays and Wednesdays.

Continue up the south aisle and enter the **Presbytery**. Above the screens are six mortuary chests containing the bones of early English kings, and behind the **High Altar** a magnificently carved 15th-century ornamental screen. Adjoining this is the **choir** with some outstanding early-14th-century stalls and misericords. The tomb of William II Rufus is under the tower. At the east end of the cathedral is the 12th-century **Chapel of the Guardian Angels**, and the modern **Shrine of St. Swithun**, the patron saint of British weather. If it rains on his day, July 15th, you're in for another 39 soggy days. Other sights include the crypt and the treasury.

Leave the cathedral and stroll through the Close, partially surrounded by the ancient monastery's walls. An arcade of the former Chapter House links the south transept with the Deanery. Dome Alley has some particularly fine 17th-century houses. Pass through the **Kingsgate** (6), the second of the two surviving medieval town gates. Above it is the tiny 13th-century **Church of St. Swithun-upon-Kingsgate**, which should definitely be visited.

Winchester College (7), the oldest "public" school in England, was founded in 1382 and is associated with New College at Oxford. You may visit the chapel or wander around the courtyards on your own whenever the college is open. Guided tours are available from April through September.

Continue down College Street to the ruins of **Wolvesey Castle** (8), begun in 1129 and destroyed in 1646 by Cromwell's forces during the Civil War. They are enclosed by part of the old city wall, but you can enter and take a look from April through October, Tuesdays through Saturdays, from 2–5 p.m. The adjacent Wolvesey Palace, thought to have been designed by Sir Christopher Wren, is now the bishop's residence.

From here there is a wonderfully picturesque **riverside walk** to the venerable Hospital of St. Cross, the oldest functioning almshouse in England. It is about one mile away and can be reached by bus along St. Cross Road, but the delightful stroll along the stream is too lovely to miss. You can always ride back. To get there, just follow the map.

The ***Hospital of St. Cross** (9) has always had a tradition of providing a dole of bread and ale to weary wayfarers, which includes you. Ask and ye shall receive. Founded in 1136 by Bishop Henry de Blois, grandson of William the Conqueror, the institution cares for 25 brethren who live in 15h-century quarters and wear medieval gowns. There is a 12th-century Norman chapel and a 15th-century hall and kitchen that can be visited. It is open all year, except on Sundays and Christmas Day, from 9 a.m. to 12:30 p.m. and 2–5 p.m.; with shorter hours in winter. Don't miss this.

The Hospital of St. Cross

Those returning on foot can take the alternative route via Garnier Road. St. Catherine's Hill, across the river, has an Iron Age fort and the foundations of an early chapel at its summit, as well as an excellent view.

Back in Winchester, the footpath leads across the River Itchen alongside the medieval walls to the **City Mill** (10), now a youth hostel. There has been a mill at this location since Anglo-Saxon days. The present one, built in 1744, may be visited between April and mid-October, Tuesdays through Saturdays, from 1:30–4:45 p.m.

Turn left and follow **The Broadway** past the statue of King Alfred, who made Winchester a center of learning over a thousand years ago. The huge Victorian **Guildhall** of 1873 houses the tourist office. From here, High Street leads to The Castle, an administrative complex that includes the **Great Hall** (11), the sole remaining part of Winchester Castle. Dating from the early 13th century, the hall was the scene of many important events in English history. Go inside and take a look at the famous Roundtable, once associated with King Arthur but now known to be of 14th-century origin. It is open daily from 10 a.m. to 5 p.m., closing at 4 p.m. on winter weekends. From here it is only a short stroll back to the train station.

Southampton

Great seaports are exciting places, having been touched by the world in ways that inland cities never experience. Despite the decline in passenger traffic, Southampton has maintained its cosmopolitan character and continues to thrive on international trade. There is a certain fascination to watching its ever-changing harbor scene and another to exploring its colorful past.

Southampton's recorded history begins with the Roman garrison of *Clausentum*. This was followed by the Saxon town of *Hamwih* where, in 1016, Canute was offered the crown of England. Large-scale trade with the Continent developed after the Norman Conquest, and in the 12th century the port became an embarkation point for many of Richard the Lionhearted's Crusaders. During the Hundred Years War the town was often raided by the French, most notably in 1338. A serious decline, lasting 200 years, began in the 16th century. The Pilgrims departed from here in 1620, making a stop in Plymouth on their way to the New World. A few decades later, in 1665, Southampton was decimated by the plague.

Great places have a way of bouncing back. At its low point, Southampton suddenly discovered the spa business, becoming a fashionable seaside resort, a position it held until losing out to Brighton during the Regency. But there was still the harbor with its deep channels and four high tides a day. In the 1840s the railway came and vast docks were built. Southampton had become England's gateway to the world. Millions of troops left from here during both world wars. The city was devastated by bombs in the early 1940s, and largely rebuilt in the decades that followed. Miraculously, most of its ancient treasures survived and are now part of the modern city.

GETTING THERE:

Trains depart London's Waterloo Station at least hourly for Southampton. The trip takes 70 minutes or so, and return service operates until late evening.

By car, Southampton is 87 miles southwest of London via the M-3 and A-33 highways.

South Side of Bargate

LINKS:

If you're traveling from point to point, instead of making daytrips, Southampton offers direct rail service to **Chichester, Portsmouth, Winchester, Salisbury, Bath,** and **Oxford**. By making two changes you can also reach **Windsor**. All of these destinations are described elsewhere in this book, and can also be readily reached by car.

PRACTICALITIES:

Avoid coming on a Monday, when virtually all of the sights are closed. The local **Tourist Information Centre**, phone (0703) 221-106, is in the middle of Above Bar Street, north of the Bargate. Southampton is in the county of **Hampshire**, and has a **population** of about 210,000

FOOD AND DRINK:

There are plenty of restaurants and pubs in the central business area, including:

La Brasserie (33 Oxford St., 2 blocks north of the main gate to the docks) One of Southampton's best restaurants, French cuisine. X: Sat. lunch, Sun. $$

The Solent (Herbert Walker Ave., opposite Mayflower Park) Good food in the modern Post House Hotel. $$

Golden Palace (17 Above Bar St., just south of the tourist office) An upstairs Chinese restaurant specializing in seafood and dim sum. $ and $$

The Star (26 High St., near Holy Rood Church) Bar lunches and
full dinners in an 18th-century inn. $ and $$

The Red Lion (High St., near the Holy Rood Church) A famous
old historic pub with lunches. $

Duke of Wellington (Bugle St., near the Tudor House) Lunch in
an ancient pub. $

SUGGESTED TOUR:

Leaving the **train station** (1), follow Civic Centre Road to Above
Bar Street and turn right. The tourist office is straight ahead. Continue
on to **Bargate** (2), a particularly fine example of an early medieval
fortification, once part of the ancient town walls. There is an interesting **museum** of local history inside, which can be seen on Tuesdays
through Fridays, from 10 a.m. to noon and 1–5 p.m.; on Saturdays
from 10 a.m. to noon and 1–4 p.m.; and on Sundays from 2–5 p.m.

From here, Bargate Street leads along remnants of the walls to the
Arundel Tower. The western section of the ramparts, originally dating
from Norman times, is still in good condition. Take a look at it, then
follow the map to Bugle Street.

The **Tudor House** (3) is a handsome half-timbered 16th-century
structure that now houses a museum of life in old Southampton. Be
sure to see the 12th-century Norman merchant's house in its garden,
adjoining the town wall. The museum is open during the same times
as the Bargate Museum, above. On the other side of the square is St.
Michael's Church, also dating from Norman times but heavily altered
in the 19th century.

Follow Bugle Street to Westgate and turn right. The 14th-century
West Gate opens onto Western Esplanade, once the quay from which
the Pilgrims departed in 1620. Turn left and enter **Mayflower Park** (4).
There are good views of the harbor here.

Return to Town Quay and visit the **Maritime Museum** (5) in the old
14th-century Wool House, once a warehouse and later a jail. Its attractions include a maritime history of Southampton, models of famous
ships, and an interesting collection of seafaring artifacts. Visits may be
made during the same times that the Bargate Museum, above, is open.
From here you can explore the nearby piers.

God's House Tower (6) on Platform Road is a 15th-century fortification that is now used as a museum of archaeology. Step inside to
see the fine displays of prehistoric, Roman, Saxon, and medieval finds.
Again, the hours are the same as those of the Bargate Museum, above.

From here you can walk to the **Itchen Bridge** (7), a modern high-
level span offering incomparable views of the entire harbor complex
all the way out to the Isle of Wight. Along the way you will pass Gate
4 to the Ocean Dock, where the big liners call, just opposite Latimer

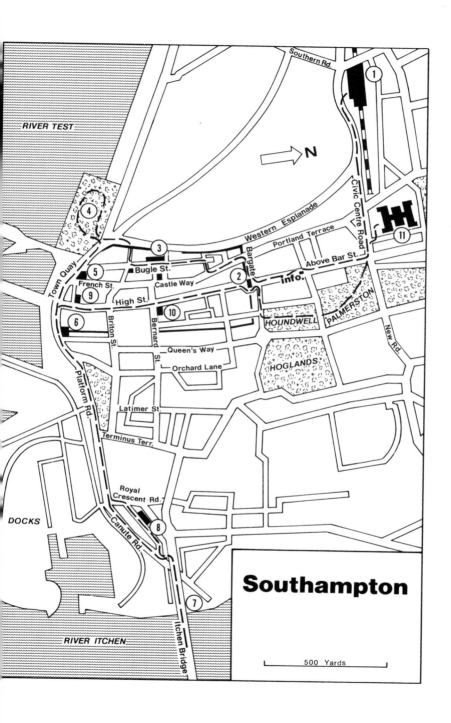

RIVER TEST

Southern Rd.

N

1

Civic Centre Road

11

Western Esplanade

Portland Terrace

Bargate

Above Bar St.

info.

2

PALMERSTON

HOUNDWELL

New Rd.

3

Bugle St.

Castle Way

Town Quay

5

French St.

9

High St.

10

6

Briton St.

Bernard St.

Queen's Way

Orchard Lane

HOGLANDS

Platform Rd.

Latimer St.

Terminus Terr.

DOCKS

Royal Crescent Rd.

Canute Rd.

8

7

Itchen Bridge

RIVER ITCHEN

Southampton

├─────── 500 Yards ───────┤

In the Hall of Aviation

Road. Permission to enter the dock area is usually given without any problem.

Return and follow the map to the **Hall of Aviation** (8) on Albert Road South. The fascinating displays here include a World War II Spitfire and an actual Sandringham flying boat, once used for passenger service in the Pacific, that may be boarded. Ask for permission to climb up into the flight deck. These marvelous old airplanes may be seen on Tuesdays through Saturdays, from 10 a.m. to 5 p.m.; and on Sundays from noon to 5 p.m.

Continue on and make a right up High Street. The remains of a long Norman structure incorrectly known as **"Canute's Palace"** (9) are in Porter's Lane. High Street leads past the historic Red Lion Inn to the ruined **Holy Rood Church** (10) of the 14th century.

Now follow the route through Houndwell and Palmerston Park to the ***Art Gallery** (11) in the massive Civic Centre. One of the very best art museums in all of Britain, it specializes in British painting, and also has an excellent collection of Old Masters, Impressionist, and Post-Impressionist works. The museum is open on Tuesdays through Fridays, from 10 a.m. to 5 p.m.; on Saturdays from 10 a.m. to 4 p.m.; and on Sundays from 2–5 p.m. From here it is only a short stroll back to the train station.

*Salisbury and Stonehenge

The cathedral city of Salisbury is a relative newcomer as English towns go. It was first settled in 1220 when the local bishop moved his cathedral down from a hilltop stronghold known as *Sarum.* Dating from prehistoric times, this earlier site was of great importance to the Romans, who called it *Sorviodunum.* Later becoming the Saxon settlement of *Searoburh,* it acquired a Norman castle and a cathedral during the 11th century. Frequent clashes between the clergy and the military, as well as harsh conditions imposed by a dry, windswept location, led to the establishment of a new town in the more hospitable meadows along the River Avon, just two miles to the south. After this, Old Sarum gradually died out. Its abandoned cathedral was demolished in 1331 and the stones reused for building a wall around the new town's cathedral close. By the 16th century the site was completely deserted although, as the rottenest of the Rotten Boroughs, it continued to send two members to Parliament until 1832.

The new town of Salisbury has always been a peaceful place that escaped the vicissitudes of history. Since its cathedral was one of the few to be based on a chapter of secular canons rather than a monastery, it quickly became a worldly center with all of the features of a thriving provincial capital. Salisbury today is an extraordinarily beautiful town made all the more fascinating by its proximity to the mysterious Stonehenge, one of England's most popular tourist attractions.

GETTING THERE:

Trains depart London's Waterloo Station at hourly intervals for the $1\frac{1}{2}$-hour ride to Salisbury, with return service operating until mid-evening. Schedules are somewhat reduced on Sundays and holidays. There is bus service for Stonehenge from Salisbury.

By car, Salisbury is 91 miles southwest of London via the M-3 and A-30 highways. To get to Stonehenge, take the A-345 north to Amesbury, then the A-303 and A-344 west to the site. Stonehenge is about 10 miles from Salisbury. Old Sarum is along the way, about two miles north of Salisbury on the A-345.

LINKS:

For those following an itinerary, Salisbury offers good direct rail service to **Southampton** and **Bath,** along with easy connections to **Winchester, Portsmouth,** and **Oxford.** It is also possible to reach **Windsor** or **Woodstock** without too much difficulty. All of these destinations are featured elsewhere in this book, and can just as easily be reached by car.

PRACTICALITIES:

Salisbury may be visited on any day, although some sights are closed on Sundays. Getting to Stonehenge without a car may be difficult in winter or early spring, or on Sundays or holidays. The local **Tourist Information Center,** phone (0722) 334-956, is in the Guildhall on the Market Place. A colorful outdoor **market** is held there on Tuesdays and Saturdays until mid-afternoon. Salisbury is in the county of **Wiltshire,** and has a **population** of about 37,000.

FOOD AND DRINK:

The town is famous for its ancient pubs. Some of the best of these, and restaurants too, are:

Haunch of Venison (1 Minster St., near St. Thomas's Church) A very famous pub with meals, dating from the 14th century. $$

Old Mill (Town Path, Harnham) A delightful old mill by the River Nadder, with a great view and good food. $$

King's Arms (9 St. John St., just east of the cathedral) A half-timbered inn with lots of character. $ and $$

Pheasant Inn (Salt Lane, north of Market Place) A pub and a restaurant, dating from 1400. $ and $$

New Inn (41 New St., near North Gate) A pub with good food, in a 15th-century building. $

Michael Snell (5 St. Thomas Sq., near St. Thomas's Church) Light meals in a coffee shop, with homemade sweets. X: Sun. $

Mainly Salads (18 Fisherton St., near the bridge) Light vegetarian meals and snacks in pleasant surroundings. X: Sun. $

SUGGESTED TOUR:

Depending on your arrival time, it is probably best to head out for Stonehenge immediately, getting there before the crowds get too thick. Buses leave from the train station (1) a few times daily except on Sundays or holidays, from mid-April to mid-December. More frequent service is available from the bus station near the Market Place (9). Those driving their own cars should just follow the directions in "Getting There," above.

Stonehenge

*Stonehenge (2) is a massive circular group of standing stones, erected in several stages between the Late Neolithic and Middle Bronze ages. It seems to have been a temple of sorts, but anything beyond that is speculation. What is truly marvelous about the place is that you can believe anything you want about it, no matter how outrageous, and no one can prove you wrong. Go right ahead and indulge your imagination. Perhaps Merlin really did build it by magic, or maybe it actually was an astronomical observatory, or even a temple of the Druids. Who knows? One thing is certain, however. What you get out of it is what you put in. To approach this site without preparation is to see a pile of rocks and little else. Pamphlets explaining some of the theories are sold near the entrance, although advance homework will make your visit more rewarding. The site is open daily from 9 a.m. to 6 p.m., closing at 4 p.m. in winter.

On the way back you should try to make a stop at the ruins of **Old Sarum,** the original Salisbury, described in the introductory paragraph above. From there return to the train station and begin your exploration of "new" Salisbury.

Leaving the **train station** (1), walk down to the River Nadder and cross it. A footpath from here leads through delightful countryside to the ancient **Harnham Mill** (3), parts of which may date from the 13th century. Now an inn, its bucolic setting is a scene right out of a Constable landscape. All along the way there are wonderful views of the cathedral.

Return to **Queen Elizabeth Gardens** (4) and follow the map across the 15th-century Crane Bridge. Turn right at High Street and stroll through **North Gate** (5), a 14th-century structure that once protected the bishops from rebellious citizens. The **Mompesson House** (6) on Choristers' Green, built in 1701, has an exquisite Queen Anne interior with notable plasterwork. It belongs to the National Trust and is open from April through October, on Saturdays through Wednesdays, from 12:30–6 p.m.

*Salisbury Cathedral (7) was built over a very short time span, from 1220 to 1258, which accounts for its remarkable architectural unity. It is the purest example of the Early English style to be found anywhere in the kingdom. The graceful tower was added a century later and, at 404 feet, is the loftiest medieval spire on Earth.

Enter through the north door. The interior is somewhat disappointing for so majestic a structure. This is due to an overly zealous spring housecleaning in the 18th century that stripped it of much of the medieval clutter that make some other churches so fascinating. Despite this, there are still some interesting things to see. The most famous of these is the 14th-century **clock mechanism** at the west end of the north aisle. Still in operating condition, it is thought to be the oldest in England and perhaps in the world. The **West Window** contains some good 13th-century stained glass, as does the **Lady Chapel** at the east end. Stroll out into the **Cloisters,** the largest in England, and visit the adjoining ***Chapter House,** whose treasures include one of the four existing original copies of the **Magna Carta,** as well as 13th-century sculptures illustrating scenes from the Old Testament.

A walk around Cathedral Close makes a pleasant break before continuing on. The Bishop's Palace, now occupied by the Cathedral School, and the Old Deanery are particularly fine 13th-century buildings within the precincts. Be sure to visit the **Salisbury and South Wiltshire Museum** (8) in the King's House along West Walk. Its displays include models and relics from Stonehenge and Old Sarum, along with items of local history. The museum is open on Mondays through Saturdays, from 10 a.m. to 5 p.m., closing at 4 p.m. in winter. During July and August it is also open on Sundays, from 2–5 p.m. You may also be interested in seeing the **Military Museum,** located in another nearby historic house.

Follow North Walk to **St. Ann's Gate** where, in a room above the gateway, Handel gave his first public concert in England. Pass under this and turn left on St. John's Street. The King's Arms has been an inn since the 15th century. Just beyond it is the White Hart Hotel, an 18th-century coaching inn. Continue on to the **Market Place** (9), where a market has been held twice a week since 1361, a custom that continues today. The Guildhall of 1795 is in the southeast corner and houses the tourist office.

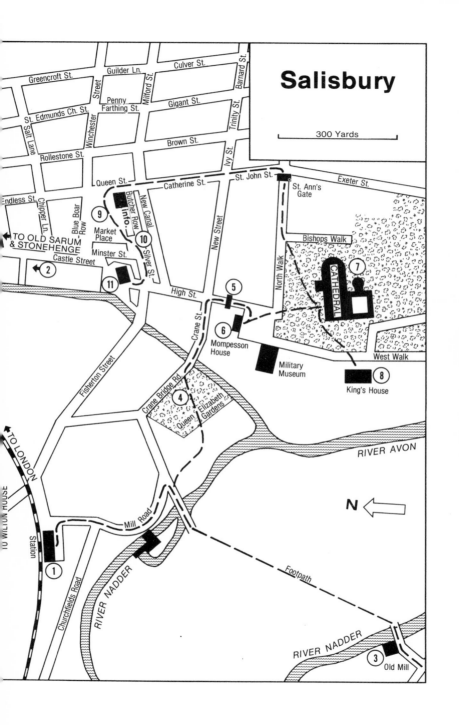

Salisbury

300 Yards

Greencroft St.

Guilder Ln.

Culver St.

Barnard St.

St. Edmunds Ch. St.

Penny Farthing St.

Gigant St.

Winchester Street

Milford St.

Trinity St.

Salt Lane

Rollestone St.

Brown St.

Endless St.

Chipper Ln.

Blue Boar Row

Queen St.

Catherine St.

St. John St.

Exeter St.

Ivy St.

St. Ann's Gate

9

Info.

Butcher Row

New Canal

TO OLD SARUM & STONEHENGE

Market Place

10

Bishops Walk

North Walk

CATHEDRAL

7

Castle Street

Minster St.

Silver St.

New Street

2

11

High St.

5

West Walk

Crane St.

6

Mompesson House

Military Museum

King's House

8

Fisherton Street

Crane Bridge Rd.

4

Queen Elizabeth Gardens

RIVER AVON

TO LONDON

TO WILTON HOUSE

Mill Road

N

Station

1

Churchfields Road

RIVER NADDER

Footpath

RIVER NADDER

3

Old Mill

Salisbury Cathedral

Cut through the market to Silver Street. The beautiful hexagonal **Poultry Cross** (10) was first mentioned in 1335 as the spot where poultry was sold. Around the corner, approached through alleyways, is **St. Thomas's Church** (11), one of the most interesting buildings in Salisbury. Founded in honor of Thomas à Becket about 1220, it was rebuilt in the 15th century and has a marvelous medieval fresco known as the *Doom Painting,* depicting the Last Judgement, above its chancel arch. This was whitewashed over during the Reformation and not rediscovered until the 19th century. The area immediately surrounding the church is the quintessence of a medieval merchants' town and the perfect place to wind up your tour.

If you decided not to go to Stonehenge, you might want to visit *Wilton House** instead. One of England's most attractive stately homes, it is filled with outstanding art and has lovely gardens. You can get there by taking a bus from outside the cinema on New Canal. Wilton House is open from Easter through mid-October, on Tuesdays through Saturdays and Bank Holiday Mondays, from 11 a.m. to 6 p.m.; and on Sundays from 1–6 p.m.

Windsor and Eton

Windsor, like Stratford, Oxford, and the Tower of London, is one of England's greatest tourist attractions. It has just the right combination of elements to make an ideal daytrip destination for first-time visitors and seasoned travelers alike. To begin with, it is very close to the capital and easy to reach. Second, it contains within a small area much of what is considered to be typically English. There is the Royal Castle, still in use after 850 years, a picturesque riverside location on the Thames, a colorful Victorian town, and in Eton one of the great public schools that have molded British character since the Middle Ages. Add these together and you have a carefree and thoroughly delightful day ahead of you.

GETTING THERE:

Trains depart London's Paddington Station frequently for Slough, where you change to a shuttle train for Windsor and Eton Central. The total journey takes about 40 minutes, with returns until late evening. Service is reduced on Saturdays, and especially on Sundays. There is also direct service from London's Waterloo Station to Windsor and Eton Riverside, taking about 50 minutes and running about twice an hour, less frequently on Sundays. Most travelers will find the route via Paddington to be more convenient.

By car, Windsor is 28 miles west of London via the M-4 motorway. Get off at Junction 6.

LINKS:

If you're following a point-to-point itinerary instead of making day-trips, Windsor has easy rail connections to **Bath** and **Oxford;** and less directly to **Winchester, Southampton, Salisbury, Woodstock,** and **Stratford-upon-Avon.** All of these are described elsewhere in this book, and can just as easily be reached by car.

PRACTICALITIES:

The castle grounds are open daily except for special events. The State Apartments are also open daily, with the exception of Sundays in winter, but closed when the Queen is in residence. If in doubt, check with the local **Tourist Information Centre,** phone (0753) 852-010, in the Windsor and Eton Central Station. Windsor is in the county of **Berkshire,** and has a **population** of about 30,000.

FOOD AND DRINK:

Some good pubs and restaurants are:

In Windsor:

> **Wren's Old House** (Thames St., near the bridge) Meals at an inn, once the home of Sir Christopher Wren. X: Sat. Lunch. $$$
>
> **La Taverna** (2 River St., near the bridge) Good Italian food in a nice location. X: Sun. $$
>
> **Carpenters Arms** (Market St., behind the Guildhall) A comfortable pub with lunches. X for meals: Sun. $
>
> **Windsor Chocolate House** (8 Church St., behind the Guildhall) Light lunches and afternoon teas. $

In Eton:

> **Eton Buttery** (High St., by the bridge) Excellent food with a French touch, in view of the castle. $$
>
> **Eton Wine Bar** (82 High St., near the bridge) Healthy, imaginative cooking with a changing menu. $$

SUGGESTED TOUR:

Start your walk at **Windsor and Eton Central Station** (1). Directly adjacent to this is the wonderful **Royalty and Empire** exhibition that re-creates moments of the Victorian era with replicas of old railway equipment, animated figures of Queen Victoria and other notables, and a 15-minute audio-visual extravaganza. This perfect introduction to Windsor, operated by Madame Tussaud's, is open daily from 9:30 a.m. to 5:30 p.m., closing at 4:30 p.m. in winter.

Cross the main street, passing the statue of Queen Victoria, and enter the castle grounds. Begun by William the Conqueror in the 11th century, *Windsor Castle has been altered by nearly every succeeding monarch. It is the largest inhabited castle in the world and remains a chief residence for the sovereigns of England.

Enter through Henry VIII's Gateway and visit *St. George's Chapel (2), one of the most beautiful churches in England. Many of the country's kings and queens are buried here. Continue on past the massive **Round Tower** and go out on the North Terrace, which has magnificent views up and down the River Thames. The entrance to the *State Apartments (3) is nearby. A stroll through them is highly worthwhile, but don't fret if they are closed because the Queen is here. Equally interesting is *Queen Mary's Dolls' House, a miniature 20th-century palace in exquisite detail, also entered from the North Terrace. Both are usually open on Mondays through Saturdays, from 10:30 a.m. to 5 p.m.; and on Sundays from 12:30–5 p.m.; closing at 3 or 4 p.m. in winter. They are also closed on winter Sundays and on some holidays. The rest of your tour of the castle can be spent just poking about any

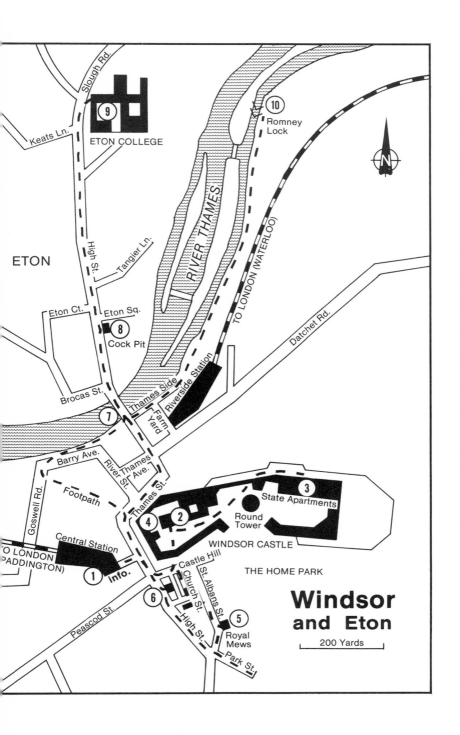

Slough Rd.

Keats Ln.

⑨ ETON COLLEGE

⑩ Romney Lock

N

High St.

Tangier Ln.

ETON

RIVER THAMES

TO LONDON (WATERLOO)

Eton Ct.

Eton Sq.

⑧ Cock Pit

Datchet Rd.

Brocas St.

Thames Side

Riverside Station

⑦

Farm Yard

Barry Ave.

River St.

Thames Ave.

Footpath

Goswell Rd.

Thames St.

③ State Apartments

② Round Tower

④

WINDSOR CASTLE

Central Station

TO LONDON (PADDINGTON)

① info.

Castle Hill

THE HOME PARK

Church St.

St. Albans St.

⑥

Peascod St.

High St.

⑤ Royal Mews

Park St.

Windsor
and Eton

200 Yards

A Statue of Queen Victoria Guards the Castle

area that is not off limits, and visiting the **Curfew Tower** (4).

Leave the castle and stroll down Church Street, perhaps stopping at the Parish Church and Brass Rubbing Centre. Walk through the graveyard to St. Alban's Street, near the foot of which is the **Royal Mews Exhibition** (5), a display of ceremonial carriages and various gifts received by the Queen. From here you might go down Park Street for a walk in the **Home Park.**

The elegant **Guildhall** (6) on High Street was completed in 1707 by Sir Christopher Wren. Step onto its porch and note that the center columns do not quite reach the ceiling they allegedly support, a trick played by the architect to prove the soundness of his design. Continue down High Street and Thames Street, making a left a the footpath to the river. Along the way you will pass a bowling green, tennis courts, and a lovely waterside park. **Boat trips,** some as short as 35 minutes, are available here.

The old **cast-iron bridge** (7) to Eton is reserved for pedestrians. Once across it follow High Street past numerous shops and pubs to the **Cock Pit** (8), a 15th-century timbered inn where cockfighting was once patronized by Charles II, the Merry Monarch. Outside it are the **town stocks** and an unusual Victorian mailbox.

Eton College (9) was founded in 1440 by Henry VI, himself a teenager at the time. It is the most famous of England's public (meaning

Boat Trips on the Thames

very private) schools and has educated many of the nation's greatest leaders. As you walk around you will notice the peculiar traditional garb of the students, which makes them look a little like penguins. Parts of the school are open to visitors, including the schoolyard, cloisters, and the chapel. The Upper and Lower schools may also be seen at times. Guided tours, led by senior boys, are available. Be sure to visit the **Museum of Eton Life,** which re-creates life among the students in bygone times. Located in the cellars of the original 15th-century buildings, it is usually open from 2–5 p.m., depending on school activities.

Return to the bridge. If you have any strength or time left you may want to take a pleasant walk along the Thames to the **Romney Lock** (10), or visit a pub before returning to London.

*Bath

Legend has it that the hot mineral springs of Bath were discovered about 500 B.C. by Prince Bladud who, suffering from leprosy, was cured and became king. Whatever truth lies behind this story, we do know that the Romans built a settlement there named *Aquae Sulis,* which served as their spa for nearly 400 years.

During the Middle Ages the waters of Bath were well known for their curative properties, but the splendor of the Romans had vanished. The town was renovated for Queen Anne's visit in 1702 and a master of ceremonies appointed to oversee the spa. This post remained after the queen's departure and was filled in 1705 by a bizarre young gambler named Richard "Beau" Nash, who in the next 40 years virtually invented the resort business.

Nash began by persuading the local leaders to invest vast sums into building a town of unmatched elegance. Much of the design fell to one John Wood, an architect with visionary ideas. Under his plan, individual houses were only components of a larger structure behind a common façade. This thinking reached its height in that triumph of the Palladian style, the Royal Crescent, designed by his son in 1767.

Today, Bath remains much the same as it was when the Georgian aristocracy made it their playground. The remains of the Roman era have since been unearthed, adding to its many attractions. Despite its stylish refinement, Bath makes a great daytrip destination largely because it is such a fun place to visit. Many travelers, in fact, consider it to be nothing less than the most enjoyable town in England.

GETTING THERE:

Trains leave London's Paddington Station at least hourly for Bath Spa Station, a ride of about 80 minutes. Return service operates until late evening.

By car, take the M-4 highway to Junction 18, then south on the A-46. Bath is 119 miles west of London.

LINKS:

For those following a point-to-point itinerary, Bath offers direct rail service to **Southampton** and **Salisbury,** along with easy connections to **Portsmouth, Winchester, Windsor,** and **Oxford.** It is also possible to reach **Woodstock** and **Stratford-upon-Avon** without much difficulty. All of these destinations are featured elsewhere in this book, and can just as easily be reached by car.

PRACTICALITIES:

Bath may be visited at any time. The local **Tourist Information Centre,** phone (0225) 462-831, is on Abbey Churchyard, next to the Roman Baths. Bath is in the county of **Avon,** and has a **population** of about 84,000.

FOOD AND DRINK:

Out of an enormous selection of restaurants and pubs, some choices are:

Popjoys (Beau Nash House, Sawclose, adjacent to the Theatre Royal) An elegant Regency restaurant with inventive English cuisine. Reservations recommended, phone (0225) 460-494. X: Sat. lunch, Sun., Mon. $$$

Royal Crescent Hotel (16 Royal Crescent) Very fine food with an outstanding wine selection. For reservations phone (0225) 319-090. $$$

Clos du Roy (7 Edgar Buildings, George St., 2 blocks south of the Assembly Rooms) Imaginative French cuisine with good-value lunches. X: Sun., Mon. $$ and $$$

Flowers (27 Monmouth St., west of the Theatre Royal) A delightfully pleasant restaurant with a reasonably priced lunch menu. X: Sun. $$ and $$$

Moon and Sixpence (6a Broad St., east of the Octagon) Simple lunches and full dinners, with outdoor tables available. $$ and $$$

Woods (9 Alfred St., near the Assembly Rooms) Famous for its good food and Georgian elegance. X: Sun. $$

The Grapes (Westgate St., 2 blocks northwest of the Roman Baths) An old-fashioned pub with good food and a lively crowd. X: Sun. $

Huckleberry's (34 Broad St., east of the Octagon) A fine place for vegetarian meals. X: Sun. $

SUGGESTED TOUR:

Leaving **Bath Spa Station** (1), walk straight ahead on Manvers Street past the bus station and in turn left on North Parade. In one block this becomes a colorful lane called **Old Lilliput Alley,** lined with some of the oldest houses in Bath. One of these is **Sally Lunn's House** (2), built in 1482 on Roman foundations, which as a coffee shop has been famous for its hot Bath buns since the late 17th century. They are still just as delicious, making this a favorite place for a break. You could also just pop in to see the original **kitchen** in the cellar, and the Roman walls. At the end of the passage is **Abbey Green,** an especially attractive spot.

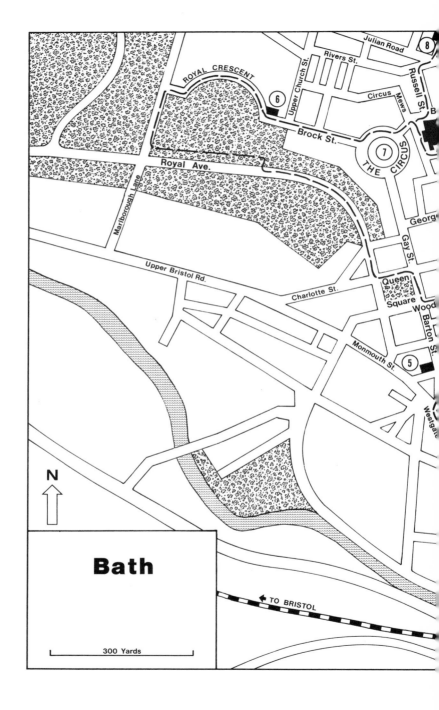

Julian Road

Rivers St.

ROYAL CRESCENT

Upper Church St.

Circus

Russell St.

Circus Mews

Brock St.

6

7

THE CIRCUS

B

Royal Ave.

Marlborough Lane

Georg

Gay St.

Upper Bristol Rd.

Charlotte St.

Queen
Square

Wood

Barton St.

Monmouth St.

5

Westgate

N

Bath

TO BRISTOL

300 Yards

8

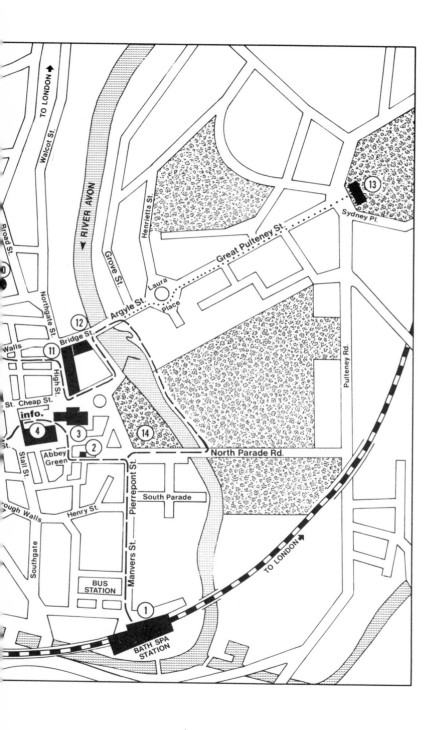

The Abbey

Turn right on Church Street and follow it for two blocks to the **Abbey** (3). This splendid example of the Perpendicular style was begun in 1499, although it did not gain a roof until the 17th century. Earlier churches existed on the same spot for several hundred years before a cathedral was built in 1088, a Norman structure that was destroyed by fire in 1137. The present abbey is noted for its enormous clerestory windows that flood the interior with light, and for its vaulted ceiling, planned from the start but not added until 1864.

Walk across the Abbey Churchyard to the entrance of the ***Roman Baths and Pump Room** (4). The tour through this ancient complex includes a fascinating **museum** of Roman and prehistoric relics, featuring the renowned gilt-bronze head of the goddess Minerva. An overflowing part of the original Roman reservoir is in the area, as is the **Great Bath,** a marvelously preserved pool that is today open to the sky. The original Roman lead plumbing is still in use, while the columns and statues above are Victorian additions. Another group of small baths and hypocaust rooms lie beyond, along with the King's Bath and the Circular Bath. A few of the ruins were discovered in the 18th century, but it was not until the 19th that the major finds were excavated. Above all of this is the famous **Pump Room,** an elegant Georgian assembly hall reflecting a gentility long vanished elsewhere. Be sure to see the wonderful equation clock of 1709, as well as the

The Great Bath

charming prints and 18th-century furniture. Needless to say, this is the perfect spot for a **tea break,** served from 10 a.m. to noon and 2:45–5 p.m., daily in summer and on Sundays in winter. The entire complex is open daily from 9 a.m. to 6 p.m., closing at 5 p.m. in winter. During August it is also open in the evenings from 8:30–10:30 p.m.

Continue down Bath Street and turn right into St. Michael's Place, then left through a narrow passage called Chandos Buildings to Westgate Buildings. Another right brings you to the **Theatre Royal** (5), first erected in 1720 but later rebuilt. It is adjacent to Beau Nash's last home, now a restaurant named after his mistress, Juliana Popjoy. Now follow the map by way of the narrow, cobbled **Queen Street** and continue through Queen Square, heading uphill through Royal Victoria Park.

From the gravel walk you have an excellent view of the ***Royal Crescent** (6), a magnificent sweep of 30 houses joined together in one continuous façade of 114 Ionic columns. Designed in 1767 by John Wood the Younger, this is regarded as the epitome of the Palladian style in England. Follow it around to **Number 1,** whose interior has been restored to its 18th-century splendor. This exquisite house is open to the public from March through October, on Tuesdays through Saturdays, from 11 a.m. to 5 p.m.; and on Sundays from 2–5 p.m. During the rest of the year it is open on weekends only, from 11 a.m. to 3 p.m.

The Royal Crescent

Stroll down Brock Street to **The Circus** (7), a circular group of Georgian houses considered to be John Wood's finest work. It is arranged so that no street goes straight through, resulting in a view from every angle. Continue along Bennet Street, from which you can take an interesting little side trip by turning up Russell Street and making a right on Rivers Street to the **Camden Works Museum** (8). The Victorian engineering shop, brass foundry, and mineral-water plant is complete with all of its original machinery and related items. An unusually fascinating place to visit, it is open daily from 2–5 p.m., March through November, and on weekends only during the rest of the year.

Now head for the **Assembly Rooms** (9). Also built by John Wood the Younger, this structure was the center of social activity in Bath, having witnessed many grand balls, banquets, receptions, and the like. The ***Museum of Costume** on its lower floor is the largest of its kind in the world. Clothes dating from as far back as the 16th century up to the present are very well displayed, many of them in period room settings. It is open daily from 10 a.m. to 5 p.m.

The route now takes you down to Milsom Street, the main shopping thoroughfare. The 18th-century **Octagon** (10) now houses the **National Centre of Photography.** This intriguing museum has displays of both contemporary and early camera work as well as an outstanding collection of antique and modern photo equipment, including a vast number of Leicas. It also serves as the headquarters of the Royal Photographic Society, and is open daily from 9:30 a.m. to 5:30 p.m.

Continue straight ahead past Upper Borough Walls and turn left through the very charming **Northumberland Place** to High Street. The building on the other side is the **Guildhall** (11), whose banqueting room is one of the finest interiors in Bath. This may be seen on Mondays through Fridays, from 8:30 a.m. to 4:30 p.m. Next to it is the **Covered Market,** which was founded in medieval times and remains very much alive in its 19th-century building.

Turning left around the Orange Grove brings you to Grand Parade. To the left, on Bridge Street, is the **Victoria Art Gallery,** which displays changing exhibitions of interest. It is open on Mondays through Fridays, from 10 a.m. to 6 p.m.; and on Saturdays from 10 a.m. to 5 p.m. The **Pulteney Bridge** (12) spanning the Avon is one of the few left in Europe to be lined with shops. Built in 1770 with obvious inspiration from the Ponte Vecchio in Florence, it makes a spectacular sight rising above the weir.

Once across it, you might want to make a **side trip** down Argyle Street and Great Pulteney Street to the **Holburne of Menstrie Museum** (13), which specializes in the arts of the Age of Elegance. Silver, porcelains, miniatures, and paintings by Gainsborough and others are among its attractions. Visits may be made on Mondays through Saturdays, from 1 a.m. to 5 p.m.; and on Sundays from 2:30–6 p.m.

Return almost to the bridge, then go down a flight of steps marked Riverside Walk to the River Avon and stroll past the weir. From the embankment on this side you can take a **boat ride** lasting about one hour. Check the tourist office for current schedules. When you get to the next bridge, climb the stairs and cross it. You are now on North Parade. The **Parade Gardens** (14) on the right are a good place to relax before returning to the station.

* Oxford

There is practically nothing you cannot learn at Oxford. Scores of independent schools compete with some 35 colleges that make up the 11,000-student university, each a closed world in itself, barricaded within its separate quadrangle. To this sheltered spot in the very center of England come thousands of visitors curious about English academic life and eager to see the countless treasures accumulated since medieval times.

The town of Oxford is older than the university, which itself dates from the 12th century. As far back as 912, *Oxenford*—the ford for oxen across the Thames—was mentioned in Anglo-Saxon chronicles. In 1071 the conquering Normans built a castle and defensive walls. Always the homes of lost causes, Oxford sided with the Royalists during the Civil War of the 17th century and to this day retains a little bit of that sense of privilege largely gone from the rest of Britain. Unlike Cambridge, with which it is inevitably compared, Oxford is also an industrial center, although you would hardly realize this from the old part of town.

There is far more to the town and its university than can possibly be seen in a single day. For this reason, the suggested tour has left out a great deal that is worthwhile and concentrated on a balanced blend of colleges, market-town atmosphere, parks, museums, and notable buildings. As a visitor, you may have to improvise somewhat as public accessibility to some of the places varies at the whim of individual colleges. This will present no problem, since if one quad is closed, another nearby will probably be open. It is always a good idea to ask the porter at each entrance about which specific points of interest are free to public inspection. Please remember that all of the colleges are private and that admission to them is a courtesy, not a right. Some are currently charging a small admission fee.

GETTING THERE:

Trains leave London's Paddington Station about hourly for the one-hour trip to Oxford, with return service operating until late evening. A change at Reading may be necessary. Service is reduced on Sundays and holidays.

By car, Oxford is 57 miles northwest of London via the A-40 and M-40 highways.

The Bridge of Sighs

LINKS:

If you're traveling from point to point instead of making daytrips from London, Oxford offers direct rail service to **Winchester** and **Southampton,** as well as buses to **Woodstock.** By changing trains once, you can easily reach such places as **Portsmouth, Salisbury, Windsor, Bath,** and **Stratford-upon-Avon.** All of these are described elsewhere in the book, and can just as readily be reached by car.

PRACTICALITIES

Oxford can be visited all year round, although it is less hectic and more accessible during the winter months between mid-October and March. The Ashmolean Museum is closed on Mondays and a few holidays, while some of the sights have shorter hours on Sundays. The local **Tourist Information Centre,** phone (0865) 726-871, is on St. Aldate's, just south of Carfax. You might want to ask them about their special-interest guided walking tours, or about renting a bicycle in town. Oxford is the county town of **Oxfordshire,** and has a **population** of about 114,000.

FOOD AND DRINK:

A few choice pubs and restaurants are:

Elizabeth (84 St. Aldate's, near Christ Church) Excellent Continental cuisine, with an outstanding wine cellar. For reservations phone (0865) 242-230. X: Mon. $$$

La Sorbonne (130a High St., east of Carfax) A long-established restaurant with classical French cuisine. X: holidays. $$$

Casa Blanca (upstairs in the Covered Market on High St., just east of Carfax) Traditional and colonial French cuisine. $$

Brown's (9 Woodstock Rd., west of University Parks) Very popular place serving spaghetti, burgers, salads, and the like along with loud music. $

Turf Tavern (4 Bath Pl., near the Bridge of Sighs) A pub in a 13th-century building on a small alleyway, with courtyard gardens. Good lunches. $

Bear Inn (Alfred St. at Bear Lane, by Christ Church) A traditional university pub in a 13th-century inn, with light meals. $

Munchy Munchy (6 Park End St., 2 blocks southeast of the train station) Spicy Malaysian and vegetarian dishes in a simple setting. X: Sun., Mon. $

SUGGESTED TOUR:

Leaving the **train station** (1), you have a choice of either walking or taking a bus or taxi to Carfax (2), a bit over a half-mile away. If you choose to walk, follow Park End Street past the **Oxford Canal.** This historic waterway was built in 1790 to provide transportation between London and Birmingham, using the River Thames from here to the capital. Until the development of the railways, it played a very important role in England's Industrial Revolution and is still navigable, being quite popular with pleasure boaters today. Look down it to the right to see the scanty remains of **Oxford Castle,** which dates from Norman times.

Continue on New Road and Queen Street to **Carfax** (2), whose name derives from the Latin *Quatre Vois,* or four ways. This crossing is the hub of Oxford. The **tower** in its northwest corner is all that remains of the 14th-century Church of St. Martin, and may be climbed from March through October for a good view of the famed "Dreaming Spires." The tourist office is just a few steps to the south, on St. Aldate's.

Cross the intersection and walk down High Street, locally known as "The High," passing the 18th-century **Covered Market** with its colorful food stalls. When you get to Catte Street, turn left into Radcliffe Square and enter the **University Church of St. Mary the Virgin** (3). While the main body of the church dates from the 15th century, its **tower** is late

The Radcliffe Camera from St. Mary's Church Tower

13th. A relatively easy climb to the top of this will allow you to see in advance the route of the walk to come.

Leaving the church, you are now facing the **Radcliffe Camera** (4), a massive domed building from 1737 that serves as a reading room for the Bodleian Library. To the left is Brasenose College, named after the 14th-century "brazen-nosed" doorknocker in its dining hall. Step into its quad for a look around.

At the far end of the square is the ***Bodleian Library** (5), the oldest in the world, originally founded in 1450 and entitled by law to a copy of every book published in the United Kingdom. It has millions of them scattered between this and a newer building on Broad Street. Walk through it, stopping to examine some of the unusual exhibits and manuscripts, which may be seen on Mondays through Fridays from 9 a.m. to 5 p.m., and on Saturdays from 9 a.m. to 12:30 p.m. To one side of its courtyard is the 15th-century ***Divinity School,** which has one of the most beautiful stone-vaulted ceilings anywhere.

A doorway leads to the ***Sheldonian Theatre,** a magnificent auditorium designed by Sir Christopher Wren in 1669 to serve the secular ceremonial needs of the university. You can usually visit this, as well as climb up into its octagonal cupola for a nice view, on Mondays through Saturdays from 10 a.m. to 12:45 p.m. and 2–4:45 p.m. (closes at 3:45 p.m. in winter). Adjacent to this is the interesting **Museum of the History of Science,** which displays early scientific instruments and

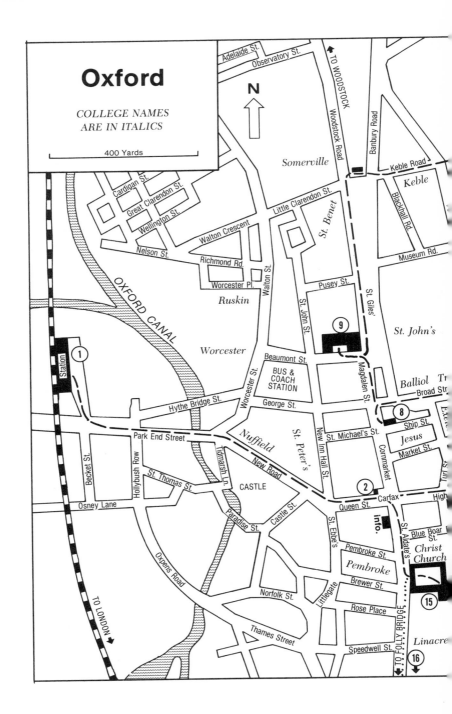

Oxford

COLLEGE NAMES ARE IN ITALICS

400 Yards

N

TO WOODSTOCK

Adelaide St.
Observatory St.

Woodstock Road

Banbury Road

Keble Road

Somerville

Little Clarendon St.

Cardigan St.
Great Clarendon St.
Wellington St.
Walton Crescent
Nelson St.
Richmond Rd.
Worcester Pl.

Walton St.

St. Benet

Keble

Blackhall Rd.

Museum Rd.

Pusey St.

St. John St.

St. Giles'

St. John's

Ruskin

Worcester

OXFORD CANAL

Station

1

Beaumont St.

BUS & COACH STATION

George St.

Hythe Bridge St.

Worcester St.

9

Balliol   *Tr*

Broad Str.

Magdalen St.

St. John's

8

Ship St.

St. Michael's St.

Jesus

Market St.

Cornmarket

Nuffield

New Road

St. Peter's

New Inn Hall St.

2

Carfax

Queen St.

High

Park End Street

Becket St.

Hollybush Row

St. Thomas St.

Osney Lane

Tidmarsh Ln.

CASTLE

Castle St.

Paradise St.

St. Ebbe's

Info.

St. Aldate's

Blue Boar St.

Christ Church

Pembroke St.

Pembroke

Brewer St.

Norfolk St.

Littlegate

Rose Place

15

Oxpens Road

Thames Street

Speedwell St.

TO FOLLY BRIDGE

Linacre

16

TO LONDON

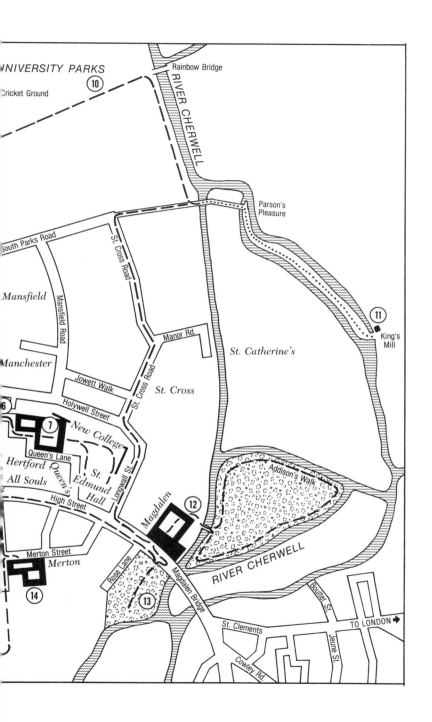

related objects. It is open on Mondays through Fridays, from 10:30 a.m. to 1 p.m. and 2:30–4 p.m.

Exit this complex of old buildings and stroll down New College Lane, with its famous **Bridge of Sighs** (6) linking two parts of Hertford College. Pass under it and amble into ***New College** (7), which is anything but new. Founded in the late 14th century by William of Wykeham, the bishop of Winchester, it has changed very little in the past 500 years. To the left of its unpretentious entrance are the cloisters, alive with a special feel of the Middle Ages. Just beyond are the **gardens,** one of the most delightful spots in Oxford. There you will find a well-preserved section of the old city walls that predate the college itself. While at New College, you should also try to see its rather remarkable **chapel,** noted for a strong modern statue of *Lazarus* by Jacob Epstein, a painting of *St. James* by El Greco, and some excellent 14th-century stained glass. New College is usually open to visitors from 2–5 p.m. during terms, and from 11 a.m. to 5 p.m. during vacation. A nominal entrance fee is charged.

Return to the Bridge of Sighs and walk down Broad Street. To your left is the Clarendon Building, which houses university administrative offices, and the Old Ashmolean Building. Blackwell's Bookshop, across the street, is world famous and makes an interesting stop. A bit farther along, to the left, is the **Oxford Story** (8), an audio-visual "experience" that uses the latest in theatrical technology to re-create eight centuries of Oxford life. It is open daily from 9 a.m. to 5 p.m., closing later in July and August.

Coming to Cornmarket, turn left for a look at **St. Michael's Church,** whose tower, dating from before 1050, was once part of the old city walls. You can climb it between 10 a.m. and 5 p.m., but not during services, on Christmas, or after 4 p.m. in winter.

Now follow Magdalen Street and make a left on Beaumont Street. Just a few steps down this is the renowned ***Ashmolean Museum** (9), the oldest public museum in Britain. In 1659 one Elias Ashmole received as a gift "twelve carts of curious things" from an incurable collector named Tradescant. To these he added his own similar collection and offered it all to the university on the condition that it erect a suitable building to house them. Since then, the acquisitions multiplied until they outgrew the Old Ashmolean and were moved in 1845 to the present structure. The collections are certainly eclectic enough. Along with the Leonardos, Raphaels, and Michelangelos; the French Impressionists; the Rubens and Rembrandts; the Hogarths and Constables; are displayed all sort of archaeological and historical curios, including the lantern Guy Fawkes carried when he tried to blow up Parliament in 1605; several mummies, ancient coins, and musical instruments. You will need at least an hour to sample this treasure. The

Punting on the River Cherwell

museum is open on Tuesdays through Saturdays, from 10 a.m. to 4 p.m.; and on Sundays from 2–4 p.m.

At this point you could cut the tour short by returning on Magdalen Street and following Cornmarket and High Street to Magdalen College (12). An enjoyable **two-mile walk** *through lovely parkland awaits those who continue on instead.*

Returning to the corner, make a left up St. Giles' until it becomes Woodstock Road. Cross the street and pass through the yard of the 13th-century St. Giles' Church, then cross Banbury Road and follow straight ahead on Keble Road. On your right is the supremely Victorian Keble College. Enter the **University Parks** (10) and follow the map past the Cricket Grounds where, if you're lucky, a match may be in progress. When you get to the Rainbow Bridge turn right and follow the banks of the River Cherwell. The walk becomes more and more picturesque as you approach Parson's Pleasure. If the weather is fine, you may see students slowly punting along the water, stopping here and there in secluded spots to enjoy a picnic. A delightful side trip can be made by following the path to the ancient **King's Mill** (11). Return to town via St. Cross Road and Longwall Street, continuing on to the most beautiful college at Oxford.

*Magdalen College (12), pronounced *Maudlen*, was built during the 15th century and has long been among the best-endowed at Oxford. Its more than 100 acres include lawns, gardens, water walks, and a private deer park. There is a small admission for entry, which is made from High Street. The adjacent **bell tower** is perhaps the town's most famous landmark. Be sure to cross the small footbridge for a refreshing stroll along Addison's Walk.

Back on High Street, turn left across Magdalen Bridge for a lovely view. If you would like to try your hand at **punting** (and are not afraid of getting wet), the boats may be rented by the hour at the foot of the bridge. The **Botanic Garden** (13), opposite, has been an inviting place to relax since 1621, especially since it's free.

Return along High Street to Magpie Lane and turn left. At its end, to the left, is the entrance to ***Merton College** (14), generally considered to be the oldest at Oxford, having been transferred here from Sussex in 1274. Its picturesque Mob Quad of 1308, Treasury of 1274, and Chapel of 1294 are the most interesting features.

Now follow straight ahead to the cricket field and turn right to the entrance of Oxford's largest college, ***Christ Church** (15). Again, there is a small admission charge. Don't miss the **Dining Hall** with its portraits of notable alumni, including 14 prime ministers and William Penn. It is reached via a staircase. The **Cathedral of Oxford,** one of the smallest in England, is on the east side of the huge Tom Quad. Its age is uncertain, but it predates the entire university. Return to Tom Quad and take a look at Tom Tower. Every night at five past nine its bell tolls a curfew of 101 strokes, one for each of the original students. But why five past nine? Because Oxford lies 1° 15' west of the prime meridian, its time is uniquely its own. Christ Church can usually be visited on Mondays through Saturdays, from 9 a.m. to 5 p.m.; and on Sundays from 1–5 p.m.

Exit onto St. Aldate's. From here you may want to make a little side trip to nearby **Folly Bridge** (16, off the map). Spanning the River Thames—called the *Isis* in Oxford—this bridge is the starting point for boat trips on the river, and is surrounded by attractive **pubs,** making it the perfect end to your walking tour.

Woodstock

Blenheim Palace is the attraction that brings thousands of visitors from all over the globe to the ancient village of Woodstock. One of the greatest of England's stately homes, it was built in the early 18th century as a fitting tribute to John Churchill, the first duke of Marlborough, who routed the French and Bavarians at the Battle of Blenheim in 1704. Before this, the vast property on which it sits was a royal hunting preserve. A manor house existed on the site since at least the time of Ethelred the Unready, everyone's favorite Saxon king. Henry I made great improvements, and his mansion remained a residence of royalty down through Tudor days. By the time Blenheim Palace was built, however, the old structure had almost fallen to ruin and all traces of it were demolished.

Woodstock itself originally grew up to service the royal manor. Several inns were established for this purpose, and today continue to provide hospitality to the many visitors who come to see Blenheim Palace. There is also a fine museum of rural life, an interesting church, and lovely old streets lined with picturesque buildings.

GETTING THERE:

Trains depart London's Paddington Station hourly for the one-hour trip to Oxford, where you change to a **local bus.** These leave at about half-hour intervals from the bus stop on Cornmarket, which can be reached by following the directions to Carfax on the Oxford trip. The ride takes less than 30 minutes. Bus service on Sundays and holidays is reduced, and may have to be taken from the nearby bus station on Beaumont Street instead. Trains return from Oxford to London until late evening.

By car, Woodstock is 64 miles northwest of London. Take the A-40 and M-40 to Oxford, then continue on the A-34 to Woodstock.

LINKS:

For those following an itinerary, Woodstock has good bus service to **Oxford,** where you can get a direct train to **Winchester** or **Southampton.** By changing trains it is also easy to reach **Portsmouth, Salisbury, Windsor, Bath,** or **Stratford-upon-Avon.** All of these destinations are featured elsewhere in this book, and can be readily reached by car as well.

PRACTICALITIES:

Blenheim Palace is open daily from mid-March through October. Fine weather will make this trip much more enjoyable. The local **Tourist Information Centre,** phone (0993) 811-038, is in the library on Hensington Road. Woodstock is in the county of **Oxfordshire,** and has a **population** of about 3,000.

FOOD AND DRINK:

The small village of Woodstock has quite a few inns, pubs, and restaurants. Some choices are:

Feathers (Market St.) Elegant dining with French overtones in a small hotel. Reservations suggested, phone (0993) 812-291. $$$

Bear Hotel (Park St.) Traditional English fare in the pub or dining room of a 16th-century inn. $$ and $$$

Marlborough Arms (Oxford St.) Dining at a small inn. $$

Brothertons Brasserie (High St.) Light meals with a creative touch. $

SUGGESTED TOUR:

Begin your visit at the **bus stop** (1) on Oxford Street opposite the Marlborough Arms Hotel. The **tourist office** (2) is located around the corner on Hensington Road. Follow the map down Market and Park streets to the entrance of the Blenheim Palace grounds. The **Triumphal Arch** (3), designed in 1723 by Nicholas Hawksmoor as a monument to the first duke of Marlborough, is a fitting introduction to so grandiose a place. On your right is a lake created in 1764 by the renowned landscape architect Lancelot "Capability" Brown.

*Blenheim Palace (4) has been continuously occupied by the dukes of Marlborough since it was begun by Sir John Vanbrugh in the early 18th century as a gift from Queen Anne. Sir Winston Churchill, grandson of the seventh duke, was born here in 1874 and is buried nearby at Bladon Church. There is an exhibition of his personal belongings in the palace, which remains the home of the present (11th) duke. To see its magnificent interior you must take one of the frequent guided tours, lasting about an hour. Blenheim Palace is open daily from mid-March through October, from 10:30 a.m. to 5:30 p.m.

Be sure to explore at least a part of the palace grounds after the tour is finished. Boat rides are usually available on the lake. The **Butterfly and Plant Center** (5), where exotic tropical butterflies live in a virtually natural habitat, is an exciting experience as well as a horticulturist's delight. You can get to it by miniature railway or on foot.

A very pleasant way to return to Woodstock is to follow the route on the map. The **Grand Bridge** (6), an extravagant span over what was

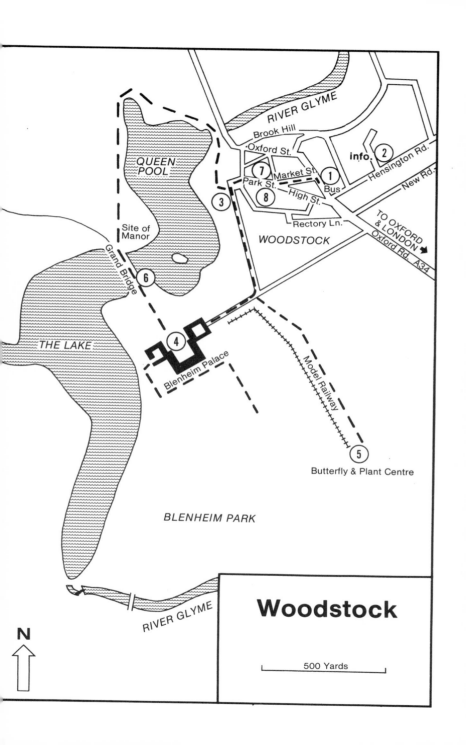

RIVER GLYME

Brook Hill

Oxford St.

QUEEN
POOL

info. ②

Hensington Rd.

⑦

Market St.

New Rd.

①

Park St.

Bus

③

High St.

⑧

Site of
Manor

Rectory Ln.

TO OXFORD
& LONDON

WOODSTOCK

Oxford Rd. A34

Grand Bridge

⑥

THE LAKE

④

Blenheim Palace

Model Railway

⑤

Butterfly & Plant Centre

BLENHEIM PARK

RIVER GLYME

N

Woodstock

500 Yards

Queen Pool at Blenheim

then only a creek, was part of Vanbrugh's original design. Most of it is now under water. The land just beyond it was the site of the old Woodstock Manor, for centuries a country residence for England's kings and queens.

Back in the village, stroll down Park Street and visit the small but interesting **Oxfordshire County Museum** (7), which features displays on local life through the centuries. It is open on Mondays through Fridays, from 10 a.m. to 5 p.m.; on Saturdays from 10 a.m. to 6 p.m.; and on Sundays from 2–6 p.m. During the winter it closes earlier. The **town stocks,** outside the museum, have holes for five legs. Was this a joke or did Woodstock have an unusual number of one-legged culprits? The **Church** (8) is often overlooked but is actually a fascinating study in changing styles, ranging from Norman to Perpendicular. Beyond this, the village offers several interesting shops and some very appealing **pubs** in which to relax.

*Stratford-upon-Avon

As someone once remarked, there's no business like show business. That, put simply, is what Stratford-upon-Avon is all about. The whole town is one vast theater, entertaining thousands of visitors a day. Despite this, it has miraculously managed to avoid the worst of tourism's trappings and still retains a quite genuine charm. Just about everyone who goes there enjoys the experience.

William Shakespeare was born in Stratford in 1564. This is also where he lived a great deal of his life and where he died in 1616. Many of the buildings associated with the Bard have been lovingly preserved and may be visited. The Royal Shakespeare Theatre, one of the greatest anywhere, is beautifully situated on the banks of the quiet Avon. There are several other attractions, some relating to Shakespeare and others not, but perhaps in the long run it is simply the atmosphere of this delightful old market town that is so memorable.

GETTING THERE:

Trains depart London's Paddington Station around 6 and 9 a.m. for Leamington Spa, perhaps requiring a change en route. At Leamington change to a local for Stratford-upon-Avon. The total journey takes about $2\frac{1}{2}$ hours, with return trains running until mid-evening. Service is poor or non-existent on Sundays and holidays.

"The Shakespeare Connection," a **train/coach** combination, leaves London's Euston Station every morning for Coventry, where you change to a special bus. The total ride takes about 2 hours. It is usually possible to make a late-night return on this *on performance days only* if you want to see a performance at the theater and first make a reservation with the coach operator. BritRail Passes cover the train portion only. Check the schedule in advance or with the coach operator, Guide Friday Ltd., at Stratford, phone (0789) 294-466.

Special Packages including rail and/or coach transportation, overnight accommodations, theater tickets, and dinner are available through travel agents in London and elsewhere.

By car, take the A-40 and M-40 to Oxford, then the A-34 to Stratford-upon-Avon, which is 96 miles northwest of London.

LINKS:

If you're traveling from point to point rather than making daytrips, Stratford offers easy rail connections to **Oxford, Winchester**, and **Southampton.** By making an additional change of trains you can readily reach **Portsmouth, Salisbury, Windsor,** or **Bath.** Those moving on to **Cambridge** or other areas in East Anglia can avoid returning to London by traveling via Birmingham. All of these destinations are described elsewhere in this book, and can just as easily be reached by car.

PRACTICALITIES:

The major sights in Stratford are open daily except Christmas and Boxing Day, with generally longer hours from April through September. Some minor attractions close on Sundays from November through March. A colorful **outdoor market** is held on Fridays at the intersection of Greenhill and Wood streets. The local **Tourist Information Centre** is at 1 High Street, phone (0789) 293-127. You might ask them about local **bicycle** rentals. Stratford is in the county of **Warwickshire**, and has a **population** of about 21,000.

FOOD AND DRINK:

Some outstanding restaurants and pubs are:

Box Tree (Waterside, in the theater) Classic food with a wonderful view of the Avon. Proper dress and reservations required, phone (0789) 293-226. X: when theater is closed. $$$

Shepherd's Restaurant (Sheep St., 2 blocks northwest of the theater) A lighter version of English country food, served with a garden view. $$

Hussain's (6a Chapel St., near New Place) Indian food, with tandoori specialties. $$

Slug and Lettuce (38 Guild St., near the Birthplace) A popular pub and restaurant combo with garden tables available. $ and $$

Black Swan (Waterside St., near the theater) Also known as the Dirty Duck, very famous with actors. Pub and restaurant. $ and $$

River Terrace (Waterside, in the theater) Self-service cafeteria. X: when theater is closed. $

Café Natural (Greenhill St., 3 blocks southwest of the Birthplace) Vegetarian and other healthy foods in cheerful surroundings. $

Shakespeare's Birthplace

SUGGESTED TOUR:

Leave the **train station** (1) and follow the map to that most logical of beginnings, ***Shakespeare's Birthplace** (2). This is actually two houses joined together, the eastern part having been his father's shop and the western half the family residence. To the left of it is the modern **Shakespeare Centre**, which houses exhibitions, a library, and a study center. Enter this and wander through the delightful **garden**, complete with flowers, shrubs, and trees mentioned in his plays. The well-marked trail then takes you into the old house itself, where you will visit the bedroom in which Shakespeare was presumably born on or about April 23, 1564. The entire house is furnished as it might have been in his youth, including an interesting period kitchen and an oak-beamed living room. Visits may be made on any day except Christmas and Boxing Day (December 26). On Mondays through Saturdays it is open from 9 a.m. to 6 p.m., closing at 5 p.m. in October and 4:30 p.m. from November through March. On Sundays from April through October it is open from 10 a.m. to 6 p.m., closing at 5 p.m. in October; and from November through March from 1:30–4:30 p.m. A reduced-price joint ticket covering all of the "Shakespeare Properties" is available.

Return on Henley Street and continue on to the **Tourist Information Centre** (3) in the former home of Shakespeare's daughter, Judith.

Walk down Bridge Street and turn right at Waterside. The **World of Shakespeare** at the **Heritage Theatre** (4) provides a good, if somewhat commercialized, introduction to Elizabethan England. This multimedia extravaganza surrounds the audience with 25 stage sets depicting such events as the London plague and Queen Elizabeth I's epic journey to Kenilworth, all brought to life through the clever use of sound, light, and special effects. The show runs continuously every half-hour. It is open daily from 9:30 a.m. to 5:30 p.m.

Stroll through **Bancroft Gardens**, going past the canal basin and locks. Overlooking this pleasant scene is the **Shakespeare Memorial**, a life-size bronze statue of the Bard with figures of Hamlet, Lady Macbeth, Falstaff, and Prince Hal. Continue on and cross the footbridge over the Avon. This span was formerly used by a horse-drawn tramway that once connected Stratford with Moreton-in-Marsh. From here you will have a beautiful view of the river and the modern Royal Shakespeare Theatre. The 15th-century **Clopton Bridge** with its 14 arches, to the left, still carries heavy traffic.

Return and walk over to the **Royal Shakespeare Theatre** (5). Built in 1932 to replace a smaller 19th-century theater that burned down, its performances of Shakespearian plays are world famous. Although tickets should be booked well in advance, they are frequently available on the day of performance. The attached **RSC Collection** has interesting mementos of theatrical personalities and other Shakespeariana. You can ask here about **backstage tours** of the theater. Near this is the new **Swan Theatre**, specially designed to present plays by Shakespeare's contemporaries and playwrights influenced by him.

Thirsty travelers can refresh themselves at the famous **Black Swan Pub**, a.k.a. the *Dirty Duck*, closeby on Waterside. From here, a path leads along the river's edge, passing the **Brass Rubbing Centre** where you can make your own inexpensive souvenir of Stratford.

Continue on to ***Holy Trinity Church** (6), the scene of Shakespeare's baptism in 1564 and burial in 1616. Copies of the church registers showing both events are on display. His **tomb** is inscribed with the famous lines ending in *"and curst be he that moves my bones."* There are a few other interesting items in this 14th-century church, particularly the humorous **misericords** under the choir seats.

Hall's Croft (7) on Old Town is the next stop. This splendid Tudor house was the home of Shakespeare's eldest daughter, Susanna, and her husband, Dr. John Hall. Its interior is well worth visiting for a glimpse of how a prosperous doctor's family lived in those days. Be sure to see the dispensary with its surgical instruments, herbs, and potions. A stroll through the **garden** in the rear is a delight. Hall's Croft is open during the same times as the Birthplace (2), except that it is closed on Sundays from November through March.

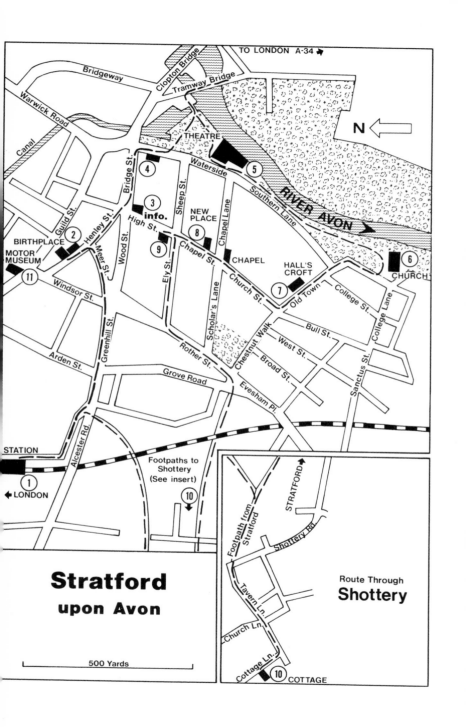

TO LONDON A-34

Bridgeway

Warwick Road

Canal

Clopton Bridge

Tramway Bridge

THEATRE

Waterside

N

④

Bridge St.

③

info.

Sheep St.

NEW PLACE

Chapel Lane

Southern Lane

RIVER AVON

②

Guild St.

Henley St.

High St.

⑧

⑨

Chapel St.

CHAPEL

⑤

⑥

CHURCH

BIRTHPLACE

MOTOR MUSEUM

⑪

Windsor St.

Meer St.

Wood St.

Ely St.

Scholar's Lane

Church St.

HALL'S CROFT

⑦

Old Town

College St.

College Lane

Arden St.

Greenhill St.

Rother St.

Grove Road

Chestnut Walk

West St.

Bull St.

Broad St.

Evesham Pl.

Sanctus St.

STATION

Footpaths to
Shottery
(See insert)

① LONDON

⑩

Stratford
upon Avon

500 Yards

Footpath from Stratford

STRATFORD

Shottery Rd.

Route Through
Shottery

Tavern Ln.

Church Ln.

Cottage Ln.

⑩ COTTAGE

The Royal Shakespeare Theatre

Turn right on Church Street and pass, on the right, the **King Edward VI Grammar School,** where the young Shakespeare learned his "small Latin and less Greek." Adjoining this is the 15th-century **Guild Chapel** with its noted fresco of the *Last Judgement* above the chancel arch. Just beyond, on Chapel Street, is the site of Shakespeare's own home, **New Place** (8), which he purchased in 1597 and in which he died in 1616. Its last owner demolished it in 1759, and today only the foundations and the **garden** remain. These can be reached by going through the **New Place Museum** in the former home of Thomas Nash, who was married to Shakespeare's granddaughter, Elizabeth Hall. It is open during the same times as the Birthplace (2), except on Sundays from November through March.

Harvard House (9) has nothing to do with the Bard, but a lot to do with Harvard University, which owns it. This outstanding example of a half-timbered Elizabethan structure was the home of the mother of John Harvard, whose donations helped found the famous institution in the U.S.A. That is why the Stars and Stripes fly from its flagpole. The richly decorated interior may be visited on Mondays through Saturdays, from 9 a.m. to 1 p.m. and 2–6 p.m.; and on Sundays from 2–6 p.m. Adjacent to this are two other buildings of similar style and age, one of them being the well-known **Garrick Inn**, named for the actor David Garrick who organized the first Shakespeare Festival here

Anne Hathaway's Cottage

in 1769. This is a great place to stop for a break.

While in Stratford you will probably want to see ***Anne Hathaway's Cottage** (10), certainly one of the prettiest (and most visited) sights in England. The home of Shakespeare's wife before their marriage, this 16th-century thatched-roof farmhouse is set in gorgeous surroundings. The furnishings are fairly authentic as the cottage remained in her family until late Victorian times. Located in the nearby hamlet of Shottery, about one mile from Stratford, it is easily reached by bus from Bridge Street, by car or bike, or better still, on foot via a country path that begins at Evesham Place. The route is well marked and is shown on the map and its insert. The cottage is open during the same times as the Birthplace (2). Return by way of the other path to Alcester Road.

There is one remaining sight in town that might interest you. This is the **Stratford Motor Museum** (11) on Shakespeare Street, near the Birthplace. A sumptuous collection of exotic cars from the 1920s and 1930s, it has no connection with Shakespeare but is still pure theater. It is open daily from 9:30 a.m. to 6 p.m., with shorter hours in winter. From here it is only a short stroll back to the station.

St. Albans

The first Christian martyr in Britain was a Roman soldier named Alban, who was beheaded for embracing the faith and sheltering a persecuted priest. The spot where this happened is now the town of St. Albans, which overlooks the site of the important Roman city of *Verulamium.* An abbey in his memory was erected during the 8th century by King Offa II of Mercia. Following the Norman Conquest this was rebuilt and eventually became the great cathedral that it is today.

Verulamium itself died out after the fall of the empire, and slowly fell to ruin. Many of its stones were used to build the cathedral, but surprising amounts still remain in what is now parkland. There is a Roman theater, the only one of its kind in Britain, a well-preserved hypocaust, and large sections of the original walls. A splendid collection of archaeological finds is displayed in the Verulamium Museum. The town of St. Albans, on the other side of the River Ver, has a long and colorful history. Its medieval streets are lined with ancient structures which, added to the cathedral and remains of the Roman city, make this a satisfying destination for an easily accomplished daytrip.

GETTING THERE:
Trains leave London's King's Cross ThamesLink Station (connected by tunnel to the regular King's Cross Station) very frequently for the 25-minute run to St. Albans. Many of these can be boarded earlier at London's Farringdon, Moorgate, Blackfriars, and London Bridge stations. Service is somewhat reduced on Sundays and holidays. Return trains run until late evening.

By car, St. Albans is 20 miles north of London via the M-1 highway to Junction 6.

LINKS:
For those following an itinerary, St. Albans is difficult to reach by train without going through London, although it is possible to get there from **Stratford-upon-Avon** via Birmingham, Leicester, and Bedford. Many of the trains to and from London also go directly to Sevenoaks for the **Knole** trip, **Brighton**, or **Guildford.** All of these destinations are featured elsewhere in this book, and can also be readily reached by car.

St. Albans Cathedral

PRACTICALITIES:

Most of the sights are open daily throughout the year, with some closing or having reduced hours on Sundays and holidays. Open-air **markets** are held in St. Peter's Street on Wednesdays and Saturdays. The local **Tourist Information Centre**, phone (0727) 726-871, is in the Town Hall near the Market Place. St. Albans is in the county of **Hertfordshire**, and has a **population** of about 77,000.

FOOD AND DRINK:

There is no shortage of pubs and restaurants, of which some choices are:

Langtry's (London Rd., a bit east of the cathedral) Makes a specialty of seafood. X: Mon. lunch, Sun. $$$

La Province (13 George St., by the cathedral) French provincial cuisine in pleasant surroundings. $$

Koh-I-Noor (8 George St., by the cathedral) Both Indian and English food. $

Ye Olde Fighting Cocks (Abbey Mill Lane, by the river near Verulamium) A very ancient inn with substantial pub lunches. $

SUGGESTED TOUR:

Leave the **train station** (1) and follow Victoria Street to Chequer Street. This half-mile walk can be avoided by taking a bus. Once there, cut through a passageway to the **Market Place** and turn left. French Row retains much of its medieval appearance, including the 14th-century Fleur de Lys Inn where King John II of France was imprisoned following the Battle of Poitiers in 1356. Just beyond this is the **Clock Tower** (2), a flint-and-rubble structure of 1412, which is one of the few remaining curfew towers in the country. It may be climbed on weekends, from 10:30 a.m. to 5 p.m., for a good view.

Cross High Street and pass through the rebuilt Waxhouse Gateway, where pilgrims going to the shrine of St. Alban once bought their candles. From here a path leads to the west front of the **Cathedral** (3), one of the largest in Britain. An abbey church dedicated to St. Alban stood here since Saxon times, but the present structure was begun in the 11th century by the Normans and incorporates many later additions. It did not become a cathedral until 1877, when a new diocese was created. The interior is rather plain but graceful. A good deal of the original **wall paintings**, once whitewashed by the Puritans, have been restored to their former splendor. Be sure to see *St. Alban's Shrine** in the chapel behind the altar screen. Dating from the 14th century, this was later destroyed and rebuilt in 1872, when over 2,000 of its broken fragments were carefully pieced together.

Leave the cathedral and stroll past the **Abbey Gateway** of 1361, at one time the town jail and now occupied by St. Albans School, founded in the 10th century. Abbey Mill Lane leads to the site of Roman Verulamium. The **Fighting Cocks Inn**, by the river, was a notorious center of cockfighting and claims to be one of the oldest pubs in England. It is also a fine place to stop for lunch or just a drink.

Cross the bridge and explore the remains of ancient **Verulamium**. The importance of this city is made obvious by the fact that it was the only town in Britain to be declared a *municipum*, a status that conferred Roman citizenship on its inhabitants. Founded shortly after the conquest of A.D. 43 and sacked by Boadicea in A.D. 61, it rose to become the third-largest city, after London and Colchester, in Roman Britain. The town flourished until about 410, when it fell into decay, and what was left after the stones were salvaged was slowly covered by earth.

Continue on past remains of the Roman walls to the **Hypocaust** (4), a preserved mosaic floor and heating system of a large house, now protected *in situ* by a modern structure. A path leads to the **Verulamium Museum** (5), which displays some of the greatest treasures of Roman Britain. These include jewelry, household utensils, pottery, wall paintings, a bronze figure, and many other fascinating objects

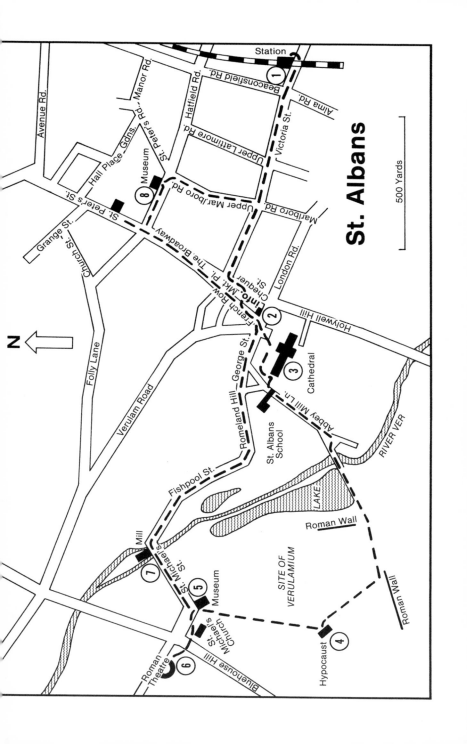

St. Albans

N

500 Yards

discovered during the excavations. The museum is open on Mondays through Saturdays from 10 a.m. to 5:30 p.m.; and on Sundays from 2–5:30 p.m.; with shorter hours in winter.

St. Michael's Church, near the museum entrance, was begun in 948 and still retains considerable traces of its original Saxon work. Inside, there is a monument to Sir Francis Bacon, who is buried there.

Walk across the road to the **Roman Theatre** (6), built to accommodate a crowd of 1,600 spectators. Semicircular in shape, it is the only one of its type in Britain. Although only the lower walls remain, visualizing what it must have looked like is not too difficult. It is open daily from 10 a.m. to 5 p.m.

Return to St. Michael's Street and turn left. At the River Ver is the **Kingsbury Water Mill** (7), which operated until 1936. There was a mill on this site since Saxon times and the present one, restored in 1970, is now a delightful museum and tea room. Visits may be made on Wednesdays through Sundays, from 11 a.m. to 6 p.m., opening at noon on Sundays and closing at 5 p.m. in winter.

Follow the map past wonderful old houses on Fishpool Street, Romeland Hill, and George Street. Turn left on French Row and continue up St. Peter's Street to St. Peter's Church. A right on Hatfield Road leads to the **City Museum** (8), whose exhibits concentrate on local crafts and industries, bygones, natural history, and regional archaeology. It is open on Mondays through Saturdays from 10 a.m. to 5 p.m., and admission is free. From here it is only a short walk back to the station.

*Cambridge

Cambridge, one of the most beautiful towns in Europe, has long been a favorite daytrip destination. For nearly 700 years its colleges have vied with one another for architectural as well as academic excellence. Taking full advantage of its delightful riverside location, it has developed an ambiance that sets it apart from any other college town in England. Inevitably a comparison with Oxford must be made, but they are actually two very different places. Cambridge is serene, dreamy in character; while its older and larger rival is more intense, more worldly. Given the chance, you should really see both.

The site of Cambridge was important in ancient times, being the only practical place to cross the River Cam for miles around. In the centuries preceding the Roman conquest, a Celtic settlement was established just north of the river. This was taken over by the Romans and enlarged, spreading south after their departure. When the Normans came they built a castle, long vanished, on the site of the Roman camp. By the time of the Domesday Book, 1086, the town had some 400 houses and was already a trading center. From Cambridge northwards the River Cam, then called the Granta, was navigable all the way to the North Sea, a factor of vital importance in a time of poor land communications.

Scholars began to gather here about 1209 after being run out of Oxford by angry townspeople. Some of them stayed on and by 1284 the first proper college, Peterhouse, was founded. This was quickly followed by others, a university evolved, and the town flourished. New colleges are still being added, with a present total of 31 not including those independent of the university.

It is impossible to see all of Cambridge in a single day. The suggested tour was designed to include only the most notable highlights of the colleges, some of the town, a few museums, gardens, and the famous Backs along the river. Please remember that all of the colleges are private, and that admission to them is a courtesy, not a right.

GETTING THERE:

Trains leave London's Liverpool Street Station hourly for the one-hour ride to Cambridge. There are also locals taking $1\frac{1}{2}$ hours. Return trains run until late evening, and service is somewhat reduced on Sundays and holidays. In addition, there is good direct service from London's King's Cross Station as well.

By car, Cambridge is 55 miles north of London via the M-11.

LINKS:

For those traveling from point to point rather than making day-trips, Cambridge offers direct rail service to **Bury St. Edmunds**, and direct buses to **Oxford**. By changing trains once you can easily reach **Stratford-upon-Avon** (via Birmingham) or **Colchester** (via Ipswich). Rail travel to the other destinations described in this book requires making connections in London. They can all, of course, be readily reached by car.

PRACTICALITIES:

Cambridge may be visited in any season, although many of the colleges are closed to the public during student exams between May and mid-June. Most museums are closed on Mondays. The local **Tourist Information Centre**, phone (0223) 322-640, is on Wheeler Street just south of the Market Square. You might ask them about renting a **bicycle**, a nice way to explore this flat countryside. The town is in the county of **Cambridgeshire** and has a **population** of about 88,000.

FOOD AND DRINK:

Cambridge has a wide selection of restaurants and pubs, especially in the budget range. Some choices are:

Don Pasquale (12 Market Hill, by the Market Place) An upstairs Italian restaurant and a downstairs pizzeria. $$ and $

Anchor Pub (Silver St., by the Mill Pond) An upstairs restaurant and a downstairs pub. $$ and $

Browns (23 Trumpington St., opposite the Fitzwilliam Museum) Fresh, simple food in cheerful surroundings. $

Pentagon (Art Theatre, 6 St. Edward's Passage, a block east of King's College Chapel) A self-service place with a good salad bar. X: Sun. $

Nettles (5 St. Edward's Passage, a block east of King's College Chapel) Wholesome health and vegetarian dishes, mostly to take out. X: Sun. $

Hobb's Pavilion (Parker's Piece, 5 blocks southeast of the Market Square) Crêpes and other light meals. X: Sun., Mon. $

Fitzwilliam Museum Café (in the museum) An unusually good museum cafeteria. X: Sun., Mon. $

SUGGESTED TOUR:

Leaving the **train station** (1), you can either walk or take a bus or taxi to **Market Square** (2), a distance of about a mile. If you walk, just follow the map up Regent and St. Andrew's streets, then make a left on Petty Curry to the square. A colorful **outdoor market** is held here on Mondays through Saturdays.

The Ceiling of King's College Chapel

Great St. Mary's Church, next to the square, is the University Church. You can enter it and climb to the top of its tower for an excellent view.

Make a left onto King's Parade and enter the Great Court of **King's College** (3). Founded by Henry VI in 1441, the school originally occupied a site directly to the north. Henry's ambitions grew, however, and what was then the center of medieval Cambridge was ruthlessly torn down to make way for a monumental college. At that point the War of the Roses intervened and Henry was deposed, leaving only part of the chapel finished and the rest an open field. It was another 280 years before any new buildings were erected. In the meantime, the chapel was completed during the reign of Henry VIII. This is, quite simply, the finest building in Cambridge and arguably the greatest Gothic structure in England.

Enter the ***Chapel** and look up at the miraculous fan vaulting on the ceiling, then at the dark wooden choir screen, and finally at the sheer expanse of glass. The total effect is breathtaking. Stroll through the choir and examine the **Adoration of the Magi* by Rubens that hangs behind the altar. An experience never to be forgotten is to return in the late afternoon for Evensong, a service held daily during terms, except on Mondays.

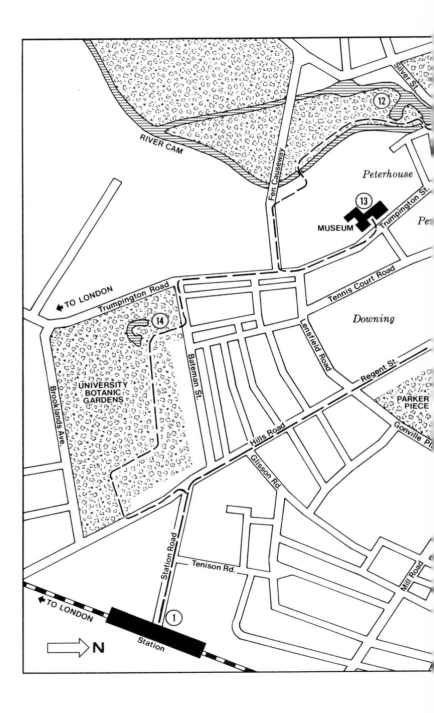

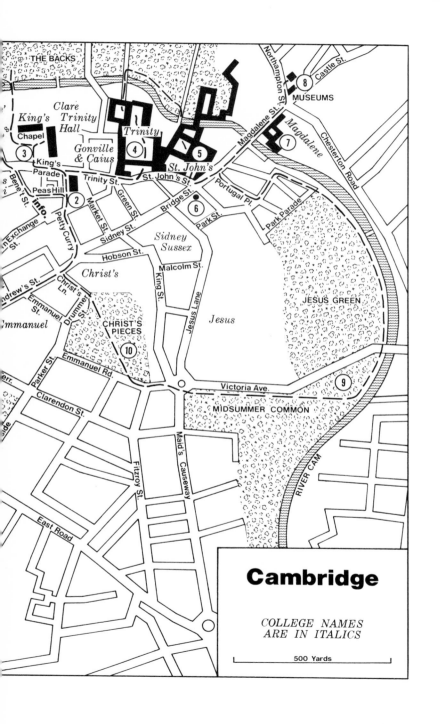

THE BACKS

King's
Chapel

Clare
Trinity
Hall

Trinity

Gonville
& Caius

King's
Parade

PeasHill

Trinity St.

St. John's

St. John's St.

MarketSt.

GreenSt.

SidneySt.

HobsonSt.

Bridge St.

Park St.

Portugal Pl.

Park Parade

Sidney
Sussex

Christ's

Christ's
Ln.

Andrew's St.

Emmanuel
St.

Emmanuel

Drummer St.

Malcolm St.

King St.

Jesus Lane

Jesus

CHRIST'S
PIECES

Emmanuel Rd.

Parker St.

Clarendon St.

East Road

Fitzroy St.

Maid's Causeway

Victoria Ave.

MIDSUMMER COMMON

JESUS GREEN

RIVER CAM

Northampton St.

Magdalene St.

Magdalene

Castle St.

MUSEUMS

Chesterton Road

Bene't St.

PettyCurry

Exchange
St.

info.

3

2

4

5

6

7

8

9

10

Cambridge

COLLEGE NAMES
ARE IN ITALICS

500 Yards

Leaving the chapel, walk straight ahead past the Fellows' Building of 1724 and turn right into the ***Backs**, those idyllic gardens and meadows along the River Cam that give Cambridge its special character. Cross the bridge for your first sight of this, then return to King's Parade and turn left. Passing the Senate House and Gonville & Caius College, continue up Trinity Street to Trinity College.

With over 800 students, **Trinity** (4) is the largest college in Cambridge. It was founded by Henry VIII in 1546 and has long had connections with royalty. The Great Gate leads into the **Great Court**, so vast that the lack of symmetry along its sides is hardly noticeable. An extremely different atmosphere permeates the cloistered Nevile's Court, reached by passing through the hall at the west end. The magnificent ***Library**, built by Sir Christopher Wren in 1676, completes the west façade of the cloister. Containing such treasures as early editions of Shakespeare and the original manuscript of *Winnie-the-Pooh*, it may usually be visited on Mondays through Fridays, from noon to 2 p.m.; and on Saturdays from 12:30–2:30 p.m. Continue through a third court, turn right to the Backs, and cross a footbridge over the Cam.

Follow the map and cross another bridge into **St. John's College** (5). To your left is the famous **Bridge of Sighs** that connects two halves of the college. Continue to the first courtyard and cross the bridge into New Court, a Victorian Gothic structure of 1831. Beyond this lies the contemporary Cripps Building, which makes good use of the river. Return over the Bridge of Sighs and stroll through two more courts to the main entrance at the junction of Bridge Street and St. John's Street.

The fascinating **Round Church** (6) of 1130 was inspired by the Holy Sepulchre in Jerusalem. It is one of the very few medieval circular churches surviving in England. Restored during the 19th century, it still conveys the character of early Norman architecture.

Now follow Bridge Street across the Cam and turn right into **Magdalene College** (7). Pronounced *Maudlen,* it was founded in 1542, using the buildings of a former Benedictine monks' hostel. Samuel Pepys was a student here from 1650 to 1653 and left behind his collection of books, including an original manuscript of his immortal diary. These can be seen, kept in Pepys' unique bookshelves, in the library facing the second court on Mondays through Saturdays, from 11:30 a.m. to 12:30 p.m. and 2:30–3:30 p.m., with shorter hours off-season.

Magdalene Street is lined with restored 16th- and 17th-century houses. Turn right and follow it to the **Folk Museum** (8), which features re-created room settings of bygone years as well as other memorabilia relating to Cambridge's past. It is open on Tuesdays through Saturdays from 10:30 a.m. to 5 p.m.; and on Sundays from 2:30–4:30 p.m. While there, you might want to stop in at the famous **Kettle's Yard**, an important collection of modern art in a nearby house on

Punting on the Cam

Northampton Street.

At this point you can skip ahead to Queens' College (11) by following the map, or continue on for a lovely walk along the river and through a park. To do this, turn left into Portugal Place, make another left at New Park Street, and a right on Thompson's Lane.

Stroll along the picturesque footpath by the river's edge. Once beyond Victoria Avenue turn right through **Midsummer Common** (9). Crossing the Four Lamps intersection, walk down Short Street and into a pleasant park called **Christ's Pieces** (10). Arriving at Drummer Street, continue on Christ's Lane, then turn right to Petty Curry and return to Market Square (2). A left here leads down Peas Hill to Bene't Street. Make a right and then a left onto Trumpington Street. In another block turn right and pass through St. Catherine's College.

Across Queens' Lane is the imposing entrance to ***Queens' College** (11), often regarded as the most charming in Cambridge. Little changed over the centuries, Queens' appears today much as it did in the 15th century when it was founded by two separate queens (thus the spelling). Enter the medieval Old Court, built in 1449, and pass through the Cloister Court of 1495. From here cross the so-called **Mathematical Bridge**, a curious wooden span over the Cam, first erected in 1749 without the use of nails or other fasteners. Unfortunately, some one took it apart to "discover" its secret, and nobody has ever been able to put it back together correctly. The present bridge is a near copy, except that its builders cheated by using bolts.

Turn right and stroll down along the river to the Grove, a garden with lovely views. Returning to the Cloister Court, walk through the Walnut Tree Court and the Old Court, then exit onto Queens' Lane. If you have had enough walking by now, you could go directly to the Fitzwilliam Museum (13) or return to Market Square (2) and take a bus or taxi to the station.

If you choose to carry on, make a right on Silver Street and a left at Laundress Lane. This leads to the **Mill Pond** (12), where punts (flat-bottomed boats) may be rented for a cruise on the Cam. It looks easy, but inexperienced punters often wind up in the drink, so be careful!

Now walk along the path, crossing a footbridge to the left, and turn right to the Fen Causeway. Follow this to Trumpington Street. To the left is the ***Fitzwilliam Museum** (13), one of the most important art museums in England. Its collection ranges from ancient Egyptian to Impressionist art and includes, besides paintings, drawings, and sculpture, a vast assortment of armor, silver, porcelains, and manuscripts. You could easily spend the better part of a day here, but a quick tour can be done in an hour or so. The museum is open on Tuesdays through Saturdays from 10 a.m. to 5 p.m.; and on Sundays from 2:15–5 p.m. Not all of the galleries are open at the same time.

Now follow Trumpington Street to Bateman Street and turn left. To your right is the entrance of the **University Botanic Gardens** (14), a delightfully varied area devoted to research but open to the public on Mondays through Saturdays, from 8 a.m. to 6 p.m. or dusk, whichever is earlier; and on summer Sundays from 2:30–6:30 p.m. Stroll through it and exit onto Hills Road, which is close to the train station.

Bury St. Edmunds

Bury St. Edmunds has been called the nicest town in the world. An exaggeration perhaps, but this really is a delightful place to explore. The ruins of its great abbey are wonderfully picturesque, and Bury itself, spared the effects of industry, is an elegant reminder of what prosperous country towns were once like.

Its history began during the late 9th century when Edmund, the last king of the East Angles, was defeated by marauding Danes, shot full of arrows, and beheaded. Later made a saint, the martyr was buried at *Beodricesworth*, today's Burt St. Edmunds. An abbey was founded there in 945 and rebuilt by King Canute in 1021. For centuries this remained a place of holy pilgrimage. It was there that the English barons met in 1214 to demand that King John ratify the Magna Carta. In 1539, the great abbey was disbanded by Henry VIII and gradually became the romantic ruin that it is today.

GETTING THERE:

Trains depart London's Liverpool Street Station several times in the morning for Cambridge, where they connect with a local for Bury St. Edmunds. The total journey takes about 2 hours, with return trains operating until early evening. It is also possible to go by way of Ipswich. Service is greatly reduced on Sundays and holidays.

By car, Bury is 75 miles northeast of London. Take the M-11 and A-11 to Newmarket, then the A-45 into Bury.

LINKS:

If you're following an itinerary, Bury offers direct rail service to **Cambridge** and easy connections to **Colchester.** It is also possible to reach **Stratford-upon-Avon** by train via Peterborough and Birmingham. Rail travel to the other destinations in this book requires making connections in London. They can all, of course, be easily reached by car.

PRACTICALITIES:

Bury may be visited at any time, and is especially interesting on Wednesdays and Saturdays, when **outdoor markets** are held. The local **Tourist Information Centre**, phone (0284) 763-233, is at 6 Angel Hill, near the Abbey Gate. Bury is in the county of **Suffolk**, and has a **population** of about 30,000.

FOOD AND DRINK:

Bury is noted for its Greene King ales, especially their Abbot Ale. These are served, among other places, at **The Nutshell** on The Traverse, which claims to be England's smallest pub. Some good places to eat are:

The Vaults (in the Angel Hotel by the Abbey Gate) Traditional English fare in the vaults beneath an ancient inn. $$$

Suffolk Hotel (38 The Butter Market, near Moyse's Hall) Lunch in a former coaching inn, now a hotel. $$

Masons Arms (Whiting St., near the Guildhall) A favorite old pub with meals. $

SUGGESTED TOUR:

Leave the **train station** (1) and follow the map down Northgate Street to the **Abbey Gate** (2), erected in 1327 following an uprising of the townspeople. Stroll through the lovely Abbey Gardens to the 13th-century **Abbot's Bridge**, then walk along the River Lark to the ruins of the **Abbey** (3). A plaque marks the location of the high altar where in 1214 the assembled barons of England swore they would compel the despised King John to grant them their rights by signing the Magna Carta, which he finally did a year later at Runnymede. The largest surviving part of the 11th-century abbey is its **West Front**, now incorporated into a very strange row of houses. Walk over the ruined **Charnel House**, whose crypt is filled with ancient bones, then leave the abbey grounds.

The **Cathedral Church of St. James** (4) dates from the early 16th century, but did not become the seat of a bishop until 1914. Since then, major modifications have been made to render it more suitable as a cathedral. The 12th-century **Norman Tower**, opposite, serves as its bell tower.

Turn left on Crown Street and visit **St. Mary's Church** (5), one of the finest in the region. Built in the 15th century, it houses the tomb of Mary Tudor, sister of Henry VIII. The church is famous for its magnificently painted ceiling.

Continue down Crown Street to the **Theatre Royal** (6), a Regency structure from 1819 that has been thoroughly restored by the National Trust. You may visit its delightful interior when it is not in use. From here follow the map past the medieval **Guildhall** on Guildhall Street, and the Victorian Corn Exchange on Cornhill. The Traverse is a colorful lane featuring the smallest pub in England, The Nutshell, and a fine 17th-century inn, the Cupola House.

The **Market Cross Art Gallery** (7) features changing exhibitions and is open on Tuesdays through Saturdays, from 10:30 a.m. to 4:30 p.m. Cross the open square to the 12th-century **Moyse's Hall** (8), one of

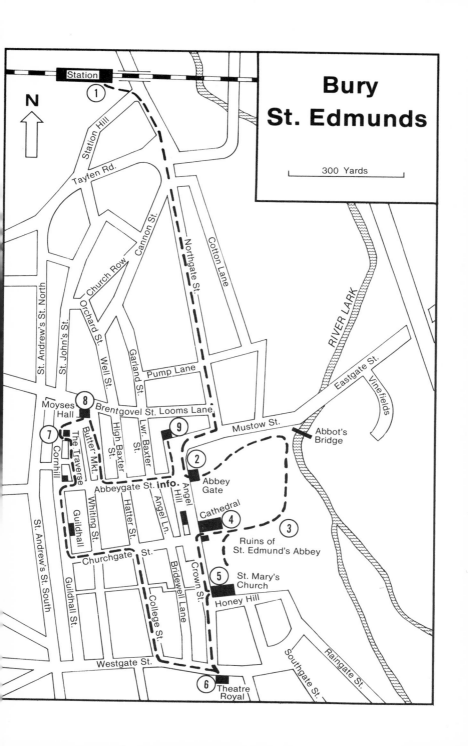

Bury
St. Edmunds

300 Yards

N

Station

1

Station Hill

Tayfen Rd.

Cannon St.

Church Row

Orchard St.

Well St.

Garland St.

Pump Lane

Northgate St.

Cotton Lane

RIVER LARK

Eastgate St.

Vinefields

St. Andrew's St. North

St. John's St.

Moyses Hall

8

Brentgovel St.

Looms Lane

Mustow St.

Abbot's Bridge

7

Cornhill

The Traverse

Butter Mkt.

High Baxter St.

Lwr. Baxter St.

9

2

Abbey Gate

Angel Hill

Cathedral

4

3

Ruins of St. Edmund's Abbey

Abbeygate St.

info.

Whiting St.

Guildhall

Hatter St.

Angel Ln.

Churchgate St.

St. Andrew's St. South

Guildhall St.

Bridewell Lane

College St.

Crown St.

5

St. Mary's Church

Honey Hill

Westgate St.

6

Theatre Royal

Southgate St.

Raingate St.

Ruins of the Abbey

the oldest domestic buildings in England. Previously used as a house, an inn, and a jail, it was converted into a museum in 1899. All manner of fascinating junk is on display, including items of historical interest, bygones, and archaeological finds. These may be seen on Mondays through Saturdays from 10 a.m. to 5 p.m.; and on Sundays from 2–5 p.m.

Return via Butter Market and Abbeygate Street to Angel Hill. On your right is the **Athenaeum**, a Regency social center where Charles Dickens once gave readings. He also immortalized the nearby Angel Hotel in his *Pickwick Papers*. Beyond this is **Angel Corner** (9), a Queen Anne house maintained by the National Trust, that houses the splendid **Gershom Parkington Collection of Clocks and Watches**, one of the finest museums of its kind in the country. Its collection of ingenious old timepieces, all ticking together, can be seen Mondays through Saturdays from 10 a.m. to 5 p.m.; and on Sundays from 2–5 p.m. From here you can walk back to the train station.

Colchester

No other town in England has a recorded history quite as old as Colchester's. Beginning as a small settlement in the Bronze Age, it had already become an important place by the 1st century A.D. when Cunobelin, Shakespeare's "Cymbeline," made it his capital. This was captured by the Romans in A.D. 44 and became their first colony in Britain, *Colonia Camulodunum*. After the fall of the empire, the town was taken over by the Anglo-Saxons, who called it *Colneceaster*. William the Conqueror built a mighty castle there, and all through the Middle Ages the town thrived on its cloth trade.

Colchester is still a flourishing place, and a very attractive one at that. Its handsome streets are lined with an absorbing mixture of the old and the new, including Roman walls, a surprisingly well-preserved Norman castle keep, many medieval houses, and structures of every age since.

GETTING THERE:

Trains leave frequently from London's Liverpool Street Station for the one-hour trip to Colchester, with returns until late evening. Service is reduced on Sundays and holidays.

By car, Colchester is 56 miles northeast of London via the A-12.

LINKS:

For those following an itinerary, Colchester has easy rail connections to **Bury St. Edmunds** and **Cambridge**. Reasonable travel by train to the other destinations in this book requires making connections in London, or can be done by car.

PRACTICALITIES:

Several of the attractions are closed on Sundays, while the colorful **outdoor market** is held on Saturdays. The local **Tourist Information Centre**, phone (0206) 712-233, is at 1 Queen Street, opposite the Hollytrees Museum. Colchester is in the county of **Essex**, and has a **population** of about 88,000.

FOOD AND DRINK:

Colchester has been noted for its oysters since Roman times. Some good places to eat are:

> **Red Lion Hotel** (High St., near the castle) Traditional fare in an old half-timbered inn. $$

George Hotel (116 High St., near the castle) A renovated medieval inn with a carving restaurant and grill. $$

Bistro 9 (9 North Hill, north of High St.) Imaginative cooking, with vegetarian alternatives. $$

Rose and Crown (East Hill, beyond the river) A 15th-century inn with a fine restaurant. $$

Norfolk (North Station Rd., on the way to the station) A popular pub with meals. $

SUGGESTED TOUR:

The **train station** (1) is nearly a mile from High Street, where the sights begin. You can cover this partly uphill distance by bus, taxi, or on foot. Once there, turn left past the wonderfully Victorian Town Hall and left again on West Stockwell Street.

This quiet and charming old area is known as the **Dutch Quarter**, where refugee Flemish weavers settled in the 17th and 18th centuries. **St. Martin's Church** (2) has an interesting 12th-century tower. Turn right through the churchyard and follow East Stockwell Street and St. Helen's Lane, passing several fine old houses, to the 13th-century St. Helen's Chapel. A left on Maidenburgh Street leads to the remains of the ancient **Roman walls.** Stroll along these, and then make a right to the castle.

The only part of ***Colchester Castle** (3) that survives today is its enormous keep, the largest in England. Built by the Normans about 1085 on the foundations of a Roman temple, it now houses the fabulous **Colchester and Essex Museum** of late Celtic and Roman antiquities. Visits may be made on Mondays through Saturdays from 10 a.m. to 5 p.m.; and also on Sundays from April through September from 2:30–5 p.m. Don't miss seeing this, especially the underground vaults.

Walk over to the **Hollytrees** (4), a Georgian mansion dating from 1718. This is occupied by a splendid museum of 18th- and 19th-century bygones, costumes, and military objects. It is open on Mondays through Saturdays from 10 a.m. to 1 p.m. and 2–5 p.m. Two other nearby museums are the **Natural History**, housed in the former All Saints' Church and having the same hours as the Hollytrees; and the **Minories Art Gallery**, which features a collection of works by Constable and other artists but is primarily known for its changing exhibitions. It has a café serving light lunches, and is open on Tuesdays through Saturdays from 10:30 a.m. to 5:30 p.m.; and on Sundays from noon to 5 p.m.

Continue down High Street to the 15th-century St. James's Church near the corner of Priory Street. From here you can make a side trip down East Hill to the half-timbered **Siege House** (5) on the River Colne,

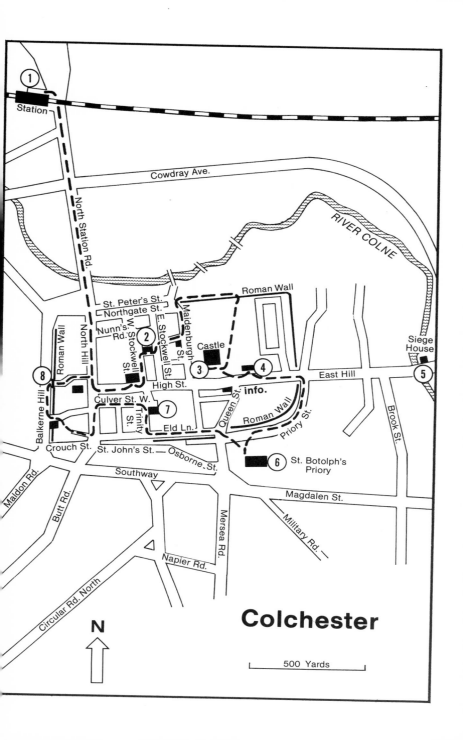

Holy Trinity Church

which still bears bullet marks from the 17th-century Civil War and is now a restaurant.

A stroll down Priory Street will take you past a fine section of the Roman wall. Turn left into the very romantic ruins of **St. Botolph's Priory** (6), a 12th-century Augustinian foundation destroyed during the siege of 1648. From here follow the map along Eld Lane, passing some inviting pubs, and turn right on Trinity Street.

Holy Trinity Church (7) has a Saxon tower made of Roman bricks. Its 14th-century interior, well worth a visit, is home to an interesting museum of rural life and crafts. It is open during the same hours as the Hollytrees Museum, above. Nearby, on Trinity Street, is a small **Clock Museum** where locally-made timepieces can be seen.

Make a left on Culver Street West and follow the map to the **Balkerne Gate** (8), originally built in the late 1st century A.D. by the Romans. Turn right and stroll down a passageway past the modern Mercury Theatre and the fantastic Victorian water tower, known locally as "Jumbo." From High Street you can either walk or take a bus back to the station.

Index

Boat Trips, Castles, Cathedrals, Country Walks, London Attractions, Museums, Roman Relics, and Stately Homes & Palaces are listed individually under those category headings. *Names of persons are in italics.*

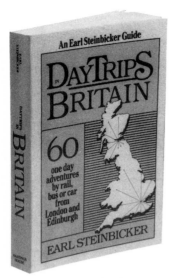

An Earl Steinbicker Guide

DAYTRIPS
BRITAIN

60
one day
adventures
by rail,
bus or car
from
London and
Edinburgh

EARL STEINBICKER

DAYTRIPS
IN BRITAIN

For travelers venturing farther afield,
this popular guidebook describes daytrips to 60 of the most exciting destinations within range of London, Edinburgh, and Glasgow. Among the
highlights are: a preserved steam railway near London, resorts on the Isle
of Wight, the Welsh capital of Cardiff,
the maritime memories of Exeter and
Bristol, a great medieval castle at War-
wick, the restored early industrial village at Ironbridge,
a steam-train excursion through northern Wales, the Roman and medieval towns of Chester and York, a walking tour of Edinburgh (and
one of Glasgow, too), the origins of golf at St. Andrews, the poetic
Burns Country, a cruise on Loch Lomond, and a scenic train ride
through the West Highlands of Scotland. 65 large maps, 107 photos,
352 pages.

Soon, a New Companion to the Series:

DAYTRIPS FROM NEW YORK

100 One-Day Adventures by Car

by Lida Newberry

6th Edition, Revised by Joy Johannessen and Earl Steinbicker

For the past twenty years this well-known guidebook has led thousands of year-round travelers on delightful excursions through
nearby New York State, New Jersey, Pennsylvania, Connecticut, and
Massachusetts. 352 pages, maps, photos.

DAYTRIPS

TRAVEL GUIDES BY EARL STEINBICKER

● **OTHER TITLES NOW AVAILABLE** ●

DAYTRIPS IN GERMANY
55 of Germany's best attractions can be enjoyed on daytrips from Munich, Frankfurt, Hamburg, and Berlin. Walking tours of the big cities are included, as are glossaries. 62 maps and 94 photos. 3rd edition, 336 pages.

DAYTRIPS IN FRANCE
Describes 45 great one-day excursions—including 5 walking tours of Paris, 23 daytrips from the city, 5 in Provence, and 12 along the Riviera. Glossaries, 55 maps, 89 photos. 2nd edition, 336 pages.

DAYTRIPS IN HOLLAND, BELGIUM AND LUXEMBOURG
There's more to the Low Countries than just Amsterdam, Brussels, and Luxembourg City. Many unusual destinations are covered on the 40 daytrips described in this guidebook, along with all of the favorites including the 3 major cities. Glossaries, 45 maps, 69 photos, 288 pages.

DAYTRIPS IN ITALY
Features 40 one-day adventures in and around Rome, Florence, Milan, Venice, and Naples. It includes walking tours of the major cities as well as many smaller destinations such as the hill towns of Tuscany. Glossaries, 45 maps, 69 photos, 288 pages.

● **IN PRODUCTION** ●

DAYTRIPS IN EUROPE
75 one-day excursions from the great cities of a dozen European countries. Heavily illustrated with maps and photos.

"Daytrips" travel guides by Earl Steinbicker describe the easiest and most natural way to explore Europe on your own. Each volume in the growing series contains a balanced selection of enjoyable one-day adventures that can be taken from a major base city, or even within that city. Some of these are to famous attractions, while others feature little-known discoveries.

For every destination there is a suggested do-it-yourself tour, a local map, full travel directions, time and weather considerations, restaurant recommendations, photos, and concise background material.

Since all of the daytrips can be made by public transportation, the books are especially useful to holders of the various popular railpasses. Road directions are also included. These guides are ideal for business travelers as they make the most of limited free time.

SOLD AT LEADING BOOKSTORES EVERYWHERE

Or, if you prefer, by mail direct from the publisher. Use the handy coupon below or just jot down your choices on a separate piece of paper.

Hastings House
141 Halstead Avenue
Mamaroneck, NY 10543

Please send the following books:

_____copies   **DAYTRIPS LONDON** @ **$12.95**   _____
                (0-8038-9329-9)
_____copies   **DAYTRIPS IN BRITAIN** @ **$12.95**   _____
                (0-8038-9301-9)
_____copies   **DAYTRIPS IN GERMANY** @ **$12.95**   _____
                (0-8038-9327-2)
_____copies   **DAYTRIPS IN FRANCE** @ **$12.95**   _____
                (0-8038-9326-4)
_____copies   **DAYTRIPS IN HOLLAND, BELGIUM**   _____
                AND LUXEMBOURG @ **$12.95**
                (0-8038-9310-8)
_____copies   **DAYTRIPS IN ITALY** @ **$10.95**   _____
                (0-8038-9293-4)

New York residents add tax: _____

Shipping and handling @ $1.50 per book: _____

Total amount enclosed (check or money order):   _____

Please ship to: _____

_____

_____